Knave of Spades

ALAN TITCHMARSH has his own daytime ITV show, *The Alan Titchmarsh Show*, and is also known to millions through his popular BBC TV programmes *British Isles: A Natural History*, *How to be a Gardener*, *Ground Force* and *Gardeners' World*. He has written more than forty gardening books, as well as seven best-selling novels including his latest, *Folly*, and two previous volumes of memoir, *Trowel and Error* and *Nobbut a Lad*. He was appointed MBE in the millennium New Years Honours list and holds the Victoria Medal of Honour, the Royal Horticultural Society's Highest Award. In 2009, he was made a Vice President of the Royal Horticultural Society. He lives with his wife and a menagerie of animals in Hampshire where he gardens organically.

ALAN TITCHMARSH

Knave of Spades

HODDER

First published in Great Britain in 2009 by Hodder & Stoughton
An Hachette UK company

First published in paperback in 2010

3

Typeset in Bembo by Hewer Text UK Ltd, Edinburgh
Printed and bound by CPI Mackays, Chatham ME5 8TD

Hodder & Stoughton policy is to use papers that are natural, renewable
and recyclable products and made from wood grown in sustainable
forests. The logging and manufacturing processes are expected to
conform to the environmental regulations of the country of origin.

Hodder & Stoughton Ltd
338 Euston Road
London NW1 3BH

www.hodder.co.uk

In memory of Harry Rhodes without whose encouragement none of this would have been possible.

Acknowledgements

Writing is a solitary business but not, in my experience, a lonely one. I enjoy the solitude of committing thoughts to paper day after day, but find that the task is made much easier by a handful of people whose opinions, expertise and support make the process even more fulfilling and enjoyable. Independence is one thing; working in a vacuum is quite another.

To my editor Rowena Webb I am grateful for a continuous supply of encouragement and valued advice. Her sunny yet discerning approach is of tremendous value, and her assistant Ciara Foley has the patience of a saint. To my literary agent, friend and sounding board Luigi Bonomi I again offer my heartfelt thanks for his tireless enthusiasm. He is the world's best bolsterer. Juliet Brightmore made picture selection great fun, and Kerry Hood is matchless when it comes to marshalling me 'on the road', along with Andrew Smith who knows just when to chat and just when to sit quietly and drive. He has all the perspicacity of Jeeves without the loftiness – a real treasure. This merry band are the people who remind me how lucky I am to do the job that I do.

As to my family; words fail me, in the nicest possible way. As Margaret Thatcher said: 'There is no such thing as Society. There are individual men and women, and there are families.' I've been rather blessed with mine.

Contents

Whoever could make two ears of corn or two blades of grass to grow upon a spot of ground where only one grew before would deserve better of mankind and do more essential service to his country than the whole range of politicians put together.

Dean Swift

knave noun. Old English *cnafa* – boy, servant

At the Beginning . . .

'I want to be a gardener.' That's what I told my parents. As aspirations go it was a pretty simple one. Compared with the desire to study Eng. Lit. or PPE (whatever that was) at Oxford it was off the bottom of the Richter scale. 'The man who could call a spade a spade should be compelled to use one. It is the only thing he is fit for,' wrote Oscar Wilde, emphasising the belief that gardening was a job for those who were a bit lacking upstairs to tackle more intellectual pursuits.

Back in 1964 gardening was something most folk did at weekends – down our end of town it consisted of Dad mowing the bit of grass 'out the back' and clipping the privet, while Mum scattered a few annual flower seeds over a grey ribbon of dust in spring – marigolds or love-in-a-mist – in the earnest hope that the dog would not scratch them up before they germinated. Up the posh end, where walls of sandstone replaced the privet, and striped greensward lay like a verdant Wilton carpet around the formal rose beds, gardening consisted, as Charles Barr put it, 'of putting on a wide straw hat, holding a gin and tonic in one hand and a trowel in the other and telling the man where to dig.' That sort of person could, for four guineas, have the initials FRHS after their name, indicating their Fellowship of the Royal Horticultural Society, like Mr Moffatt, who owned the florist's shop on The Grove and had those four letters in gilded copperplate after his name on the glazed front door. Me? I just wanted to grow things. The interest in quotations came later.

I liked growing things mainly because I found I could. And because it made me feel good about myself. And because it made my surroundings look better. Not that it impressed the other lads in the street, who clearly thought I was a bit odd. All except Mick Hudson who scattered seeds with me, in between games of kick-can and cricket against the bus garage wall at the bottom of our street. By and large they left me alone to get on with it. Best that way really. Apart from the one lad who called me Petunia. It should have left me scarred. It didn't. Not really.

Today gardening is infinitely more fashionable. Lawyers and bankers, worn down by the metropolitan grind and nervous of their future, sell the house in Primrose Hill and move out with Olivia and Zac to an estate in Herefordshire to grow a new life. Rarely a month goes by without the 'girl in pearls' on the frontispiece of *Country Life* being described as a 'garden designer'. She'll have done a course at one of the fashionable London gardening schools and been booked to sort out the gardens of her friends . . .

Oh, but that's no way to start. It makes me sound bitter and twisted when, in reality, I'm thrilled to bits that gardening has become more popular, more acceptable, more revered. That's *gardening*, rather than *garden design*. Becoming a garden designer before having been a gardener is akin to painting in oils without the faintest knowledge of the medium.

Enough. Time to get on with the story. I hope it will at least fire your enthusiasm for a way of life that I have found more rewarding than I could have ever imagined. I don't mean financially – well, at least not in the first twenty years – but then as real gardeners know, patience usually pays off.

It's curious that a miserable childhood is assumed to give a life more validity. That, I suppose, is why 'misery memoirs' have been so popular. I can't claim that there was much misery in mine, apart from the occasional deadly boring Sunday afternoon with aged relatives and an uncomfortable time at secondary school. I'm not exactly a prime candidate for top-drawer tragedy. And, anyway, if life had been miserable my mum wouldn't have let me drone on about it – a trouble shared being a trouble dragged out till bedtime. Get up and get on was her motto. It became mine, too. Luckily.

But, misery or not, we all have to battle. Nothing comes on a plate. I'm genuinely bewildered by the course my life has taken, but then I have stuck at it – tenaciously rather than ruthlessly – and been lucky enough to encounter just a handful of people who have said 'yes you can' at those vital moments when all I could say was 'no I can't'. I'm thankful for their intervention, and that in the end I did have the nerve to fly in the face of accepted wisdom – and critics – and battle on.

By leaving school at the age of fifteen and 'following my bliss', I have found, eventually, rather a pleasant place to be. Is it unfashionable, do you think, to be content? That's content, rather than smug or self-satisfied. I'm always ready for it to go wrong – at any second – but it would be churlish of me to pretend that I have not enjoyed the journey so far. It's been a long and an unexpectedly varied one. I didn't imagine, back then, that I would end up presenting television programmes or writing novels, hosting the *Last Night of the Proms* or editing Percy Thrower. Well, I might have *imagined* it, but that was as far as it went. It is difficult to express surprise at the course of one's own life without sounding like a clone of Uriah Heep, disingenuous, falsely modest, or possessing the two attributes already mentioned – self-satisfaction and smugness. You need self-confidence for those two and in spite of outward appearances, there's not a lot of that in my store cupboard.

If I am honest I never really expected to get anywhere. Yorkshire in the 1950s and 60s – my part of it anyway – was not the hub of the universe, more of a distant outpost. Newsworthy things happened elsewhere. This was not something that worried me overmuch at the start of my journey, travelling hopefully, if realistically, on a route of whose direction I was uncertain and which would turn out to be peppered with frustrations, disappointments, irritations, worry, grief and all those other negative emotions that occur, after all, in most people's lives.

I have been blessed with the kind of life I could never have dreamed of when I left school – a varied and unexpected series of events, many of them totally unrelated to gardening, but all of them built on a foundation stone that consists of a love of nature and a willingness to be interested. I suppose that is the secret. That and the fact that I had the knack of being able to grow things . . .

Green Shoots

His slow beginnings who can trace?
He springs from a peculiar race.
The child of hope and second sight,
Born of despair and of delight.
          'How does a gardener grow?', Fay Inchfawn

It could have gone either way. I could have been a carpenter,
rather than a gardener. The thing was, I was so desperate to
leave school I almost didn't mind what I did. Almost.

The combination of my science teacher's bellowing, my
English teacher's lack of faith in my imaginative prose, my
geography teacher's matchless aim with a blackboard rubber and
my failure to either understand or care about the intricacies of
French verbs sealed my fate. The only thing 'irregular' that I
knew of was my Auntie Alice and it was clear there was no
cure for it. The journey home at four o'clock every weekday
afternoon, with my homework-filled brown 'leather' suitcase
trailing along the ground and revealing the grey and fibrous
nature of its true cardboard self, was akin to an assault on Everest.
I was not, as Cookie, the Croydon-born and spherical widow
next door, observed, 'as happy as Larry'.

I had failed my eleven-plus. Not spectacularly, just positively.
I'd gone from the sooty Victorian stonework of Ilkley All Saints
Junior School in Leeds Road to the brand new glass-and-painted-

panel work secondary school on Valley Drive. They pulled it down last year, so at least I have the satisfaction of knowing that I outlived the place that caused me so much grief.

It came as a shock that, having been called 'Alan' by my teachers for the first seven years of my scholastic life, I was now 'Titchmarsh'. Soft beggar. But it is so much more difficult to hide with a name like that than it is with Robertson, Smith or Brown. I'm sixty now and deep down I still shudder slightly at the sound of my own name. I could have changed it to something less obtrusive when I started doing television, but the moment passed and so now I'm stuck with it. Does Cliff Richard, I wonder, still feel like Harry Webb? Does Michael Caine feel a traitor to the memory of Maurice Micklewhite? A good name for a gardener, that. Alan Micklewhite. A missed opportunity.

Not that all the blame for my slow start can be laid entirely at the door of the school, or the teachers, come to that. I was a classic late developer. A bit of a dreamer. I meant well but, as one of my school reports remarked, 'Alan has very good intentions; what a pity they are not always fulfilled.'

Well, I tried. I just seemed to be on a different planet – to the rest of the pupils as well as the staff. An odd lad, I suppose. Not what would nowadays be called a geek, or a nerd, just . . . well, not quite fitting in. Too sensitive for my own good, as well. My dad, while not by nature a gruff person, did have his concerns. When you're a Yorkshire plumber and your only son seems to be interested in art, nature, model theatres, acting in school plays and gardening, you could be forgiven for thinking that he might turn out to be closer in temperament to Liberace than Sean Connery. His relief when I brought home my first girlfriend was palpable. As was my mother's apprehension.

The memories of those early years are as vivid as a stained-glass window. I cannot watch the film *Kes* without pangs of anxiety at young Billy Casper's feelings of isolation on the football pitch – always the last to be picked along with the 'fat boy'. I was the smallest in the class until I left school at fifteen and went to work in the greenhouses where I grew ten inches in the first year.

As inferiority complexes go it was fairly well developed. But I cannot claim that I was ever mistreated. Both parents were loving – my father in that understated Yorkshire way – and concerned to instil in my sister Kath and me a sense of duty, good manners, kindness and honesty. To write them down now makes them sound strangely old-fashioned and, frankly, many of the traits they embodied are rather ancient. I was taught to walk on the outside of the pavement when accompanying a female – I still do – and to take off my school cap whenever I passed a lady, whenever a funeral cortege passed me and whenever I went indoors. The wearing of baseball caps in the house still makes me uneasy.

I could not leave the table without asking to do so, was not permitted to talk with my mouth full, went to church on Sunday and knelt by my bed each evening to say my prayers. I don't kneel any more.

Neighbours were 'Mr So-and-so' and 'Mrs So-and-so', aunts and uncles never referred to by their Christian names alone, and until I was well into double figures I never dared to answer my parents back. On the first occasion I disagreed with my mother's pronouncement on something, I don't know who was the more shocked, her or me.

By the time I was fifteen I was perhaps a little more assertive than it would appear from this confessional, but not much. The one thing I did know was that I was determined to leave school, even if the words of one of my teachers would ring in my ears for the rest of my life – 'He'll never amount to much.' At least I have that much in common with Einstein.

Now if, at this point, you have come to the conclusion that I have laboured for years under the weight of an inferiority complex the size of a small African country, or that I have a chip on my shoulder comparable to a London Routemaster bus, you could be forgiven. But I haven't really. I have simply bumbled along through life trying, like most folk, to make sense of it all, though there are times when a little more self-confidence might have come in handy. Being apologetic is all very well, but it can be tiresome. It can also be confused with wimpiness, and I'd like to think that I wasn't a wimp.

Dad wasn't at all sure that leaving school at fifteen – before taking my O levels – was a good idea. Once it became clear that my mind was set on doing so, he took up a rearguard position: 'You'll need a trade.'

He had noticed that over the previous five years I had become more and more interested in gardening. I had built a polythene greenhouse in our back garden where a selection of plants from geraniums to false castor oils had been cultivated, along with a cage of pet mice. Nature had always been an interest of mine. For a while it was touch and go whether I would be a gardener or a vet, but then the appearance of a cat in my greenhouse scared the mice literally to death and so plants started to seem like a more viable career path than animals.

What's more it was a well-known fact that to be a vet – or anything to do with the natural sciences – you needed O levels, A levels and a university education. The latter was never even breathed about; it was clear that my academic career was all but over at fifteen and the prospect of a university education was not even considered.

My interest in nature had developed early on. It was so ingrained that I cannot say for certain when it began. I have always been fascinated by 'natural history', to use the more academic term that I never thought of using during my childhood and adolescence. I could lie on the lawn under a sheet of blackout material for hours on end, watching birds coming down to feed on the crumbs I had scattered on the lawn. I would scoop handfuls of frog spawn from the tarn on Ilkley Moor each spring and watch the full stops turn to commas and the commas into wriggling crotchets every year, even growing on the froglets in a small vivarium that Dad made for me from an old orange box and a sheet of glass left over from repairing the kitchen window. My required television viewing was *Zoo Quest* with David Attenborough, *Look* with Peter Scott and *On Safari* with Armand and Michaela Denis.

I joined the Wharfedale Naturalists' Society at the age of eight – their youngest member – and went to 'lantern lectures' about butterflies and birds, fungi and mammals in winter, and up the Dales on field trips in spring and summer in the back of some obliging older member's Renault R8 Deluxe. He wore a tam-o'-shanter and a kilt, but apart from that he was quite normal and never attempted to feel my knee when he changed gear.

Gardening seemed a natural extension of this passion for everything that flew, crawled, swam or grew. I still think of gardeners as the only truly interactive naturalists. Birdwatchers watch birds, botanists look at flowers, but gardeners grow them, working hand in hand with nature rather than simply spectating.

Not that my wish to be a gardener impressed my father. He could never see gardening as 'a trade'. I found it hard to see why until, several years after I had taken up the spade, he confessed that both his father and his grandfather had been 'jobbing gardeners' and had made him weed for a penny a bucket. His own boredom with that soulless, repetitive task, and observation of the fact that neither of his male forebears had ever had more than a couple of ha'pennies to rub together had put him off gardening for life. My grandfather's spade – which I use to this day – was employed by my father to mix concrete. It still carries the telltale traces.

Worried that he might not countenance my being a gardener, I offered joinery as an alternative trade, reasoning in my own mind that if I could not grow things for a living then at least I could spend all my spare time doing so. I had always been good with my hands – whether that meant knocking together my own greenhouse from timber off cuts my dad brought home, or building model stage and television studio sets from balsa wood and cardboard (strangely prescient as it turned out), so joinery was not such an odd choice.

Dad, probably worn down by both my unhappiness at school and my constant nagging about gardening and joinery, finally made an appointment for him and Mum to see the headmaster. Not that he told me about it. Not until he returned home anyway.

'We think,' he said, 'that it might be better if you left school early.'

My joy at the prospect of being released from Purgatory was tempered by the fact that they clearly thought the further education of this academic failure would be futile.

'To be a joiner?' I asked.

'No.'

'What then?'

'The headmaster said that there were plenty of joiners about but not enough gardeners, and that if you had your mind set on it then we should let you be a gardener.'

'Oh.'

If the high five had been invented I would have given him one. Instead, I wandered off into the garden. Birds sang, bees buzzed and the leaves of the old sycamore up at the top end rustled in the summer breeze, but I don't think I heard them. Dad's words just echoed in my ears over and over again. Some massive weight had been lifted from my shoulders. I blundered in a kind of delirium into my little polythene greenhouse among the geraniums and the spider plants, the false castor oils and the busy lizzies. For a while I could not see much. I think I must have got something in my eye. I reached for the hanky in my left-hand pocket. I still have one there. It dates back to the taking off of the cap, the asking to get down from the table and the walking on the outside of the pavement. An ancient tradition, but one that still comes in handy – in cold weather, when eating spaghetti Bolognese, and in moments when life throws up things that catch you unawares.

Green Fingers

She grew them with rough, almost slap-dash love, but her hands possessed such an understanding of their needs they seemed to turn to her like another sun.

Cider With Rosie, Laurie Lee

Do I believe in 'green fingers'? Completely. Not that I think there is anything remotely mysterious or fanciful about the condition. It is instinctive, the ability to grow things; present in all of us, though clearly nearer the surface in some than in others. Those who claim to be able to kill anything they touch probably lack any real determination to make things grow, coupled with an inability to uncover any kind of 'feel' for plants; the basic skill, though deep-seated, is masked by the accumulated sophistication of a technological age that has relieved them of the necessity to grow things. The knack has been lost. That is what 'green fingers' is – a knack.

If you look at the way plants behave, notice their likes and dislikes and act accordingly the chances are that they will grow for you. They are innately willing to do so and capable of doing so. Most of them grow in spite of us, rather than because of us, so it is up to us not to get in the way. Oh, and you'll also need a bit of patience. In a world of instant gratification, the pleasure involved in anticipation is sometimes difficult to get across.

While my dad had no patience at all with the garden in Nelson Road, where I spent the first sixteen years of my life, my mum pottered about in it in between washing and ironing, cooking and bringing up two children. She inherited her growing skills from her father, Herbert Hardisty, a council 'ganger' from the highways department, whose allotment on the banks of the River Wharfe initiated me, aged one, into the delights of home-grown food.

Blackberries scrambled with fruity abandon over brass bedsteads; a tank of soot water was dipped into with a large brass syringe to repel caterpillars from Brussels sprouts and Savoy cabbages, and sweet peas were grown up tented rows of bean poles, the sparrows being scared off by the glittering silvery lids of Cadbury's cocoa tins strung among them. Mum would push me there in my pram and park me among the bean rows while she helped her horny-handed father pull carrots and beetroots for summer salads.

For a few years a small veg patch graced her own garden at Nelson Road, but soon her tastes became more ornamental. Not that she was into anything that remotely approached garden design. The area that passed for the lawn was rectangular, the washing line ran down its centre like a semi-permanent spine and the yard-wide borders that surrounded it were stuffed with a mixture of goldenrod, montbretia and shasta daisies – perennial plants that were happy to hold their own come drought, deluge or badly-aimed football. For several years our garden must have looked like that of Polly Garter in *Under Milk Wood* – 'Nothing grows in our garden, only babies. And washing.' There were only two babies, me and my younger sister Kath, but Mum was, unlike Polly Garter, scrupulously hygienic.

A brave 'Dorothy Perkins' rose scrambled over the chain link fence at the bottom, offering us privacy from the two nosey spinster sisters whose garden in Wellington Road backed on to ours, until black spot robbed it of its leaves in August and their curiosity was once again satisfied.

The heroic nature of the street names was part of my childhood litany – Nelson Road, Wellington Road, Trafalgar Road and Nile Road. Only Brewery Road stood out as letting the side down. My mother, though not exactly a snob, was acutely aware of what she thought was 'common'. She could never have brought herself to live in Brewery Road.

Like Laurie Lee's mother, my own mum's way with plants was instinctive. When I started attending day-release classes and night school to learn my craft, I would come home and tell her what she was doing wrong, with the benefit of my newly acquired knowledge and all the confidence of youth.

'Oh,' she would say. 'I see.' And go on doing things in just the same way as she always had. Age and experience have since taught me that there is more than one way to root a cutting, and my mother could root the spokes of an old umbrella.

When, at long last, I was allowed to follow my instincts and become a gardener, Mum decided that what I wanted to be was a propagator. It sounded, probably thanks to its first two syllables, like a 'proper' gardening job. One involving a deal of skill. I think she thought that it meant you were called in, rather like a consultant surgeon, when any plant was in need of resuscitation and duplication. Should any species (not a word I ever heard her utter) be in danger of exhaustion or extinction, in would come the propagator to offer emergency care and attention. To Mum the doctor – always referred to as 'doctor' without the definite article – was the earthly manifestation of God, and the propagator was clearly the horticultural equivalent. She rather liked the thought of that. So did I.

My first job, rather more menial in nature, came about as a result of a happy accident. Dad, though a plumber by trade, was also a part-time fireman and would be called out by the siren that wailed over the town, or by the ear-splitting ring of the bell at the bottom of our stairs, causing him to drop whatever he was doing, swap his slippers for his shoes and run to the fire station four streets away. He would spend Tuesday evenings on maintenance work there with the other part-timers – carpenters and electricians, decorators and council workmen – among them Wally Gell, who worked in the local parks department. One Tuesday night – presumably while they were checking that the hydrants were fully functional, or polishing the chrome on one of the two gleaming scarlet 'appliances' – Dad mentioned that his lad wanted to be a gardener.

'Oh,' said Wally. 'We've a vacancy if he wants to apply.'

So one day in the summer of 1964 I put on a pair of jeans, a clean shirt and tie and a check sports jacket, polished my shoes and went on my bike to the council nursery half a mile away on Little Lane to meet the Parks Superintendent, the very man whose name was painted on the door sill of the grey Austin A30 van that trundled him around town.

Hector Mutlow F.Inst.P.R.A (Fellow of the Institute of Park and Recreation Administration – a qualification that could not be purchased even by those who lived up the posh end of town) was a small, bird-like man with a shortie raincoat and a flat tweed cap. His voice had a tremulous, reedy quality that made him sound like a bassoon in need of tuning, with an occasional hint of the bagpipes.

I stood in front of him, in the rough gravel drive of the nursery, hoping that my appearance, at least, would not let me down. It seems odd, now, to think that even to be a gardener I needed to wear a collar, tie and sports jacket and have shiny shoes. Standards no doubt slipped over the next few years, but in July 1964 I needed all the help I could get to secure the position for which I was desperate: Apprentice Gardener for Ilkley Urban District Council.

Hector Mutlow looked me up and down. It did not take long. There wasn't much to look at.

'So you want to be a gardener?'

'Yes.'

'Are you sure?'

'I think so, yes.'

'Well, I don't want you to do anything hasty, so why don't you come and work for me for a fortnight for nothing, and if you like it I'll take you on.'

I thanked him profusely. I think I heard bells ringing. Maybe a heavenly choir.

'Are you alright?'

The voice seemed to be coming from elsewhere. I pulled myself together. 'Yes. Fine. When do I start?'

'Right now if you want.' He looked over his shoulder and called to the man in the doorway of the old brick potting shed. 'Kenneth, do you want to show this lad what he'll be doing?'

Ken Wilson nodded. He was the parks department foreman, Hector Mutlow's number two, a wise and gentle man, balding, with kind eyes and a face that lit up when he smiled. In all the years I knew him he was always scrupulously fair, though if a job was not done well he would let you know, in that quiet-spoken but firm way he had. 'There are some plants over here saying "Alan, why don't you water me?" was one of his favourites. He had been a Japanese prisoner of war, not that he spoke about it much. Occasionally he'd let slip something about his days in a concentration camp – swapping a blanket for cigarettes and then, when he had got his hands on the cigarettes through the fence, pulling both them and the blanket back. But when questioned further he would neatly change the subject and you knew it was time to move on. I could not forsee that later in life, due to Ken's mapping out of my early career, I would stand within a few feet of the man ultimately responsible for his incarceration – the Emperor of Japan.

Ken came over, on that first day, and shook my hand, looking into my eyes and no doubt trying to work out how long I would last. He, too, wore a tie, but the jacket was off and the sleeves rolled up, his grey flannel trousers (he never wore jeans) protected by a denim apron.

'You'd better follow me,' he said softly.

He led the way to an old Victorian greenhouse that was divided into three – two long, low, white-painted houses, joined by a higher central section. Following him, I climbed the two stone steps up to the first greenhouse and heard the clinking of the loose brass ferrule as he turned the knob and pushed open the door. Inside, carefully arranged on the shingle-topped staging were row after row of geraniums – scarlet, orange, pink and magenta, many of them with coloured leaves as well as bright flowers. The music of their names I would come to know well in the years that followed – 'Verona' and 'Majestic', 'Mrs Quilter' and 'Flowers of Spring,' 'Happy Thought' and 'Harry Hie-Over' and the foreign-sounding 'Paul Crampel' and 'Gustav Emich'. Alongside them stood a swathe of neat, upright plants with feathery plumes of red and yellow – Prince of Wales' feathers, or celosia. They seemed to me to be unbelievably exotic.

The cathedral-like atmosphere – the stillness of the air and the silence, except for the rhythmic drip-drip-drip of water from the staging into the sunken concrete tanks beneath them – was awe-inspiring. My only experience of greenhouse gardening was in the tiny polythene lean-to I had built at home against the stone wall of the midden at the bottom of the garden, which was barely six feet by three. The one where the mice died but the geraniums and the spider plants grew.

Having walked me through these floral cathedrals, Ken Wilson said the three words which, at that point in my life, were the most thrilling I had ever heard: 'These are yours.'

At first I thought I must have misheard. 'Are you sure?' I asked him.

He raised his eyebrows, and I realised the stupidity of my reply.

'Right,' was the best response I could manage.

'I'll leave you to get on with your watering then.' And with that he was gone.

I stood there, in that first greenhouse, quite still for a few moments, gazing at the colour on all sides, looking up at the white-painted rafters and down at the deep and seemingly bottomless tanks of rainwater beneath the staging. Gloop, drip, gloop, drip were the only sounds I heard in this otherwise silent haven. Then I walked on towards the higher central greenhouse and opened the door to discover tall grevilleas, the Australian silk-bark oak, in pots on the floor, shooting upwards and diffusing the rays of the summer sun with their ferny fronds. The wall at the back of this tall lean-to that backed on to the potting shed was lime-washed bright white. In front of it were serried ranks of *Primula obconica* in pots on the staging. The next door led to the final greenhouse and more geraniums, not yet in flower. I turned and retraced my steps to the bottom door, suddenly aware of a thumping sound that was coming from my chest. It was definitely my heart, there was no doubt about that. But it was beating with fear as well as excitement. What if I got it wrong? What if they all died? But I took a grip of myself. Come on. I could grow plants. Here there were just more of them.

The bellowing voice of the science mistress echoed in my ears no longer. French verbs counted for nothing here and there was no need to duck the blackboard rubber. I was in my element. In my greenhouses, and if I managed to get through the next two weeks they'd let me keep them. I was fifteen. And all this was mine for the asking.

Gardener's Boy

There's not a pair of legs so thin, there's not a head so thick,
There's not a hand so weak and white, nor yet a heart so sick.
But it can find some needful job that's crying to be done,
For the Glory of the Garden glorifieth every one.

'The Glory of the Garden', Rudyard Kipling

I got the job. I think they all knew from day one that I thought it was the best thing that had ever happened to me. Confidence is a wonderful thing. Elusive often, but delivered, sometimes, from the most unexpected sources.

Up until that point my performance, academically, had been distinctly average. I had managed the A stream in secondary school, but my class position was usually in the lower half of the thirty-odd pupils that made up class 4A. Only in spelling did I come out top (and nowadays even that doesn't count for much thanks to the spell-checker on my laptop). I was good with words though. Less so with numbers which have always seemed to me to be some kind of code. But the dictionary always appealed. Finding unusual words and using them gave me some kind of armoury that my muscle power could not provide, not that saying 'desist' to a B-stream bully would be any more likely to stop him from bashing you up than if you said 'gerroff'. Still, I did have the small consolation of knowing, as I nursed my bruised ear, that I knew what 'reciprocate' meant and he didn't.

From being twenty-something in the class at school, I shot into the top two or three at Shipley Art and Technical Institute, a grim-looking Victorian building in Saltaire, near Bradford. The philanthropic industrialist Titus Salt had built the houses, mills and factories a century previously. They have been cleaned up of late and now house the David Hockney Museum among other things, but back in the 1960s the imposing, soot-blackened building was home to students of engineering and mechanics, secretarial work and horticulture. I went there one day and one evening a week on day release to study for my City and Guilds examinations. The other four days of the week I worked in the parks department nursery with a varied bunch of men who tended the flower beds and bowling greens, tennis courts and playing fields. The nursery staff – three of us plus a driver, with occasional input from the foreman – grew all the plants necessary for spring and summer bedding out in the flower beds and roundabouts in the town and pot plants for floral decorations in the town hall and library, the Kings Hall and Winter Gardens, Ilkley's two statuesque Edwardian assembly rooms.

There were a dozen or so men, mainly middle-aged, who made up the motley crew responsible for beautifying the 'Heather Spa', as Ilkley was referred to in its Victorian heyday. It had grown in size a century and a half previously thanks to the smelly yet health-giving properties of the chalybeate waters that erupted from natural springs on the moor. Massively daunting and castellated hotels called 'hydropathic establishments' were erected to cater for the gentry who wanted to 'take the waters', and with them developed all kinds of gruesome treatments. With the passing of the hydropathic fad in the early twentieth century Ilkley had become the preferred residential area, along with Harrogate, for the wool merchants of Leeds and Bradford, and the 'hydros' had become hotels and colleges or else been pulled down to make room for more houses.

The rough north/south dividing line between the posh end and the working-class area of Ilkley is Brook Street, the town's main shopping thoroughfare. We lived in the working-class bit to the east – parallel streets of stone-built, slate-roofed terrace houses with back lanes between house and garden. Pleasant, but utilitarian. To the west of Brook Street is The Grove, the Bond Street of Ilkley (well, that might be pushing it a bit – it is more Regent Street than Oxford Street though) where Betty's Cafe – other branches in York, Harrogate and Northallerton – is the jewel in the crown, along with, among others, Studio 68 – contemporary knick-knacks – a fine jewellers, the independent Grove Bookshop doing battle with neighbouring W.H. Smith and the local optician.

Up King's Road and Grove Road to the west are larger detached houses, with spacious gardens and grounds backing on to the moors. The River Wharfe bisects the valley running east to west, at right angles to Brook Street, and on the higher slopes of both sides of the valley are the smartest houses of all, hidden from view by copses and woodland, and reached via curving gravel or Tarmac drives.

In these houses, many of the men who worked by day for the parks department would earn a few extra shillings by working on summer evenings or Saturday mornings mowing and weeding, clipping hedges and digging vegetable plots.

My wage, as far as I can remember, amounted to £3.7s.6d (that's £3.37 and a half pence). I gave it all to my mum, and she gave me back ten bob pocket money (50p).

While I was the lowest of the low in my newly appointed position, with indentures for a five-year apprenticeship and therefore a smaller sum of money since my employment was guaranteed, Mickey Ware was classed as a labourer and earned rather more. He was a year or so older than me, with a stubbly beard and a liking for Helen Shapiro.

In charge of us both was Ron Jeavons, the propagator, married with two kids, tall and gangly, with thick glasses and, said the rest of the guys, the gift of the gab. He earned his few extra bob by lecturing to the W.I. and assorted other groups eager to learn how to become a consultant surgeon for plants. It was Ron who gave me the budding knife I still use today. An apron and a budding knife were the regulation equipment of an apprentice in the nursery. The dark-blue denim apron (it took a while to stop my mother calling it my 'pinny') came wrapped up in brown paper. The budding knife came in a small cardboard box labelled 'The Burbank'. But I never did lay my hands on it. Instead, Ron took his old one out of his apron pocket and gave me that. 'I could do with a new one,' he said. I would be lying if I said that I did not feel disappointed, but if I had known that the old knife he gave me would last – to date – forty-five years, then I might not have felt so bad. Under Ron's tutelage, and that of one or two of the rest of the team, I spent the next few years learning my trade.

Dad would wake me at around seven since we both needed to leave early for work. I didn't need to shave every day at fifteen, neither did we shower every morning in the 1960s – anyway, we hadn't got one, only a bath and that was for Friday nights or special occasions – so I was out of the door and on my bike for the ten-minute ride to the nursery on Little Lane once Dad had got a bowl of thick porridge down me. His fallback position in summer was Weetabix or Shreddies. He'd have done me a cooked breakfast if I'd have asked for it, but Dad's problem was that whenever he cooked anything, he found it impossible to eat it. Not because it was in any way substandard; simply that the act of preparing it had robbed him of any appetite. He was a martyr to his digestion until the end, in the days before they had invented Irritable Bowel Syndrome.

I went through a range of bikes over the four years I worked at the nursery. Mick Hudson always had a new one courtesy of Kensitas gift coupons, but since neither of my parents smoked that brand (Dad was a Senior Service man and Mum could manage only a single Peter Stuyvesant on special occasions before looking slightly green) it was not an option open to us. Having grown out of the maroon Hercules bought from someone snooty in the Scout group, I graduated to a drop-handlebar racing machine that Mum bought in the saleroom at the bottom of Nelson Road. The gears kept crashing when I'd cycle uphill, slamming my crotch into the crossbar with such ferocity that it was traded in in the interests of prospective fatherhood. 'It'll have to go; the lad's done himself a mischief again.'

There followed a series of machines of varying quality until I managed to save up for a new one with small wheels. Not a Moulton – they were on the pricey side, having independent front suspension – but a Raleigh version in British racing green with fatter white tyres. A bit showy, really; not a proper gardener's bike, but it served me well until I finished at the nursery, and was then left to gather dust in the outhouse along with the childhood scooter and the trike.

The nursery itself was situated just outside the centre of town and surrounded by council houses and small cul-de-sacs of pebble-dashed semis with names like Wheatlands that nodded an acknowledgement to their rural past. It comprised about eight acres, I should think, with areas of ground for growing wallflowers and shrubs, neatly arranged white-painted timber greenhouses and a series of sheds and lean-tos housing tools, vehicles and stacks of loam, peat and sand.

It was entered through large wrought-iron gates that were supported on imposing stone piers, and the foreman's house – a modest little detached cottage with a definite 'urban district council' air about it, complete with regulation U.D.C. cream and green paint – stood just inside them. Ken Wilson and his wife and daughter lived there, and in the four years I worked on the nursery I never went inside. I had been at school with

Ken's daughter, Rosemary. Even had a bit of a crush on her years before. Not that I ever told her dad that. Ken would retire there for lunch every day, while the rest of us nibbled on our sandwiches or munched our pies in the mess room.

Work began at 7.45a.m. Only a handful of the dozen or so men who worked in the parks department had cars; the rest would arrive on various modes of transport from bikes to mopeds, scooters to ancient vans and, once gathered together, would be ferried out to the various roundabouts, open spaces and flower beds in and around the town in the back of a Land Rover, sitting facing each other like schoolboys in church.

Then the nursery would fall quiet, and the trio of us that remained would begin our daily rounds. The thirteen greenhouses, in which grew geraniums and ferns, hydrangeas and chrysanthemums, were heated by a coke-fired boiler the size of a small van, situated in a sunken boiler house in the centre of the nursery. Mickey and I took it in turns – week on, week off – to maintain and fuel this temperamental beast. In these days of automatic gas- or oil-fired central heating it is hard to believe just how labour-intensive were these earlier heating methods.

Each morning on 'my week of boilers' I'd descend the dozen or so steps and open the boiler house door to be greeted by the loud hum of the pump, shifting the hot water around what must have amounted to a couple of miles of four-inch cast iron piping. The warmth of the dimly lit cellar, whose contents were covered in black dust, would tell me whether or not the boiler had stayed lit during the night – a matter of life and death for tender plants in the middle of winter. I'd open the front door of the boiler to look at the glowing bed of cinders and then begin the hardest job of all – removing the clinker. The coke, which was delivered every couple of weeks in several ton loads from the gasworks in Bradford, would make its way down a hopper into the boiler house. It would move under its own weight at first, but after a few days would have to be encouraged with a shovel. The burnt fuel would cake hard on the bottom of the boiler overnight, leaving behind an unburnable residue, clinker; that had to be removed if the fire were not to go out.

Picture me, then, on a cold winter's morning, clad in a donkey jacket (the sports jacket wore out) and will power, bouncing all of my seven stone on the end of a six-foot-long steel poker trying to break up this intractable four-inch layer of metallic crust that seemed welded to the bottom of the boiler. Once broken up, it would be removed, while still red hot, with a large pair of tongs, and deposited in a metal dustbin that sat alongside the boiler. When it filled up – every couple of days – the bin had to be carried up the steps of the boiler house and the contents dumped outside, sometimes being used to create an ash path down the side of one of the greenhouses.

Once clinkered, it was then a matter of closing the front door for half an hour and opening up the damper to get the fired bed roaring orange. Then I'd shovel in more coke and ram it right to the back of the boiler with another long metal tool that looked like a gigantic draw-hoe. Once full, the damper would be left open for a while to get the coke going, and then shut down so that it did not burn too fast. Throughout the day this beast with a life of its own would be checked every couple of hours to make sure that it was burning evenly, and more fuel added until the final stoking up at night, when it was filled once more and left to burn, with threats and crossed fingers.

On the occasions when the boiler did go out – due to temperament on its own part or neglect on the part of the stoker – it had to be cleared of all its unburnt coke with a shovel in the morning, stuffed with paper and broken wooden seed boxes, and then lit once more. On the days when it was sluggish you were allowed to go to the lawnmower shed, borrow a can of diesel fuel and give it a helping hand. I did this one morning only to pick up, in my sleepy state, a can of petrol instead of diesel. The flickering blend of paper, wood and coke was reluctant to do anything constructive until I threw in a couple of pints of the fluid encouragement. It worked a treat – after it had blown me off my feet, hurled me on to the back wall of the boiler house and removed my fringe and eyebrows. I didn't make the same mistake twice.

It was a relief when summer arrived and the boiler could be allowed to go out, although then that all-consuming task was just replaced with another one – watering.

Ron and Mickey had five greenhouses apiece, each around 30 feet long, and I had three. They would be checked for watering morning and evening, and for the first couple of years I worked there we were not allowed to use hosepipes.

'If you use a hosepipe you don't look at what you're doing', was Ken's reasoning. Neither did we, in those first few years, use plastic pots. Each and every pot in which the thousands of plants we grew were planted was made of terracotta.

'Clay pots keep the roots cool,' Ken told me. They did, but being porous they also took a deal of watering. The technique of finding out which plants needed watering was simple and effective, but hugely time-consuming. We would dip a metal, two-gallon, long-spouted Haws watering can into the rainwater tank beneath the staging and, with this in one hand and a small long-handled mallet in the other, work our way down the staging on one side of the house and back up the other, checking to see which plants were thirsty. A smart tap on the rim of each pot with the mallet would produce either a dull thud (the rootball was moist) or a ringing sound (the plant was dry). If it rang, you watered it; if it went 'clunk' you didn't.

Each of these pots, when a plant outgrew it, would be saved and washed to use again. Imagine me, then, on a freezing day, sitting in the poorly heated potting shed, cleaning hundreds of clay flowerpots in a tank of cold, muddy water with a scrubbing brush suffering from increasingly acute creeping alopoecia, its bristles reducing in number until my fingers alone were removing caked-on compost from the clay. One day, exasperated by the number of pots I was expected to wash, I engineered a stumble up the stone steps of the potting shed, sending dirty pots flying and breaking as many of them as possible. Ken, who was doing a spot of potting up at the bench by way of relief from managing the workforce, looked round. His face bore an expression of total calm. 'Oh, dear,' he said, looking at me spread-eagled on the floor. 'Never mind. Plenty more where they came from.' I didn't do it again, and the graze on my shin reminded me of my folly for the rest of the day.

I left the nursery before the oil-fired boiler arrived, but I did live to see the advent of hosepipes and plastic pots. It speeded up our watering no end – you can't tell from tapping a plastic pot whether it is dry or not – but I don't think Ken ever quite trusted them.

All those pots. It doesn't take a mathematician to work out that the plants that fill thirteen 30ft greenhouses are going to need a lot of compost. Especially when they have to be given a new and larger pot and more compost every few months.

We got through so much on the nursery that we mixed our own – much cheaper than ordering the plastic bags of John Innes compost available from 'horticultural sundriesmen' like Joseph Bentley of Barrow-on-Humber, from whom we got our fertilisers. And anyway, the stuff might have been stale. 'It goes off, you know,' was Ken's dictum. Neither could we have obtained it from a garden centre. In the early sixties garden centres had not yet arrived in the UK – small nurseries provided the locals with their plants. Only in the late sixties did these larger emporiums arrive, with the advent of container-grown trees and shrubs that could be planted at any time of year, as opposed to the nursery-grown plants that, until then, could only be dug up and transplanted when they were dormant, between November and March.

The John Innes composts, from a 1939 book by W.J.C. Lawrence and J. Newell, were a series of different formulae that would suit a much wider range of plants than in the past, when brick dust, crushed oyster shell, osmunda fibre, silver sand, charcoal and other such quirky additives were thought essential for the wellbeing of anything growing in a pot.

And so, aged fifteen, when others were learning by heart the words of 'Twist and Shout', 'Needles and Pins' and 'I Can't Get No Satisfaction', I was learning that the formula for John Innes Potting Compost No. 1 consisted of 7 parts by bulk partially sterilised loam, 3 parts by bulk granulated peat and 2 parts by bulk sharp sand, plus 4oz John Innes base fertiliser (2 parts by weight hoof and horn, one-eighth-of-an-inch grist; 2 parts by weight superphosphate of lime and 1 part by weight sulphate of potash) plus three quarters of an ounce of ground limestone or chalk per bushel. This was doubled for John Innes No.2 and trebled for John Innes No.3. The impressive (or sad) thing, though I have no way of proving it to you, is that I was able to write this down from memory without looking it up.

The loam arrived by the lorryload (though not from Kettering in Northamptonshire, which had, according to Lawrence and Newell, the perfect kind of loam. I can only assume that Kettering, and the appropriately named village of Titchmarsh just outside it, are now fresh out of loam.) This revered kind of soil had to be shovelled into an electric steriliser – a metal box about 4ft square situated under one of the corrugated iron lean-to sheds – where it was heated to a temperature of 180F for ten minutes before being emptied out and allowed to cool. There would be the odd night at home when, at eight o'clock, I would remember that I had left the steriliser on and would rush out of the house and cycle at full speed to the nursery to switch it off, emptying out the burnt earth that now smelled like cocoa.

The peat (at that time there were no thoughts of conserving it as a non-renewable resource, and anyway we lived on the moors where it was plentiful) came from Ireland in bales, held together not by polythene bags but by timber battens and taut wires. The sharp sand came by lorry and the John Innes base fertiliser and lime in paper sacks.

It would take Mickey and me half a day to mix a six-foot-high and eight-foot wide heap of John Innes, and to this day I have never seen a better mix of compost in any bag that I have bought. Formulaic it might be, but it still varies. When we ran out, usually after a couple of weeks, we'd mix some more.

All this manual labour needed fuelling. Dad's fortifying porridge would wear off after an hour or so, which meant that at around half past nine, when the driver had returned from distributing the men around town, I was grateful for the pork pies he handed round. These were not the sad, cold and damp, grey-gunge-filled apologies that pass for pork pies today, but freshly made, oven-warm raised pies with golden-brown crunchy pastry and pink, peppery pork made by Michael at Thirkell's the pork butchers on Railway Road. I could manage two of them as a mid-morning snack, drinking the liquefied jelly through the hole in the top, then crunching into the meat and pastry. At noon I'd be ready for lunch, sometimes nipping home on my bike for a poached egg or beans on toast, or else tucking into a sandwich and a KitKat washed down with a mug of sweet tea in the potting shed. At a quarter to five I'd head home for my tea – a hot main course followed by pudding – and Mum would usually knock up a sandwich or two for supper around ten. My waistline remained at 28 inches until I was twenty-six years old. The combination of youthful metabolism, manual work and regular cycling was probably responsible for my consistently wiry form, though I suppose I also owed some of it to my dad, who remained slight until the day he died.

You might think, from all this, that life on the nursery was an arduous sort of existence – slave labour, monotony and predictability in equal measure – not to mention a diet that fell something short of the now recommended five-a-day. But the funny thing is, although we worked our socks off, it was one of the most enjoyable times of my life, simply because the reason for our hard graft was the plants we were growing. Every one of the men I worked with over the years, tough and unsentimental souls though they might be, would, at some point, let the uncompromising mask that they wore slip and say, 'Now just look at them! Don't they look wonderful?' And that was why we did it.

The Men of the Soil

'How very odd.'

'Odd? Not at all,' said Mrs Charteris. 'Pinnegar was a gardener . . . just a gardener . . . and all gardeners are a little like that.'

Old Herbaceous, Reginald Arkell

There were around a dozen of them I suppose; all men, the majority of them over forty, some fast approaching retirement age. They mostly looked their years and had weather-beaten complexions from being out in all weathers. Only when it was really pelting down or the ground frozen solid did they stay in the nursery, and then we had to find jobs for them – pot-washing for those not acquainted with the finer points of propagation, or a bit of potting up for those who were more accomplished. Looking back I see what a mixed bag they were: Harry Hollings was the grand old man of the parks department, who had worked for War-Ag during the war, growing food rather than being sent to the front. He was a robust man with horn-rimmed glasses that sat on a hooked nose, white hair just visible under his flat cap, and a considerable 'corporation' out front. If ever Harry dropped something he would generally ask me to pick it up, it being easier for a young lad with a wiry framework to reach the ground than someone with Harry's years and waistline. One day his back went and he lurched perilously into the potting shed with a brown paper bag under his arm. I was alone at the bench, potting up some coleus plants. Harry motioned me to follow him into the tiny cubby hole next door where the telephone stood. I did as he asked and was surprised to discover him undoing his thick leather belt and dropping his trousers. He opened the paper bag and pulled out an aerosol which he thrust into my hand. 'Spray this on will you?' he asked. Pulling down a large pair of Y-fronts, he bent over and exposed the base of his spine as well as the tops of a pair of very large white buttocks. 'It's fair giving me some gyp.' I pressed the nozzle of the spray can and, in the interests of decency, looked the other way. 'On me back, not me bum!' he bellowed.

Like many of us, Harry would cycle to work, in his case on a large black machine whose pedals seemed to turn excessively slowly. I never saw Harry in anything except fourth gear on his Sturmey Archer, bending double to apply his not inconsiderable weight in the interests of forward motion. His children were grown up, with children of their own. By the time I arrived, Harry's wife was terminally ill and a resident of a care home up on the edge of the moor. He took her misfortune stoically and never spoke about it in anything other than matter-of-fact tones. It was accepted that she would die before long, but Harry visited her every evening without fail and without complaint, though some days he was quieter than others. Miles away.

Harry Brumfitt was the younger of the two Harrys in parks department employ. Sturdy and ruddy-cheeked with a high-domed head and a waistline that did not quite rival Old Harry's, he lived in Otley with two children and a wife who was a nurse. She was a small, pretty woman and Harry always referred to her as 'the golden voice'. Thirty years before the advent of the mobile phone, he would receive the occasional call from her on the big black telephone in the little cubby hole adjacent to the potting shed. 'Yes, dear. Yes, dear,' was all he ever seemed to say. Harry

B was slightly shy, would colour up occasionally when something embarrassed him, but we would have conversations from time to time when I seemed to be getting to know him better, only for him to end the conversation abruptly, if politely, and move off. There was something about him that raised him above the rest. He seemed quite bright and clearly had two equally bright children and an intelligent wife whom he adored. It was never spoken about in so many words, but I wondered why he did not have a job that required more of him. And I never did ask . . .

Dick Hudson was one of two drivers who ferried the men out to work in the massive dark blue Land Rover, equipped with a trailer for the lawnmowers, and who spent the rest of the day mowing the playing fields down by the river. Ancient as the hills, bandy-legged with a large flat cap underneath which sat a creased and squashed face that could rival W. H. Auden's for wrinkles, he chain-smoked Capstan Full Strength and had a cough that could rattle the windows of the mess room, the wooden shed in which he took his refreshment. Dick's working day was a source of fascination and disbelief to me. I was in at 7.45a.m Monday to Friday, along with Mickey and Ron. We allowed ourselves a five-minute teabreak mid morning and one hour for lunch – noon till 1p.m – and then worked solidly until a quarter to five, taking an afternoon mug of tea on the job. Dick would arrive around eight in the morning, take the men out to their jobs in the Land Rover and return to the nursery, where he would make himself a pint pot of caramel-coloured tea. Sitting in his old armchair, darker brown even than the tea, with horsehair stuffing bursting from every seam, he would smoke, drink and read the *Daily Mirror* for half an hour before evacuating his bowels loudly and extravagantly in the lavatory next to the potting shed. His morning ritual begun, he would mount his dirty red tractor and drive slowly down to the riverside with his gang mowers held aloft behind him, greeting any driver who hooted at him impatiently with a two-fingered salute, a Capstan held between those raised fingers. Once there he would cut the grass for an hour – leaving a wide margin around every tree to reduce the area he had to mow – before pulling up by the hedge and having his lunch. A little more mowing would follow his repast, before he returned to the nursery by 3.45p.m to hose off his gang mowers and retire to the mess room for more tea and fags until it was time to go home. On a winter's day the timetable was adjusted, since there would be little need for mowing, and as a result the fug in the mess room revived memories of Bradford pea-soupers for those members of staff old enough to remember them.

As astonishing as Dick's daily timetable was his ability to transform himself on weekend evenings from the boiler-suited tramp into a smart-suited elderly gentleman as he went for his refreshment at the Sailor in Addingham, the village outside Ilkley where he lived. I saw his wife only once, a large lady who had difficulty walking, thanks to what Dick referred to as flea-bitis.

Dick's way with words was wonderfully inventive and punctuated with expletives. My favourite was 'indifuckingstinguishable'. But each evening, when he arrived home from work, he would flop down in a chair and say to his wife, 'Tek me booits off lass; I've 'ad a grueller.'

Albert Croft was the quiet, diffident one. He was frequently teased by the others on account of his gentle disposition and his sensitive intestinal condition. He ate tablets a lot and frequently sported a white line around his lips, the residue of one or other of his preparations. He had a round, clean-shaven, cherubic face, always flushed pink, and when he took off his cap he revealed a head as smooth as a doorknob. Not shaven, just naturally hairless except for a thin semicircle of grey down around the back. Albert would occasionally let off his exasperation in my direction, me being the youngest, but always in the gentlest of ways. I never once heard him swear. Well, only once, but that was much later. Whenever I was a bit uppity with him he'd say, 'Look sunshine, I've been on the globe a bit longer than you have . . .' and there the matter usually rested, with me feeling that I'd overstepped the mark and upset him. He lived in a tiny whitewashed house at the back of The Grove, next door to the cinema. 'Fern Cottage' it said on a small plaque by the front door. This image of bucolic calm was tempered by the fact that the local prostitute lived next door. A fact to which Albert never alluded, but which did not escape the notice of the men he worked with. I had an image of him, sitting quietly reading *Amateur Gardening* in an armchair by his what-not with the aspidistra on the top, while her next door was at it into the wee small hours.

Francis Marjoram arrived late in life from a career I'm not sure where. A pipe smoker, he was rosy-cheeked, bespectacled and, like Dick Hudson, rather bandy. Perhaps they'd both ridden horses in their youth. He changed his name to Frank when he joined us, since he thought that the men might think Francis too affected. His son worked in the treasurer's department in the town hall, and brought us all our wages in a van on Friday afternoons. Frank need not have worried; he was not remotely affected and fitted in well. He had a wonderful belly laugh and I discovered when I revealed my own fondness for drama that he directed and appeared in plays for a drama group in Poole, near Otley. It was with Frank that I had the most rapport, and every now and again he and his wife would take me off in their car to see a production he had directed. *Pools Paradise* I remember – a farce that had something to do with a vicar winning the football pools – and he shared photos of himself in past productions, taking care to put them away when those of less refined sensibilities were around.

While Frank was short, bandy and thoughtful, and Dick was short, bandy and voluble, John Dale was tall, diffident and taciturn. A good 6ft 6in tall when erect, he seldom was, preferring to adopt the posture of a tortoise, stooping from the shoulders under the weight of his imagined shell. He had a large beak of a nose and a long, red face underneath the regulation flat cap. He wore a thick, stiff, black serge overcoat tied at the waist with thick twine, and his baggy grey trousers were fastened over his hobnailed boots with bicycle clips. This was so that they did not flap when he journeyed to and from work on the slender NSU Quickly moped that seemed in danger of falling over, so slowly did he travel. It added to his tortoiselike appearance that he moved slowly and deliberately even when he had dismounted his machine. His voice was low and rasping, and he spoke in measured lugubrious tones as though he were an undertaker addressing a bereaved client. Sometimes, when he leaned on his hoe and explained something to me, I would be convinced that any moment he was about to burst into tears. His eyes lit up only when he saw a pretty girl, and Mickey reckoned that when at home John loved nothing more than to watch the *Black and White Minstrel Show* on television, picking up his binoculars when the dancing girls came on in order to get a closer view. I don't know what his wife made of it.

There were other older men, some staying for a few months and then moving on to other jobs – like the fisherman who kept maggots in the back of his Hillman Imp, only to find when he returned from his day's work in the summer sun that his car was full of bluebottles. He got bored of working and went back to sitting on the riverbank and claiming the dole.

There was the Geordie know-all whose wife had a new child every year (he said he was a poor sleeper) and who baited Mickey by boasting that he could grout more bathroom tiles in an hour than ever Mickey could. (It escapes me why this was important.)

Then there was the twenty-year-old with the harelip, the son of a bank manager in the town, who came smartly dressed with Brilliantined hair, a bright yellow waistcoat, sports jacket, collar and tie, smoking a pipe. I think he had mistaken Ilkley for Cirencester. He was, Mickey and I discovered, unsure of the precise nature of the birds and the bees, and seemed to think, worryingly, that it had something to do with his dog licking his private parts. On his last day, while we were washing down the central greenhouse in my range, he jumped on to a plank set across the water tank in the middle of the floor. It snapped and he disappeared from view, to emerge like the creature from the deep a few seconds later, draped in green slime with his pipe still clamped firmly between his teeth and stains on his yellow waistcoat. Shortly afterwards his father found him an office job.

It was in such an environment and among such a rich mixture of assorted folk that I had my introduction to the real world. A world of geraniums and potting compost, Helen Shapiro and NSU Quicklys, talks about sex and drama, fags and booze, strange men and, occasionally, rather nice girls.

Hearts . . .

Where one goes wrong when looking for the ideal girl is in making one's selection before walking the full length of the counter.

Much Obliged, Jeeves, P.G. Wodehouse

Mickey was always very cagey about girls. He didn't give a lot away. When we were mixing potting compost or taking cuttings he'd let slip enough to let me know that he was playing the field – going to a dance at the King's Hall in Ilkley, or the Queen's Hall in Burley-in-Wharfedale and having a snog afterwards round the back. Maybe even a bit of a fumble. But he never said much. I wondered how successful he was. Was he keeping quiet because he felt sorry for me, or simply because nothing really happened? After a year or two he went completely silent on the subject and it wasn't long before he announced he was getting married. It seemed to me, from this experience, that when you met the right one you knew it straight away. I'd have been grateful to have met anyone.

There was the odd flirty dalliance at school – a kiss behind the curtains at a dance – but nothing serious. Not until Rosemary Pickering, the slender little redhead from Guiseley for whom I fell hook, line and everything else. I met her at a dance at the King's Hall and we held hands and kissed before she caught the bus home. She made my stomach feel funny – the first time it had been caused by something that hadn't been served up by Grandma. Our tune was 'Groovy Kind of Love'. It still makes me wistful.

To my father the encounter came as something of a relief. He made his complimentary remark from behind his newspaper one evening: 'That Rosemary . . . very nice.' Mum in the kitchen just muttered to herself something about redheads and wielded her tea towel with more than usual energy.

I suppose we 'went out' – if you can call the odd youth-club encounter and Scout-hut dance 'going out' – for about three months, maybe once a week, but in the end she dumped me – just after my sixteenth birthday party. Looking back I think *I'd* have dumped me after that party. It consisted of eight of us sitting round our front room in chairs having a chat, eating crisps, nuts and Twiglets and drinking Coca Cola. It was meant to be grown up. In reality it was deadly. I could see from the way she was sitting, opposite me, that Rosemary was wearing suspenders. It was of academic interest. She apologised for forgetting to bring me a present and said good-bye at the front door after doing her best to make polite conversation along with the other equally bewildered members of the youth club. I never saw her again. Well, not until seven years ago.

I'd written about this encounter in *Trowel and Error*. Not content with the energy one expends in the writing of a magnum opus, publishers also expect you to 'do a tour' – visiting bookshops up and down the country in the hope that keen fans will feel better disposed to buy a signed copy than one sitting unadorned and unattended among the works of greater authors.

I was somewhere in Leicestershire, sitting at a table in a bookshop with, thankfully, a long queue in front of me. I looked up and smiled every few seconds and asked the question one always asks: 'Who for?' (The answer is, invariably, 'me', and it is usually a further few seconds before the questioner can recall their own name, allowing you to pen the dedication with a personal touch.)

I handed up a signed book and then looked for the next person in the queue. In front of me stood a cuddly middle-aged lady in a long black suede mac. She smiled. I smiled back, and then the penny dropped.

'Rosemary,' I murmured.

'Hello,' she said.

'How are you?'

'I'm fine. I'm married now, with one son and one daughter.'

'Good heavens!' Not an original remark, or a very complimentary one, but the best I could manage under the circumstances.

We chatted for a few moments. 'Is it for you?' I asked. She nodded. I wrote something that I hope was meaningful, wondering if she would mind the fact that I had made reference to her in the book and revealed our short, innocent relationship to the wide world. I didn't have to wonder for long. As I handed her the book she smiled at me.

'I've read it already . . .' she said.

'Oh.' I stood up and kissed her gently on each cheek. She looked a little embarrassed, glanced away, then turned and walked slowly down the side of the queue. I watched her go. When she had walked about halfway down the line I saw her stop, then slowly turn and look back at me. She smiled. 'Thank you for page 93,' she said.

Joe Roe, who was in charge of the cemetery down on the banks of the River Wharfe, was always popping into the nursery on his old bike, to ask us to send down more wallflowers for the graves, or to moan about something or other. His general demeanour suited his job. His mouth always seemed to have rather more saliva than it could comfortably contain, so he dribbled and slavered rather a lot. I noticed that his black lace-up boots, unlike the leather ones worn by the rest of the men, were of rubber. Perhaps he needed the extra waterproofing.

He wasn't especially well disposed to me, for some reason. 'How's the council weedster?' he'd ask of me. I'd shrug. 'You know that's what they call you – all them others you left behind at school? Got a girl yet?' I'd always try to change the subject, but Joe would bait me until he once again mounted his bike and rode back to the cemetery to dig a hole for some other departed soul. 'The council weedster can't get a girl.' It wouldn't have hurt so much if it hadn't been true. Miserable old sod.

Mickey, to his credit, did his best to snap me out of it. 'Decoration this afternoon. Concert Club. You're coming.'

That perked me up. The floral decorations in the Town Hall, King's Hall and Winter Gardens were our only chance to get out. The Ilkley Concert Club was a rather upmarket organisation that organised monthly recitals using world-class artists. It was one of those rare occasions when the outside world came to Ilkley, putting it on the cultural map.

We loaded up the back of the Land Rover with peat-filled troughs, pots of primulas and celosias, ferns and pelargoniums, a few taller grevilleas for height and one or two spares of this and that, with the aim of making the front of the local stage look a little more like the Albert Hall but without obscuring the artist.

It was the middle of the afternoon. The concert was due to take place in the evening and the star of this particular performance was the clarinettist Janet Hilton. As Mickey and I entered the hall, one of us at each end of a heavy peat-filled trough, I could hear the soaring notes of the clarinet. The artist was rehearsing for the evening's performance. I glanced at Mickey. He pulled a face. Silently we walked up the steps at the side of the stage with the long black trough, and gently slid it into place.

We went out and brought in the other trough, sliding it on to the opposite side of the stage. The rehearsal was still underway. I don't think I had ever been in such close proximity to a world-class musician, and since my preference was for Handel and Schubert rather than Helen Shapiro I found myself quite carried away. Mickey, on the other hand, seemed rather taken with the soloist's legs. Her skirt, while not quite a mini, did show them off well.

We went back and forth the while, bringing in more plants, and when we had assembled our selection we began, on all fours, scooping holes in the peat and inserting them in what we considered to be a pleasing arrangement.

So it was that we both found ourselves at the feet of, and within a few feet of, the clarinettist as she finished one piece and prepared to begin another. I prayed that Mickey wouldn't say anything. That we would just carry on with our job silently while Janet Hilton ran through her pieces.

He glanced across at me with a glint in his eye and I knew that my wish was not to be granted.

Cocking his head in her direction, as if to make clear to me to whom the remark was directed, he said, 'There's someone here who's cleverer than you and me, Alan.'

Janet Hilton smiled indulgently. I could see she was embarrassed. But not nearly as embarrassed as me. Why did he have to use my name? Why couldn't he make his remark on his own account without having to rope me in? What did he mean, 'cleverer than us'? I wasn't stupid. I wasn't a concert performer but . . .

There was absolutely nothing I could say to redeem the situation. I could feel myself turning puce, and simply busied myself with making another hole in the peat for another pelargonium.

Janet Hilton began to play something by Weber, but she might as well have been playing Helen Shapiro's greatest hits for all I cared. After a few more minutes – the piece being mercifully too long to afford Mickey a second crack at a chat-up line – we slunk out of the hall with our spare plants and headed back to the nursery in the Land Rover. Mickey had about him the air of a man who had added to his list of conquests another name; I, on the other hand, looked like someone who was considering changing theirs.

. . . and Flowers

'Thank you for the flowers you sent,' she said
And sweetly smiled and coyly turned her head.
'I'm sorry for the things I said last night.
I was wrong and you were right.
Please forgive me.'
So I forgave her.
And as we wandered through the moonlit hours
I thought, 'What bloody flowers?'

Anon

The floral decorations were not only the high spot of the parks department nursery's life, they were the cause of its very existence. In these days of local government cuts, it is hard to imagine that there were once council employees whose job was solely to beautify the surroundings of the people of the town. Some time after I left, in the 1970s, they started raising bedding plants in a central nursery in Bradford, Ilkley having been swallowed up by Bradford Metropolitan District Council, but in my time there, between 1964 and 1968, the nursery on Little Lane grew all the plants needed for the town's beds and borders as well as the civic floral decorations. During the summer Mickey and I, Harry and Ron, with Ken occasionally coming to join us, would sit on stools around a huge square of sacking on the potting-shed floor, on which were piled hundreds of geranium cuttings that had been taken by Harry and the men from the flower beds around the town. Between July and September, the five of us would be responsible for preparing (slicing below a node and removing the lower leaves), inserting in four-inch clay flowerpots of cuttings compost topped with half an inch of sharp sand, and rooting – on the benches in the greenhouses – fifteen thousand individual pelargonium cuttings for the following year's display. By the end of the summer, each of us would have an aching back and a black groove down the centre of our thumb where the blade of the knife had run and the sap had stained our skin. Once rooted, the young plants were potted up individually in black polythene bag pots and, so tight were we for money even then, these bags would be retained after use, rinsed and used again. I can remember one winter's evening, emptying out faded plants from these pots on to the compost heap in the corner of the nursery, my fingers so numb with cold that the pain made me cry. And all in the interests of economy.

But the floral highlight of the year was the annual Civic Ball, when the King's Hall and the Winter Gardens were transformed with hundreds upon hundreds of pot-grown plants that had been raised especially for this one date in the calendar in early November.

November is chrysanthemum time, and we had two long greenhouses devoted to them. Now chrysanths are an acquired taste and are rather out of fashion at the moment, but for me they have a nostalgic appeal, quite simply because for four years my life was bound up with them. The aroma given off by their crushed leaves is redolent of autumn – a sour yet fruity tang that signifies the fading of the year.

We began by taking cuttings in February from the overwintered stools (an unfortunate name for the rootstocks of the plant, which were kept in deep wooden seed trays in a frost-free greenhouse). When these unpromising lumps of root and stump yielded small green shoots, these were taken as cuttings and rooted in a propagating frame. Ron, being the propagator, had charge of the 'propagating house', a long, low greenhouse with heated beds of sandy compost on top of the staging and – in the later days of my apprenticeship – a 'mist propagation unit' that sprayed the cuttings with a fine mist of water whenever they started to dry out. Research in America had shown this to be a more reliable way of inducing root formation in a variety of plants. From our point of view it just meant that you got a soaking if you mistimed your walk by.

Cuttings of 'Fred Shoesmith' and 'Town Talk', 'Leslie Tandy' and 'Balcombe Perfection' – varieties eventually producing large, tightly packed heads of incurved or shaggy reflexed petals – would be rooted and potted on into small containers before finally being moved on at the rate of three to a ten-inch clay flowerpot. In these final pots the John Innes No. 3 compost had to be rammed so hard around the plants' roots that a foot-long lump of broom handle was needed, fingers alone being unable to achieve the required effect.

Once the danger of frost was past, the plants, now in their final pots, would be stood outside on a firmed and levelled bed of ashes from the boiler, and equipped with bamboo canes that would be attached to overhead wires to prevent them from being blown over by unseasonal gusts of wind. Here they would sit for the summer, being tied in to the canes as they grew, watered almost every day and fed once a week with manure water (lumps of muck floating in it to block the nozzle of your can) or a proprietary lurid orange liquid called Solufeed. In September, when the weather became unstable, these four-feet high potfuls would be brought into a cool greenhouse to flower, the smaller side buds being removed so that the single central one would make a massive bloom perfectly timed for the Civic Ball in early November. And all because the councillors liked to waltz among the flowers. What an extravagance! And how proud we were of our achievements! What plants! What growing skills!

One greenhouse was filled exclusively with ferns, a humid corridor of *Nephrolepis exaltata* banked on either side. The plants themselves would be sprayed over daily, and so would the heating pipes beneath the staging, until clouds of steam obscured them from view. How they loved it! Verdant fountains of fronds cascaded over the front of the stone benchwork like some fantasy scene from *Lord of the Rings*.

Another house would boast hydrangeas – great domes of pink and white and electric blue – and yet another fibrous-rooted begonias, 'Mrs Clibran' and 'Optima', foot-high beauties with luscious pink and pale salmon flowers. Those were temperamental plants whose stems had to be tied individually to split green canes with thin strands of raffia so that they could be held upright. It was one of Ken's 'unwinding' jobs.

Keeping all these plants free of pests was a full-time job. All manner of noxious fluids and smokes would be brought into play. The chrysanthemum cuttings were dipped in a nicotine solution, hydrangeas were sprayed with a white oily preparation called Volck that made them shine and made it more difficult for insects to gain a foothold. Smoke bombs were let off in the greenhouses when an outbreak of red spider mite or whitefly was noticed, but for common or garden aphids – greenfly and blackfly – we would use nicotine shreds.

Like the other noxious preparations we used, these were generally purchased from Mr Moffatt's flower shop on The Grove. Not that he would let you take them away without suitable ceremony.

'Two tins of nicotine shreds and some BHC smokes please Mr Moffatt.'

He would peer at you over the top of his half-moon specs to see if you had the sort of demeanour to be entrusted with such a responsibility. Then he'd straighten his tie to emphasise his authority.

'Just a moment.' He would disappear into the back of the shop and you would hear the jangling of a large bunch of keys and the shooting of a bolt or two before he reappeared with two large tins and two boxes of fireworks.

He would ostentatiously count the goods – 'One, two, three, four' – then open a ledger similar in size and weight to the one kept by St Peter at the Pearly Gates and enter into it in his best copper plate: 'Two tins of nicotine shreds and two boxes of BHC canisters.' He would swivel the book round on the wooden counter and instruct: 'Sign here please,' before opening the door and seeing you off the premises with your deadly haul.

And deadly it was. Not just for the insects. Looking back I am astounded at how cavalier we were with those chemical preparations, in the days before health and safety took hold. Look up 'nicotine' in the dictionary and you will discover that it is 'a toxic colourless or yellowish oily liquid which . . . acts as a stimulant in small doses, but in larger amounts blocks the action of autonomic nerve and skeletal muscle cells'. It is, in common parlance, nasty stuff.

Picture us then, Mickey and I, deciding of an evening that the insect infestation in our greenhouses had got to the stage where it needed to be brought under control. We always fumigated, according to the instructions, in dull weather, not bright sunshine. As a result, it would be the last thing we did before we went home, so that the smoke could do its work overnight and we could open up the ventilators in the morning and allow in fresh air.

The technique with nicotine shreds, was to prise off the lid of the tin with a screwdriver, and then use the same implement to loosen the tightly packed shreds of grey paper inside it. These would have been impregnated at source with the nicotine.

A couple of piles of these shreds, about a foot across and six inches high, would be arranged on the path of the greenhouse – evenly spaced – and then set alight with a match. It was important that the shreds smouldered rather than blazed, so that the maximum amount of smoke was produced.

Having lit the two piles, we would beat a hasty retreat and then watch from outside the closed door of the greenhouse to make sure that they did not flare up. If they did, we would run back inside, with a handkerchief over nose and mouth, and gently stamp out the offending blaze until the heap smoked gently once more.

It was a literally eye-watering job, but we were conscientious about our work. It is down to good luck rather than judgement that to this day I'm able to walk without infirmity. I did not take much convincing to become an organic gardener.

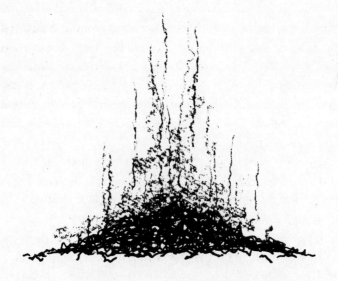

Our reward for all this came in the form of appreciative comments from those who attended the Civic Ball, which took two full days to dress with flowers. The entire balcony of the King's Hall would be filled with a bank of several hundred chrysanthemums, our two long greenhouses emptied for the occasion. The stage boxes down either side of the hall would billow with primulas, poor man's orchids and ferns, threatening to engulf the dancers below, and the stage would sport a waterfall of foliage and flowers that would not have disgraced the Winter Gardens at Scarborough.

At the end of our preparations, late on the Friday afternoon, we would leave behind this botanical cornucopia, having transformed an elegant but urban Edwardian assembly hall into a magical wonderland.

Old Harry would stagger out with the last box of raffia and split canes, dump it in the Land Rover and then return for one last look at our handiwork.

He'd nod to himself. 'Aye. Not bad. Not bad at all.' Then, satisfied that we had done our best, he would turn and leave the hall to those important enough to attend the Civic Ball in an official capacity – the surveyors and the treasurers, the lawyers and the town clerks. None of us ever got to go. Not while the band was playing anyway. We just went back in on Monday morning and took it all apart, when the sound of the music was no more than an echo, and the petals of the chrysanthemums littered the dance floor like confetti.

Rules and Regulations

The first rule of opera is the first rule of life, a very simple and possibly unexciting rule, for which I shall receive no thanks. That is, to see to everything yourself.

Melodies and Memories, Dame Nellie Melba

At least we were spared health and safety back in the 60s. We were expected to fall back on that old stalwart 'common sense', a facility much neglected in the twenty-first century. Nowadays all workmen must wear fluorescent jackets and all reversing lorries make that dreadful beeping sound that plays havoc with my tinnitus. The net result is that when everyone wears a fluorescent yellow jacket absolutely no one stands out, and when the beeping is continuous the lorry might just as well be playing 'Land of Hope and Glory'. Packets of peanuts must now bear a warning that tells the unwary that they are likely to contain nuts (which will come as a surprise to those who were expecting to find crisps), and it can only be a matter of time before signs are put up on our beaches warning all who approach the sea: 'Contains Salt' or 'Prolonged immersion may cause drowning.' Oh, you may think I exaggerate, but it cannot be far off; not when packets of sleeping tablets are already printed with the words 'May cause drowsiness.'

I wouldn't mind if it were really done in the interests of *our* safety, but we know it's not. It's simply so that we don't have a leg to stand on when it comes to suing those who are responsible. Not that I'm a natural litigant. Those adverts on Classic FM for firms of solicitors who claim they can get you a fortune if you fall off a pavement leave me frothing with despair. Have we really come to that? I cherish the sign put up in a maternity ward: 'The first ten minutes of life are the most critical.' Underneath which some sanguine soul had penned: 'The last ten are pretty tricky, too.'

Being a man of the soil and a child of nature, I have a much more straightforward solution to two of the world's problems – overpopulation and litigation. I suggest that no warnings are printed on anything, all fluorescent jackets are consigned to a furnace and lorries stop beeping tomorrow. That way, all those who are stupid enough to take a sleeping tablet before they drive, tuck into the cashews when they know they have a nut allergy and walk under a lorry without looking both ways will be bumped off quite quickly, thus usefully reducing the population and leaving behind only those who possess the commodity that I am bemoaning – common sense. Darwin called it natural selection.

Ken Wilson called it 'using your noddle'. I did just that. Most of the time. Except when I said that of course I knew how to disbud carnations (for fear of looking stupid). I methodically took off *all* the flower buds, not just the small outer ones to let the large, central one develop, which is the more usual course of action. The look on Ken's face when I proudly stated that I had done the job is etched in my memory. My actions set back one of our floral displays by a good three months. I didn't do it again.

There were other rules that I learned more quickly – like 'Do not use your thumbs when potting up plants'. How pathetic it seems now, but if I *did* use my thumbs to push the compost around the roots instead of my fingers, I would hear a tut-tutting in my ear and get a swift telling-off. Ken would also remind me that when he was in 'private service' the foreman would rap his knuckles with a bamboo cane if he caught him doing so – the reasoning behind this being that you can feel the pressure you are applying with your fingers much more sensitively than you can with your thumbs. His instructions stayed with me – I still can't bring myself to use my thumbs when potting up.

Neither can I leave doors open. It comes of working in greenhouses where heat cost money; a door left open in winter would send heating bills soaring and chill tender plants to the marrow. And so I shut doors, and drawers, and cupboards every time I pass them. It drives my family mad.

Ken's other rule was 'Every plant has a front and a back'; especially useful to know when 'staging up' – arranging plants on the greenhouse benches. Plants grow towards the light, as a result of which they tend to lean in one direction. A counsel of perfection is that you turn them regularly so that they develop evenly and in more rounded form, but no one has time to do that, unless they have finished stuffing their mushrooms, and so as long as the 'fair face' – the front – is presented to the viewer the plants look right. I cannot plant anything in my garden without 'facing it up'.

One thing I did notice, within a few weeks of starting work, was the difference between people who were comfortable with plants and those who were wary of them. There is a sort of instinctive ease about handling plants. Sometimes it may seem rough or heavy handed, but those who know plants know how robust they can be, and when their constitution is such that the gardener needs to be more careful. Those who are less certain seem almost ungainly in their actions – cack-handed, if you like.

Seedlings need treating with tenderness – the slightest squeeze of their fragile stems can kill them, which is why they are always held by the fat seed leaves or cotyledons when they are pricked out. That was another rule learned. But larger plants are surprisingly tough. Ken used to test the health of a mature cyclamen plant before it came into flower by turning the plant and the pot upside down and balancing the dome of foliage on the palm of his hand. It told him if the plant had enough but not too much water, and showed that it was in the peak of health.

It's funny how some folk don't really understand watering, imagining that if you keep tipping the stuff on a plant then it will be happy. Some are – azaleas and ferns prefer to be damp at all times – but most other plants need watering only when the compost in the pot begins to feel dry to the touch. That is the key – *feel* the compost with your fingers. If it feels dusty it is dry, and you should apply water thoroughly until it runs out of the bottom of the pot. If, on the other hand, it feels like a freshly wrung out flannel, then it is moist and the plant will be happy. If you can't see or feel the compost because of the covering of foliage, get used to weighing the plant in your hand and – like the good cook who can always guess the weight of the cake – you'll get to know whether it is wet or dry by how heavy or light it is.

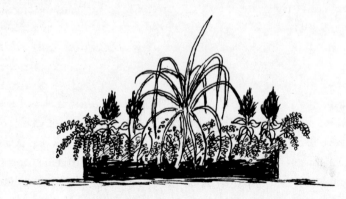

One plant in particular was regarded as the supreme test of cultivation skills when it came to watering – the cineraria. These annual pot plants with their soft green sycamore-shaped leaves are susceptible to both underwatering and overwatering.

Ken would take a fiendish delight in seeing if you could manage to grow a bench full of cinerarias. Forget to water them and they would wilt, although they'd quickly recover once visited with the watering can. But, if this wilting due to underwatering happened two or three times, then the plants might pick up again, but the edges of the leaves would start to show the tell-tale signs of browning due to drying out, and the flowers would be not nearly so spectacular.

If, on the other hand, you decided to avoid this situation and keep the plants watered well at all times, then there was a real and present danger that they would wilt due to overwatering. From this wilting they would never recover. Not ever. The answer was to have eyes like a hawk and to catch them just on the edge of wilting, watering them well and not returning until they just began to wilt once more. Result? Happy cinerarias and happy foreman.

There were other rules about watering. 'Never water when the sun is shining' was one that I had heard often at home. I offered this advice to Ken. 'So you'd leave your plants asking for water all day would you?' he asked. 'They'd be dead by evening'. Plants, I learned, need water when they are dry. It is best not to wet the foliage of hairy-leaved plants in sunny weather since they might scorch, but more harm is done by letting plants go thirsty than by watering them in bright sunshine. Watering morning and evening is better, which is what we always aimed to do on the nursery since evaporation is slower at those times and plants can consequently absorb more of it, but if a plant wilts due to dryness at the roots, cut your losses and give it a soak right there and then. It will be deeply grateful.

Some folks think all plants should be watered from below. Old Harry, on the nursery, had no time for this one. 'God waters from above doesn't he?' There was no satisfactory response. Only when plants do not permit the insertion of the spout of a can – cyclamen sometimes – or when their downy rosettes will not enjoy being saturated in water – as with African violets, or saintpaulias – need you fill a saucer with water and stand a plant in it. It will take up what it needs within half an hour and the rest can be tipped away. Few plants like to be left standing in water, though I do find that maidenhair ferns, whose fronds are excessively thin and susceptible to desiccation, are happy standing in an inch of water at all times.

Rainwater or tap? Rainwater – or cooled boiled water – if you can, but most plants can cope with tap water, unless they are lime-haters and you live in an area of hard water. Potted azaleas and rhododendrons prefer rainwater, but many other plants are too tough to care.

New gardeners can start with easy-to-grow plants and progress to the trickier kinds. Today the moth orchid – phalaenopsis – is sold in garden centres and DIY stores all over the country. It is happy in any reasonably-lit room, needs watering only once every two weeks and will keep its flowers for three or four months. Virtually indestructible, provided you don't try to kill it with kindness. Gardenias, on the other hand, are absolute stinkers – insisting on a degree of humidity and a diet of rainwater, they will drop their flower buds and turn their leaves yellow if you do anything that is not to their liking. Geraniums are, I think, much more forgiving. Or pelargoniums, as I learnt to call them.

Latin names are, for many aspiring gardeners, a nightmare. An impediment to the enjoyment of horticulture. To most of us a plant name is only of use when we want to tell someone else about it and make sure they know what we are on about. But that can give rise to confusion. Look up our native wild flowers in that wonderful book *The Englishman's Flora* by Geoffrey Grigson and you will discover that one man's lords and ladies (the common name for *Arum maculatum*) is another man's parson-in-the-pulpit. In Warwickshire they call it moll of the woods and in Wiltshire great dragon. Cross to the Isle of Wight and they'll talk about cocky baby, while in Devon they refer to it as cows and calves. It is pokers in Somerset and toad's meat in Cornwall. Confusing.

That's why we have these botanical names derived from Latin and Greek – a system devised by a Swede, Carl von Linne (Linnaeus) in the eighteenth century – so that gardeners and naturalists the world over could call a plant, or an animal for that matter, by the same name. It is a universal language, allowing, of course, for the vagaries of pronunciation. I went to the Bavarian Alps once and discovered that the plant I thought was *Saxifraga aizoides* was, to botanical-speaking Germans, *Sassifragga ite-so-ee-dez*. It took me ages to work out what they were on about. I hesitate to tell you how they pronounce the Latin name of the pine tree, *Pinus*.

In the days of my apprenticeship, armed with an increasing plant vocabulary from my City and Guilds course, I used to sit up late into the night, to the exasperation of my father, writing down these Latin names. The process was akin to writing lines as punishment. But it did help to din them into me and, having always loved words, it gave me an even richer form of language in which to indulge myself.

Some plant names have a delightful euphony: *Metasequoia glyptostroboides* and *Clematis viticella* 'Purpurea Plena Elegans' are two favourites. I love the swift and parasitic plangency of *Viscum album* (mistletoe) and the Greek scholar echoes of *Aesculus hippocastanum*, the horse chestnut.

I began to learn the descriptive qualities of these names. That the dahlia was named after Dr Dahl and so we should really say 'darlia', and that helianthus – sunflower – means quite literally 'sun-flower'. *Alba* means white and *nigra* black, *viridis* green and *rubra* red. Anything ending in '*ii*' is named after a man, and in '*ae*' a woman. The suffix '*ensis*' denotes a place. There are totally baffling epithets as well, with which to catch out friends who regard themselves as keen and well-informed gardeners. *Rhododendron ponticum* is a common plant, even a pest in many places. But ask for the meaning of its second name and you will invariably find the cognoscenti stumped. *Ponticum*? Simple – it means 'growing on the shores of the Black Sea.'

But there is a downside to plant names. It comes with age. There is a moment in life when they become more easily recalled than the names of people. It is a worrying time . . .

Under Cover Work

Who loves a garden loves a greenhouse too.
Unconscious of a less propitious clime,
There blooms exotic beauty, warm and snug,
While the winds whistle and the snows descend.

William Cowper

I can remember with crystal clarity the moment I discovered the particular brand of deep, saturating peacefulness that is to be found in a greenhouse. It is distinct from any other kind of enclosed tranquillity. It has not the cluttered dustiness of a garden shed, nor the lofty intimidation of a church or cathedral, though its peacefulness can rival both. It possesses a special kind of silence. It is a distinct form of sanctuary where plants grow, concentrating their efforts on thriving, and so it has a kind of latent energy, possessed by no other structure. Pevsner would have had a field day – not architecturally, but spiritually – had he turned his attention to palaces, and more modest structures, made of glass.

Not that my very first greenhouse was made of glass. That would have been way beyond my means. No, my first lean-to construction, made with boyish hands and fatherly timber (spare lumps of two-by-one left over from his work, and the framework of his and Mum's old double bed) was erected during a weekend in the early 1960s against the stone wall of the midden at the bottom of the garden. This soot-blackened and forbidding structure –

really no more than a flat-topped, stone-built shed used, at one time, to store rubbish, and for as long as I could remember out of bounds to my sister and me – had no use now other than to house old bikes that had been left to rot. It was a safe haven for spiders and beetles, unopened and unloved from one end of the year to the next. But its back wall abutted the garden and, facing east, it was bathed in the early-morning sunshine. I reasoned that if I used that as the small wall at the far end of the greenhouse I could build away from it in a westerly direction, alongside the privet hedge, and have a greenhouse that faced south, provided I could find something to use as the back 'wall', privet not being a particularly favoured material. I asked permission and, after a few questions as to the seriousness of my intentions, and earnest promises to 'mind the hydrangea' (we only had the one), I was given the go-ahead by my mother. Sir Joseph Paxton cannot have been more thrilled at the prospect of creating the Crystal Palace.

Over that weekend I hammered and banged (a screwdriver not being a part of my armoury – much too slow) until a relatively sturdy framework had appeared. Holes were dug in the ground to support four upright posts – left over from a rustic framework built at the top of the garden out of pity for 'Dorothy Perkins' – and the bedhead and footboard were fastened to the two rear posts to make the back wall in front of the privet. I was all set now – I had the framework in place and all I needed was something to cover it. For a rare moment in my life, maths came in useful. I calculated the amount of polythene I would need to cover the structure and took a trip to Hothersoll's in Leeds Road, where Mr Hothersoll, looking over the top of his glasses and with his tongue poking out of the corner of his mouth, the better to concentrate, cut off the required length with a large pair of scissors, rolled it up and handed it over in exchange for a few shillings. I cannot, even today, inhale the aroma of new polythene without being whisked back fifty years to that special weekend when I made my first greenhouse.

Back home I set to with drawing pins and covered the framework with the polythene. The door posed a bit of a problem. How to make it? I settled for a strip of polythene with a batten pinned along the bottom that could be rolled up to allow access and ventilation, and which could be held halfway up on a loop of string to allow a greater or lesser amount of air circulation. (It was this flimsy door that allowed in the neighbour's cat and so, a few weeks later, adjustments were made and I managed to acquire a timber frame which would make a proper hinged door.)

Cookie next door furnished me with rooted cuttings of busy lizzies (she nipped them off her plants and popped them in jam jars on her windowsill, where they rooted in a few weeks), plantlets from her spider plant (chlorophytum – one of my first Latin names), a false castor oil and several geraniums from plant stalls at the church bazaar. Orange boxes and a couple of floorboards formed the staging, and I fastened a couple of shelves against the end wall to hold more plants as my collection grew. Woolworths supplied a small plastic watering can and a packet of strong-smelling grey powder called Sangral which was, apparently, the last word in plant food.

But as any gardener will tell you, however large your greenhouse, you will always fill it. Mine was very small; it filled up very quickly. And it also filled my heart. You may remember, in *Citizen Kane*, the story of Rosebud. The great media baron, on his deathbed, having built a vast publishing empire and an enormous and luxurious mansion sitting in a grand estate called Xanadu, is heard to murmur 'Rosebud' as his life ebbs away. As the contents of his house are dispersed we see a small, painted sledge being thrown into the furnace. Upon it is painted the name 'Rosebud'. Citizen Kane was never happier than when he was a child, playing with that sledge – a time when life was true, and simple, and innocent –

and that first little greenhouse will remain my personal 'Rosebud', so much pleasure did it give me, and so many doors did it open onto a world that would become increasingly absorbing.

There, in my own domain, I would spend as much time as I was allowed – between chores and homework – tending to my plants and finding myself in a place that offered me more contentment than I had ever imagined possible. It was, in short, a revelation. An epiphany. A Damascene experience.

But polythene is not durable, and the time came when I needed more space for my plants and a more permanent structure in which to grow them. I had started work now, and the enjoyment of looking after larger, proper greenhouses made of glass had turned my head. Mum and Dad gave the nod to a fully-fledged greenhouse at the top of the garden. If I could find one that I could afford.

I asked around at work. Albert's eyes lit up. 'I've got one on the allotment,' he said. 'I'm looking to sell it.'

'What's it like?' I asked, doing my best not to sound too excited, lest the price should escalate.

'It's sectional,' offered Albert.

I misheard him. Albert had sinus trouble (another of his tablets) and his speech was not always the clearest. I thought he'd said 'It's a Sexton,' – a proprietary brand of greenhouse I assumed. If it was a Sexton, I reasoned, it must be a proper greenhouse. A good one.

I went home and told Dad. 'We'd better go and have a look at it,' he said.

Albert had told me the precise location of his allotment on the banks of the river. Dad and I took the ten-minute walk and located it. The greenhouse was situated at one end, and it was clearly not of any brand known to man. It was constructed, both the sides and the flat roof, from old window frames. They were of different sizes and different colours, and some opened on hinges and some on sashes, which did give the structure a kind of rustic charm. But no one could have called it pretty. Or attractive, even. It suited Albert and his allotment, but I could not see Mum agreeing to let Albert's edifice – sectional or not – be erected at the top of her garden.

Dad didn't say much. He didn't need to. I knew it was a non-starter and we walked home again, disconsolate.

I didn't mention it again at work for a while, except to tell Albert that his greenhouse was not quite what I was looking for. He seemed disappointed. Crestfallen in fact. And I had that terrible feeling that I still get when I am aware I have let somebody down. Disappointed them. For two pins I would have bought the greenhouse from him just to see him happy, but the five pounds he was asking was my entire budget. I felt a bit of a heel.

A few weeks later, Old Harry was working with me in the potting shed on the nursery taking geranium cuttings. 'You still looking for a greenhouse?' he asked.

'Yes.'

'You went to look at Albert's?'

'Yes.'

'Mmm. Not up to much?'

'Not really,' I muttered, guiltily.

'I might be getting rid of mine if you're still interested.'

'Oh. But I thought . . .' Harry was a keen gardener even in his spare time. He had won prizes at the local flower shows and liked nothing more than pottering in his greenhouse down Wyvil Crescent of an evening and at the weekend.

'With the missus in Arden Lea I'm going to have to move and I won't be able to take it with me.'

Arden Lea, once a large private house up Parish Ghyll Drive, was the local hospice, whose light and airy rooms looked out over Ilkley Moor. I was unsure what to say. 'I'm sorry,' was all I could manage.

My inept, brief condolences were brushed aside. In spite of the fact that Harry knew his wife was not long for this world, and that he would have to find a flat or a bungalow where he could live alone, he was not into self-pity, and that his beloved greenhouse could go to someone who would get as much pleasure out of it as he did seemed to be his main concern.

'I'll have to ask the wife. I'm going up tonight. I'll see what she says.' There the conversation ended, and Harry walked through from the potting shed into the greenhouse with another tray full of potted cuttings. I carried on, my head stuffed with a mixture of emotions – sympathy for Harry and his impending loss, and an anticipation of, at last, having my own proper place to grow things.

Harry's wife gave the go-ahead the following day and Dad and I went to look at the greenhouse. We discovered that it looked just like a greenhouse *should* look – painted dark green with a pointed roof and ventilators, and a proper door at one end. 'Better than Albert's?' asked Harry. My dad nodded and I handed over the five-pound note.

'You'll have to collect it, mind,' warned Harry.

'That's alright,' said Dad. 'I've got transport.'

I did wonder how it would fit in the Austin van, even when it came apart into sections. But I discovered that weekend that it was not the van that Dad had been referring to when he said that he had transport. It was a handcart.

Wyvil Crescent was about a mile from Nelson Road. At the age of sixteen I had reached something of a sensitive stage in my adolescence. It was difficult enough to keep my head held high when watering the hanging baskets that hung from the lamp posts in front of the smart shops along The Grove as my erstwhile fellow pupils, on their way to school, remarked 'Like the pinny!' But to have them accost me, on their way to football matches that Saturday morning, or going into town to hang out in the coffee bar, or Allen and Walker's hi-fi shop at the bottom of Cowpasture Road to listen to the latest offering from Dusty Springfield, was more than flesh and blood could stand. On that fateful Saturday, which should have been one of the happiest of my young life, we had to make that one-mile journey along one of Ilkley's busiest thoroughfares with the handcart and its iron-rimmed wheels rattling along the Tarmac. We pushed it, Dad and me, three times there and three times back. By the end of

the morning I was oblivious to any rude remarks hurled from the top deck of a scarlet West Yorkshire bus or sideswiped from a bicycle – the depths of embarrassment had been plumbed and I awaited the onset of death by shame.

But that afternoon I forgot about the journey from hell and set about admiring the best five pounds I have ever spent in my life. Not only had I acquired a greenhouse, but also all the paraphernalia that went with it. There were watering cans and syringes for spraying foliage or noxious chemicals. There were specially crafted aluminium dibbers and sieves of all sizes. There were one or two complicated-looking implements whose uses I had yet to divine, thermometers to show soil and air temperatures, and a propagating case with soil-warming cables and a real glass lid. An Aladdin paraffin heater would provide winter warmth (and a certain degree of heartache, I would later discover, in trying to regulate its performance), and a brand new automatic ventilating arm would open the top window if I was away at work and the temperature rose too high.

Having caused me the greatest amount of embarrassment in living memory, Dad redeemed himself over the next couple of weeks by replacing the rotten timber beam at the foot of one end of the greenhouse, and by building the brick foundations on which it would sit. Within the month it was freshly painted in sparkling green livery, and up and running. I was sixteen, learning about gardening faster than a cat learns to climb, and master of my own destiny. Well, I had my own greenhouse, anyway. A proper one, with real glass in the windows and real ventilators that opened on hinges. And I bet Citizen Kane never had one of those.

The Education of a Gardener

> What wondrous life is this I lead!
> Ripe apples drop about my head;
> The luscious clusters of the vine
> Upon my mouth do crush their wine;
> The nectarine and curious peach
> Into my hands themselves do reach;
> Stumbling on melons as I pass,
> Insnared with flowers, I fall on grass.
> 'The Garden', Andrew Marvell

They told me what I should do. Well, Ken did. 'You'll go to day release now – for your City and Guilds – and then to college for a year full time. Askham Bryan probably; near York. Then to Kew, Wisley or Edinburgh Botanic Garden – they do a three-year diploma course. And then on to The Grotto . . .'

'The what?' I asked. It sounded like something Father Christmas sat in.

'The Grotto. It's the headquarters of the Institute of Park and Recreation Administration. Near Reading. Down south. Then you can become a Parks Superintendent, like Mr Mutlow.' There was a twinkle in his eye.

I can't say that I was enamoured of the sound of the Institute of Park and Recreation Administration. It sounds to me now something on a par with the Ministry of Circumlocution in *Little*

Dorrit. I hadn't read *Little Dorrit* back then or I might have been more worried. As it was, I accepted the proffered career structure with gratitude tinged with apprehension.

The whole thing came as a surprise to my dad when I went home and related this ten-year plan, for that's what it would mean – a five-year apprenticeship, a year at college, three at Kew, Wisley or Edinburgh and a final year at the odd-sounding 'Grotto'. You could become a practising brain surgeon in less time.

'Oh, I see' was all Dad could manage by way of an opinion, having thought that 'a trade' was the best recommendation he could offer his son, his father and grandfather having gardened with only muscle power and determination to their name. Mum murmured, 'We'll see', and it was left at that. It was not the cost that she was worried about – a county council grant would see to that – it was probably my staying power.

But before any of those aspirations could be made reality, the most immediate was my enrolment at the Shipley Art and Technical Institute near Bradford to study for my City and Guilds Stage 1 in Horticulture. It was all a bit scary. But at least I would be learning about plants, which I was keen to do, rather than French verbs, which I wasn't.

I had never been to Shipley. Or Bradford. I'd been to Leeds, on shopping trips every couple of months with Mum, and now that I had left school I could even go on my own, should the fancy take me, to shop for clothes, which I only occasionally had to take back and change when Mum didn't think they were suitable.

Mum's view of Bradford was on a par with her view of ITV – it was a bit common. Shipley was just outside Bradford. My only knowledge of the place was its name on the front of the bus, so at least I knew how to get there and which stop to queue at in Brook Street.

Leeds is sixteen miles from Ilkley and we always went there by train. The list of stations on the way has been a litany since my childhood – Ilkley, Ben Rhydding, Burley-in-Wharfedale, Menston, Guiseley, Newlay and Horsforth, Calverly and Rodley, Kirkstall, Leeds City. I remember them by heart, still. But I had never been as far by bus – it was all of twelve miles to Shipley, or at least that's what I calculated from the little red guidebook on my bookshelf, written by M.J.B. Baddeley in 1893 (we never threw anything useful away).

I looked up Shipley and discovered that it was 'a manufacturing town of 16,000 inhabitants, picturesquely placed at the junction of the Bradford Beck and the Aire. Pursuing the valley of the former through a region teeming with mills and works we reach in 4 miles Bradford.' I assumed that in the intervening 70 years the population would have grown, but from what I had heard the 'mills and works' were still in existence.

Saltaire, just outside the town, where my place of impending education was situated, was, said Mr Baddeley, 'erected in 1853 by Sir Titus Salt (d. 1876), the first man to manufacture Alpaca woollen fabrics in England. The station is close to the mills, and equally near is the church, built in the Byzantine style.'

I saw neither, only the Art and Technical Institute which was, rather fittingly, run in the Byzantine style by a little man called Taylor whom we rudely referred to as 'Hitler' though, to be honest, his deputy Mr Hilton had the moustache. Mr Taylor was clean-shaven with receding black hair that was slicked back with Brylcreem. He was not very tall and always wore a pale grey suit, wire-rimmed glasses and a self-satisfied smile, as though he knew something you didn't.

Fortunately we students had little to do with him, meeting him only on our day of enrolment, and subsequently only ever seeing him through the plate glass window of the reception area just inside the great oak doors of the Victorian building where he addressed his secretaries surrounded by great wall charts. He looked like a pocket-sized general planning a campaign.

Our lectures took place either in lofty gloss-painted classrooms, like those I had left behind at junior school, or in the windowless basement of the building where dusty machinery which we never saw in use hogged most of the floor. There were cutaway diesel engines and disembowelled motors that bore no relation to horticulture, but then we shared facilities with a variety of engineering and secretarial subjects, and only in the third year of my course was the patch of waste ground at the rear, which overlooked Salt's Mill, turned into a garden of sorts – a series of strangely numbered sterile plots, presided over by the mysterious Mr Monkman, apparently a clone of the principal of the college, except that he wore a dark-blue apron over his suit and smoked a pipe. Quite what he did, except direct us with a spade to a particular patch of soil, I never managed to ascertain in the four years that I was there. Anyway, these little plots, with their occasional shrubs and desultory rows of crops doing their best to grow up through the bracing Bradford air, at least allowed us to get our hands dirty. That, though, was what we did at work on the other four days of the week; here at the Institute we were introduced to a world of lectures on everything from 'Decorative Horticulture' to 'Soils and Manures', 'Calculations', 'Fruit and Vegetable Growing' and the rudiments of plant growth, with *Lowson's Textbook of Botany* at our elbow.

The students – all male – were a mixed bag, drawn mostly from local authorities in the Bradford area. While intellectual pursuits might not have been high on their agenda they were, for the most part, a pleasant bunch, their broad Yorkshire accents echoing around the cavernous classrooms like booming bass drums.

We'd turn up at nine in the morning for lectures, break for coffee around 10.30a.m and then be allowed an hour for lunch at

12.30, which gave us just enough time – the three or four of us who thought we were more sophisticated than the rest – to nip down the road to the centre of Shipley so that we could patronise the Lai-Seng Chinese restaurant, situated on the first floor of the small and newly built shopping centre. A Chinese restaurant! At fifteen! They did a three-course meal for half a crown (twelve-and-a-half pence) and the first course, without fail, was the best chicken soup I had ever tasted. We hadn't heard of monosodium glutamate back then. Stuffed to the brim with spring rolls and special fried rice (the scrambled egg surprised me) we staggered back and tried not to fall asleep in the afternoon lectures and demonstrations.

In coffee and tea breaks the conversations turned to all manner of things unrelated to horticulture, if not to propagation. Keith, from a park somewhere in the depths of Bradford, sidled up to a couple of us one day and asked if we'd ever seen people 'at it'.

'What do you mean, "at it"?' I asked.

'You know. Screwing . . .'

'No! 'Course I haven't'.

I think he knew from the nervous smile that I was telling the truth. Looking around furtively, he pulled a small, grubby envelope from his inside pocket. 'Look at these,' he said, laying down a series of small black-and-white photographs on the desk in front of me. There were just eight of them – these were the days of the Brownie 127, long before the world had gone digital. The photos showed a man and a woman 'at it' in various positions on a three-piece suite. It was clearly an amateur job. I wondered if the people whose front room it was knew just what had happened on their uncut moquette. And on the hearth rug in front of the settee.

'Good, aren't they?' asked Keith.

I wasn't sure whether he meant the standard of photography or the technique of the couple involved. The best I could manage was 'Goodness!', which seemed a rather tame response to my first glimpse of what I suppose was pornography. I used to deliver *Parade* to an old man on my paper round, and one of my posher friends up The Grove had copies of *Playboy* lying around – for the articles, he said; so well written – but all these two magazines contained was pictures of nudes in various provocative poses. I had never seen people 'at it' before. It was strangely clinical, though undeniably stirring – he lying this way and she that. I did think that some of the positions must have been uncomfortable and a bit risky. But they were definitely 'at it'. It did make concentration difficult for the next hour during 'Soils and Manures'.

This was not the only kind of daring that day release introduced me to. While not quite of the winklepicker and drainpipe-trouser generation of ten years previously, I like to think that my dress sense developed in those first years at work, if not always for the better or with parental approval. The second-hand army combat jacket that I bought in Otley with my first week's wages was hastily returned and swapped for a couple of serviceable shirts. My mother and I would laugh about this later in life, though at the time the mortification I suffered on the top deck of the bus as we journeyed back there to exchange them felt as though it would scar me for life.

I did, though, manage to get away with buying hipster trousers, at Greenwood's in Ilkley. It was the only gentleman's outfitters in the town in the early 1960s that sold anything remotely trendy, apart from Addy's, the shop on the corner opposite the church, which was always regarded by my mother as a bit seedy.

You will have gathered by now that I was, up until the age of sixteen or so, somewhat under the thumb of my mum. Our relationship never descended into that of Ronnie Corbett and his mother in *Sorry!* – the TV series where at forty-something he was still at home and tied to the apron strings – but to her credit, my mum did admit that my moving away from home at the age of nineteen was probably the best thing I did. 'I'd have smothered you,' she confessed. Well, I was never smothered . . . but always aware of her opinions . . . and struggling manfully to formulate some of my own.

The hipster trousers, though, were a revelation in green tweed. Finished off with a wide brown leather belt, a pair of Hush Puppy Chelsea boots and a purple polo-necked jumper, I looked the bee's knees. I thought. The floppy fringe completed the picture. The only thing I lacked was transport. I had my bike, but longer journeys meant travelling by bus or train.

My bus journey to Shipley was a dull affair and it took the best part of an hour to cover the twelve miles up hill and down dale. Other lads had mopeds, and I envied quite desperately Dave Hollingsworth's Honda 50 with its scarlet and cream coachwork. But Chris Rigden had a proper motorbike, all chrome and throbbing saddle. I know it throbbed because he used to give me a lift as far as the bus station in Shipley, with the aim of making my journey home a little shorter. Each time I got on the back (without a crash helmet since they were not then compulsory) and wrapped my arms around his waist before he roared off down the road, I was convinced that I was about to die. I pacified myself that if I did there would at least be a certain James Dean quality to my end.

Looking back I can see quite clearly that Chris Rigden was no Steve McQueen when it came to either speed or style – his voluminous oilskins saw to that – and that in spite of my apprehensiveness I was as safe as houses.

I never did get any motorised transport, in spite of the fact that I passed my driving test first time at the age of seventeen. I was quite desperate for something better than a bike, but as my father never tired of saying, 'It's not buying a car that costs money, it's keeping it on the road.'

I did try. I spotted a 1920-something Austin Chummy in yellow and black parked down a drive on Skipton Road with a £25 price tag on the windscreen, but by the time I'd persuaded Dad to come and look at it it had gone. Then there was Ken's bible-black Ford Anglia, the old 1950s kind with the windscreen wipers that went more slowly when the car climbed a steep hill. He wanted £70 but that would have cleared my bank balance. It was clearly not to be. But you can't pull a bird on a bike, and so, instead, I persuaded Dad to let me borrow his car now and then – a lumpy old Borgward with a column gear change whose row of unmarked buttons on the dashboard I had furnished with Letraset to remind me what they all did. At least I learned to double de-clutch on it, even if its back seat was the venue for little more than a chaste peck with a very occasional girlfriend. Nothing at all worth snapping with a Brownie 127.

A Season for Everything

Therefore all seasons shall be sweet to thee.
'Frost at Midnight', Samuel Taylor Coleridge

Of all the vocations – and it is a vocation, not a job – that of gardener makes a man more aware of the seasons than any other. We have, as a race, lost the joys of what a monastic friend of mine calls 'the postponement of gratification', and while I prefer to enjoy more of the earthly pleasures than he does, I also take a deal of pleasure in anticipation.

We can eat strawberries in December now, if we want, but having been picked before they were ripe and travelled from the Far East, their flavour cannot compete with a fresh and sun-ripened berry picked from the garden in June. I want parsnips and swedes in winter, not asparagus, which belongs to April. I look forward to the first raspberries, in spite of the fact that as a fruit they freeze well and I can, if I wish, enjoy them all the year round.

Seasonality brings variety to our diet and allows us to look forward to a fresh crop of something new. It's good for the soul, I reckon, to have a little bit of Lent in every month of the year. To have anything and everything on demand might seem like an advantage, but that ready convenience has unfortunate side effects – predictability of diet, the taking for granted of the natural cycle of things, the bypassing of the seasons.

Gardeners know the seasons of the year not just for the crops they produce, but also for the effect they have on our daily work. Bitter days of winter mean more layers of clothing and frozen fingers – so cold that when run under a hot tap to thaw out they cause us such agony that we cry out in pain. It is better to let them warm up slowly than risk the gardener's version of 'the bends'.

On the nursery, when outside work had to be carried out in winter – the cleaning of greenhouse glass, for instance, or the repairing of broken panes – we would wrap ourselves up in as many layers as we could. The top one was always a tatty old gabardine overcoat, once fawn, now spattered with assorted colours of paint. It was one of several that hung behind the door of the potting shed and whose once-trim tails had so often been caught on nails and torn into shreds that Mickey and I, astride the greenhouse ridge on a windy day, looked like two distressed moths, our wings flapping in the breeze as we tried to keep our balance.

When digging in winter with the smooth-bladed spades from the toolshed (there was rivalry for the best one, worn to a shining heart shape by years of use), we would gradually shed the layers until, on even a chill February day, we were warm as toast in just shirt sleeves, digging the lumpen aromatic manure from the local stables into every spit with the eagerness and competitive spirit of youth, and wiping the sweat from our brows with our forearms as we stretched upright every few minutes to look at the rolling main of freshly cultivated earth that we left in our wake. Old Harry would look on and shake his head at our foolhardy speed, knowing that by the end of the day our backs would be finished and our spirits broken. But by the following morning, having soaked our weary bodies in a bath of Radox and fully rested, neither of us would admit to anything other than feeling at the peak of physical fitness.

What Mickey had in muscle power, I could only match in wiriness, but in the space of that first year on the nursery I grew to 5ft 9in under glass, and developed a series of upper back and shoulder muscles that are still as hard as iron.

Spring would bring a rash of weed growth to nursery paths and the beds of soil where wallflowers were sown and shrubs grown on. The once-bare earth would come to life in a haze of lime-green chickweed and yellow-dotted groundsel, and the race for survival would begin between cultivated plants and interlopers. The spade was back on its rusty nail now, and the argument would be over the favourite Dutch hoe. Only a novice went for the newest tools in the shed – old hands know that an implement broken in by years of hard labour has a handle as smooth as silk and a blade that can cut through earth like butter.

Working backwards through the rows, we would slice off the annual weeds where their stems met their roots, with the words of Lennie Best, our 'Fruit and Vegetable' lecturer at the Institute, ringing in our ears – 'Don't push it in too deep lad – skim it across the surface. You're cuttin' 'em off not diggin' em up!'

The weeds, severed in their prime, would be left on the surface to shrivel up in the sun, if we had timed it properly. If we hadn't and a shower of rain followed, we'd be back out there a few days later skimming off the ones that had re-rooted.

Repetition is always assumed to be boring, and often it is. But some jobs, by the very nature of the fact that they need to be undertaken repeatedly, give you a chance to enjoy the fruits of your labours time after time. I love creating stripes on the lawn with a mower. If, after I had cut it, the grass remained trim and never grew again, I would be deprived of the satisfaction that creating such a result gives me. The same goes for clipping hedges or edging lawns. To some these may seem moronic tasks that involve not an ounce of intellect. Skill, yes, but intellect, no. And yet they give a man time to think, time to let his mind wander, and then, when the job is completed, the deep satisfaction of a job well done. The mundanity of the task disguises its deeper pleasures.

Spring is, for any gardener, a new beginning; a chance to wipe the slate clean. 'This year will be better than last,' says the gardener, while the farmer always assumes it will be worse. Gardeners are, to a man and woman, born optimists – good gardeners, anyway.

On the nursery, spring meant seed-sowing in tray after tray of seed compost. I won't bore you with the formula, but Mickey and I had to mix that, too. Begonias would be the first seeds to benefit from our mixture – dust-fine seeds, fox-brown and glossy, worth more, ounce for ounce, than gold, said Ron. So fine and small, they are, that they need to be sown on the surface of the compost in January to give them time to grow before being bedded out in early June. Ron tries not to sneeze when he is tapping them from the palm of his hand, allowing them to bounce over the flattened surface of John Innes seed compost and spread themselves out. So delicate are they that there is no need to cover them, except with a sheet of glass and then a single sheet of newspaper to prevent the sun from burning them up.

From now on, Ron's job, first thing every morning, involves going into the humid and sequestered confines of his long, low, white-painted propagation house and seeing which seedlings have emerged, and then the glass and paper are removed from the trays and the young plants given as much light as possible, the weak rays of winter sun strengthening daily as we head towards spring.

After these *Semperflorens* begonias come the antirrhinums, the French and African marigolds, the lobelia and alyssum, the tobacco plants and the petunias, giving us week after week of pricking out seedlings into wooden trays – six in one direction, seven in the other – forty-two plants to a tray. The trays come by the dozen from the local greengrocer. Once they held tomatoes – they have 'Holland' on the sides in bright red letters – but now they hold serried ranks of embryo plants, which, when they grow up, will decorate the town with their jolly summer flowers.

The empty staging in some of our thirteen greenhouses is filled with hundreds of trays now, each sporting a rash of eager young seedlings. But some are not so eager to grow, and keel over at compost level. Fungus disease. Damping off. We prise the lid off a tin of Cheshunt Compound, a lavender-grey powder that smells strongly of ammonia – one whiff is as effective at bringing you round after a night on the tiles as a bottle of smelling salts. It is mixed with water – a teaspoonful to a one-gallon can – and the pale purple brew used to dowse the affected trays. I am never convinced that it works; it's rather like locking the stable door after the horse has bolted.

In between the pricking out of seedlings we are potting up literally thousands of rooted pelargonium cuttings. They, too, will be bedded out around the town come summer, and our greenhouses are now bursting with plants, not only on the staging, but also slung from shelves arranged on brackets above our heads on either side of the path, and in trays along the floor, too, so that to walk the length of a thirty-foot long greenhouse we need all the agility, if not the grace, of a ballet dancer. Each and every one of these pots and trays must be checked for water, morning and evening, along with the chrysanthemums and ferns, the hydrangeas and larger potted pelargoniums that we grow for floral decorations. It is an endless round of ministering to our charges, of spinning plates on sticks and making sure that none of them falls off.

With the lengthening days comes an even greater pressure on our time and a greater likelihood of plants drying out. The sun's rays are hot now, even in Yorkshire, and Mickey and I are stripped to the waist on the sunniest days, competing to see who will have the best tan by the end of summer. Mickey always wins – thicker skin, I tell him.

Our greenhouses must be shaded to prevent the plants from being scorched, especially sun-sensitive species like ferns and hydrangeas, where one day of brilliant sunshine can dry their foliage to a crisp and ruin a whole year's work. We have no blinds and no sophisticated forms of ventilation. The roof vents are on simple metal stays and we must judge how wide to open them, depending on the degree of cloud cover and the strength of the wind. On really warm days the door at the end of each greenhouse will be wedged open, too, except for the fernery, which is kept, always, as humid as a Turkish bath, its doors closed and just the merest crack of air allowed to creep through its ventilators.

'Go and put some air on,' was a frequent instruction in summer. That and damping down the floors of our greenhouses with water at two-hourly intervals was our only way of lowering the temperature, apart from shading them with a pale green version of whitewash by the name of Summer Cloud. It came in a green tin with an antiquated design, showing a man painting out the sun in a summer sky. Mickey and I would mix a bucketful apiece, whisking the green powder into water, and, armed with that and a long-handled brush, set about painting the glass of our greenhouses with a thin layer of 'green-wash' each April. From then on we could not see out of our greenhouses, and neither could others see in, until, in September, we had the deadly job of cleaning the stuff off with a scrubbing brush and a sharp jet of water. But that was a long way off yet.

Whenever the weather was warm and sunny and we had a lot of potting up to do. Mickey and I would carry a portable wooden potting bench outdoors, position it so we had our backs to the sun, and then load it up with compost and pots, continuing with the tanning competition as we worked. After long, sunny days, we would both of us admit to not being able to sleep on our backs that night, and the following day, chastened to some degree by our stupidity, we would continue our work in the shady confines of the potting shed, letting out, from time to time, muted groans as our rough work shirts abraded our stinging skin.

The pressure was relieved a little when the men had taken away our trays of bedding plants – trailers full of them distributed round the town's flower beds and bedded out in a manic four-week period at the end of May and on into June. Now we would have to clean out our greenhouses and ready them for the pelargonium cuttings. This was the least popular job of the year – scrubbing the white-painted glazing bars with a disinfectant mixture that ran down your arms, then your body, finally and inevitably making its way into your underwear and down your legs. It mattered not what you wore, the evil-smelling brew had the exploratory capabilities of Scott of the Antarctic and the slipperiness of Harry Houdini.

The shingle on the benches would be scooped up into sieves and rinsed with a hosepipe and the central path of each greenhouse scrubbed free of green algae with a stiff, long-handled broom – a job that was undertaken every Friday throughout the year, along with liquid feeding in spring and summer.

From July to September the geranium cuttings would be brought in by Old Harry and Young Harry, having been cut from the plants now growing happily in the town's flower beds and bundled into great sheets of hessian. The two Harrys would carry them over their shoulders like a pair of Father Christmases. By the end of the summer, we'd need to have taken fifteen thousand of them to ensure that next year's display was every bit as good as this year's. Some we rooted in trays, others at the rate of five to a four-and-a-half inch clay flower pot, but always the compost was topped with half an inch of sharp river sand to help guard against rotting off.

The men, now, were working without their jackets in rolled-up shirt sleeves and bib-and-brace overalls, though the flat tweed cap would seldom be laid aside. Wearily they would return at the end of the day, and even John Dale would have shed his thick, carpet-like overcoat, though he would take the precaution of putting it back on for the moped journey home, however intense the heatwave, perspiration dripping from his beak-like nose as he wobbled down the road on the overheated NSU Quickly in anticipation of an evening with the Television Toppers.

Autumn meant chrysanthemums. They would come indoors from their summer sojourn on the ash bed and need staking, tying and disbudding as well as regular watering and weekly feeding with the stinking manure-water. The newly divided pots of ferns would ask for tender nurturing and high humidity to 'get them away', and the thousands of geranium cuttings would have to be monitored for an outbreak of 'blackleg', a fungus disease that would rot off their stem bases with dire consequences. The sharp sand might help, but it did not guarantee success.

Bulbs would be potted up – narcissi and hyacinths – for a spring display in the town hall, and the flower-filled troughs from inside the town hall and the library would be replenished with fresh new flowering plants and ferns every week, regardless of the season.

And then it would be winter. A quieter time, but always with some kind of job to do – cleaning, repairing, picking off dead leaves and flowers and re-staging plants on their benches. There was always the boiler to keep topped up and clinkered, and if all else failed, there were flower pots to wash in cold muddy water and seed trays to scrub clean while we waited for the turn of the year and the days to become longer.

From November through to February it would, for the most part, be dark when we started work and dark when we finished, and on some days the sky would remain the colour of an old army blanket and we would be grateful for the warmth our greenhouses provided. This was the time of year when we, the trio of nursery workers, knew we had the best time of it.

Dick Hudson, the tractor man, would spend longer in the mess room in these darker days, drinking his tea and smoking his Capstan Full Strength, his gang mowers lying idle in their shed. What did he do in these winter months when the grass on the playing fields down by the river hardly grew at all? I glanced at his time sheet one Friday in December. It had but a single word written on it. 'MAINTAINANCE,' it said. Spelled just like that. That's what Dick did in the wintertime. He maintained himself. Come to think of it, so did we all.

Saturday Jobs

Money isn't everything: usually it isn't even enough.

Anon

Expecting a gardener to like every aspect of gardening is like expecting a musician to like all music. Only a liar could claim to do so. I can't think of many gardening jobs I really hate — except the predictable ones like battling bindweed and marestail. And growing gladioli. And pampas grass. And standard roses. But cultivating someone else's soil requires a particular kind of dedication.

My grandfather and great-grandfather had both been 'jobbing gardeners,' and Ken Wilson had been in what he described as 'private service' — working for the Vestey family — before he came into parks. Having a 'proper' job in someone else's garden does at least yield some kind of proprietorial satisfaction. Even if you do not own the patch of ground you are cultivating, your constant charge of it does give you an affinity with it. The situation is different when you are a part-time custodian whose only task seems to be that of maintenance. Such a role is totally without creativity, and maybe that's why I hated my Saturday-morning jobs.

It was Dad who got me into it, thinking, not unreasonably, that I could do with a few extra shillings to eke out my £3.7s.6d wages. He had been plumbing for the owner of a house up

Rupert Road – one of the smarter residential thoroughfares on the Middleton side of Ilkley – for some time, and the man had indicated that he was a little short-staffed in the gardening department.

It was not a large garden. The area to the rear of the smart, large semi was laid to lawn and flanked by flower borders. In front of the house was a short Tarmac drive and a shrubbery where holly and Portugal laurel, euonymus and olearia did their best to grow in dry, root-ridden soil.

I turned up at 9a.m on the first Saturday morning – I would not need any tools, I'd been told – and the owner of the house, a tall, kindly-looking gentleman, greeted me and showed me round. I admired the borders and the lawn and asked what he would like me to do. He took me to the front of the house, where the deep gloom of the shrubbery lowered over all, and asked me if I would mind 'tidying it up'. He did not need anything cut down, he said, just the soil worked over.

Every Saturday morning, for the next few months, I beavered away in the Stygian darkness with a bent garden fork, trying to rid the grey dust of its dreary carpet of weeds. I fought to find some kind of satisfaction in the job, but there is not a lot to be had in a death-defying shrubbery. Did he want me to have a go in the back garden, I asked? The answer was negative. 'No. Just keep going in the shrubbery if you would.'

Each week a few more weeds would have reared their heads and battle would commence once more. I never did get to see the back garden, with its lawn and herbaceous borders – the 'regular' gardener who turned up midweek had the satisfaction of caring for them.

The only bright moment in the morning would be the appearance of a large cup of coffee and two biscuits. It would be left for me in the utility room, which could be entered from the outside of the house; there was no need for me to remove my wellies since newspaper had been laid on the floor. After three hours of labour I would be presented with my half crown (twelve-and-a-half pence) and would cycle wearily home to begin my weekend proper.

Ken, aware of my Saturday job and of the little financial gain it offered, asked me if I could help out with his own part-time job for a widowed lady up Cowpasture Road on the other side of town. One evening a week should do it. I was not keen, but felt obliged to accept, simply to avoid letting him down.

I don't think the widowed lady took too kindly to a young lad filling in when the Parks Foreman himself could not attend. She was decidedly sniffy, and her housekeeper even more so. But here at least I got to work among the rose beds, rather than in the shrubbery, and I was even allowed to bed out in early summer. But she never seemed satisfied with what I had done. 'I'm not sure that Kenneth would have done it like that.' She never called him Ken; always Kenneth.

I smiled my most indulgent smile, and went on wielding the rusty trowel she had given me to work with (the better one was reserved for Kenneth), committing the petunias to the bare earth that bordered the roses, and trying not to mutter profanities under my breath.

The housekeeper would appear with a glass of ginger beer after I'd been at it for an hour and a half but she, too, had a look of disdain on her face. She would place the glass on a stone nearby without saying a word and beat a hasty retreat into the conservatory. Clearly, as far as she was concerned, I was the lowest form of life.

But I battled on for a year and did my best to prune the roses properly, keep the lawn edges tidy and deadhead anything that looked faded. In the end the old lady took to her bed, and it was not long before Ken told me that my services would no longer be required. I can't say that I was sorry, and from that day to this I have steadfastly avoided digging anybody else's soil. Except for *Ground Force*, of course. But that was different. At least the rates of pay were rather better, and generally speaking, the garden owners were a touch more grateful than they were in my teens.

Read All About It

Think of what our Nation stands for,
Books from Boots' and country lanes . . .
'In Westminster Abbey,' Sir John Betjeman

It's called *Simple Gardening*, it's by R.P. Faulkner and it was published by W.H. and L. Collingridge the year after I was born, 1950. It is not an impressive book to look at, and I remember thinking it a bit dull when I took it down from the little bookshelf at home and opened the first of its 160 pages. It's a small, slim volume with four intricately penned line drawings on the pale green dust jacket – taking a chrysanthemum cutting, building a dry stone wall, using a besom to sweep loam into the cracks between freshly laid turf, and planting and staking a tree. There are no photographs inside, just more line drawings, and Mr Faulkner's credentials are given on the front flap: 'After a varied experience in horticulture,' . . . well, we can all claim a few of those . . . 'Mr Faulkner became head gardener at the School of Agriculture, Nottingham, and here became well qualified to write on the practice of the art of gardening. In this book he explains clearly to the beginner' . . . that was me, so my ears pricked up . . . 'how to choose tools and dig ground and then how to plan and maintain his garden. Lawns, hedges and paths, which are the backbone of any garden design, are discussed in detail. A selection of plants for the shrub garden, perennial border

93

and rose garden is given and the suitability of plants to provide flowers for cutting is considered. Fruit and vegetable culture are fully described. Throughout the book the text is amplified by clear line drawings, plans and diagrams.'

And all in 160 pages. I read and absorbed it, noting, in my youthful keenness to do everything by the book, that rose bushes 'should be planted twenty-one inches apart', that quality tools 'are stocked by all good-class ironmongers', and that most pests could be 'controlled by spraying with DDT'. I bought a puffer pack.

Reading it now sends a shiver down my spine – not the recommendation of DDT, long since banned as being as much of a health hazard to humans as aphids, but because it can spirit me back and remind me of the excitement I felt when I first read it fifty years ago. *Simple Gardening* was the start of a lifelong addiction to books – not just gardening books – that has continued unabated.

In their eagerness to promote the speed and comprehensiveness of information that can be provided by the internet, its advocates forget one thing – the physical pleasure of books. The tactile thrill – and it really is a thrill – of actually holding one, new or old, fine leather binding or glossy dust wrapper, light or weighty. Books also have their own smell; the acrid, acidic tang of a Victorian volume; the synthetic aroma of fine colour plates. There is the long-anticipated delight of opening each book at the very beginning and then turning its pages – not at the click of a button, but by using your fingers to separate the leaves, then peeling one away. The slovenly may lick their finger to get a better grip, then turn down the corner of a page when they set the book aside. The bibliophile, on the other hand, will take inordinate care to select the best copy from the bookseller – the one with the least bumped dust wrapper, no chips to the head – and have it wrapped for the journey home. The front jacket flap will be used as a bookmark until he is halfway through reading it, then the back flap will take over – a bookmark may strain the binding at the spine. You will gather, from this, that I am of the latter persuasion.

Simple Gardening was not my very first gardening book. That distinction goes to Beatrix Potter's *The Tale of Peter Rabbit*, which I have always thought of as a gardening book. All those descriptions of vegetables, and the drawings of Mr McGregor's boot kicking over the geranium. The images have stayed with me. So, too, has the delight at feeling the glossy paper as we turned the pages – me and Mum, or me and Dad – when I was six or seven, in the twilight of the back bedroom at 34 Nelson Road.

From Mr Faulkner I graduated to Mr Thrower, having watched him on the BBC's *Gardening Club* every Friday night, when he hung his jacket on a hook on the back of the greenhouse door – the greenhouse with no glass in it. But then it was in a studio. I knew it must be, because the sun was always shining and there was never a cloud in the sky. And the soil in his flower bed always had the texture of John Innes potting compost.

Percy Thrower's Encyclopaedia of Gardening, with its glossy orange spine, shone down from my bookshelves, with Percy smiling from the front cover, crouching down in a spring border in his garden at The Magnolias near Shrewsbury. I used this A-Z reference book all the time, and then Ron, the propagator, persuaded me to buy from him two volumes of Newnes' *Successful Gardening* – big, fat green encyclopaedias that promised much in the way of information. But I found them strangely off-putting, and in spite of the fact that they sat on my shelves for forty years, I doubt that I opened them more than half a dozen times before I passed them on. Percy's book continued to offer sterling service.

Then there were the slightly strange 'Expert' books that I could buy from Woolworth's for one shilling and sixpence (seven-and-a-half pence). *Be Your Own Lawn Expert* by Dr D.G. Hessayon fell apart in the end. The 'Expert' books were not as thick then as they are now – they were more like booklets than books, but they were great value – and packed with information laid out in a unique 1950s, almost comic-book style that was soaked up by a young lad eager to learn.

Day release at the Institute meant the acquisition of more serious volumes – *Lowson's Textbook of Botany* and *Farm Machinery*, by Harris, Muckle and Shaw, the names so fitting they almost seem made up. They were worthy and earnest – reference books, rather than the sort you read for pleasure.

It was much later that I discovered the works of my now favourite gardening writer, Christopher Lloyd. That other great gardener Beth Chatto did not start writing until the 1970s, and although Vita Sackville-West was penning weekly pieces for the *Observer* as early as the 1950s, we took the *Daily Express*. The likelihood of me discovering the works of the chatelaine of Sissinghurst was about as great as me discovering Proust.

What I did discover were the monographs – books on a single type of plant. There is something about monographs that appeals to the collector, rather in the way that a collection of plants themselves holds a gardener in thrall. To have a book that deals in depth with pelargoniums, magnolias, or lavenders is akin to possessing that knowledge, or at least having it at your fingertips. The *Ladybird* books started it all when I was eight or nine – three volumes of *British Birds and their Nests* – and the *Observer* books continued the trend – *Wild Animals*, *Birds*, *Pond Life*, *Horses and Ponies* – paving the way for me to move on to grander tomes.

So it was that I came to be the proud possessor of *A Handbook of Crocus and Colchicum for Gardeners* by E.A. Bowles, *The Old Shrub Roses* by Graham Stuart Thomas and *Snowdrops and Snowflakes* by Sir Frederick Stern. These later volumes were acquired when I had a little more money and experience, and felt that I had 'grown out of' general gardening books, which, by then, I thought were

for beginners. It did not cross my mind that I would one day
write them myself.

The collection of wild flowers that I made at junior school,
sandwiched in a scrapbook between the sheets of tissue paper that
had been used to wrap our daily bread, and which won me the only
prize in my entire scholastic career, was founded on *The Observer's
Book of Wild Flowers*. For my twenty-first birthday Uncle Bert and
Auntie Edie bought me the Rev. W. Keble Martin's *The Concise
British Flora in Colour*, with a foreword by the Duke of Edinburgh.
It must be good, I thought, if His Royal Highness had put his
name to it. As it turned out, it was not misplaced confidence; the
book was – and is – a masterpiece. Written by a Devon clergyman,
it represented sixty years of painstaking watercolour painting of
almost one and a half thousand wild flowers of the British Isles, not
singly on separate sheets, but woven together on the page family
by family. Roses: dog, burnet, downy and sweet briar; vetches
alongside tares and sainfoin, medicks with clovers, figworts with
monkey flowers, mudwort and speedwell, dock with sorrel, thistles
with cornflowers. The book displayed on the page not just the
colour and beauty of the flowers, their descriptions and locations,
but also the relationships between them.

In addition to learning the Latin names of the plants, I was now learning how they fitted into the greater scheme of things – what was considered to be related to what, and those mouthfuls that were family names, which usually ended in *aceae* – *Ranunculaceae*, the buttercup family, *Iridaceae*, the iris family and *Papilionaceae*, the pea family. Of course, even here there were exceptions to the rule (one of the frustrations of botany) – *Umbelliferae* or cow parsley, *Labiatae* or deadnettles, and *Compositae*, daisies – along with the plates at the back of the book that were monochrome rather than colour, perhaps because of their assumèd dullness to the common man – plates of *Gramineae*, the grasses.

But these family names, along with genus and species, variety and cultivar, wormed their way into my affections and my conversations with the ease and regularity that a social climber might litter their conversation with the names of dukes and duchesses. Botanical name-dropping. Comforting and reassuring. They gave me, I suppose, the kind of satisfaction that the early learning of those dictionary words had given me, and became another addition to my armoury. Not that there was anyone in particular to impress with them, except myself. To others in gardening they were common currency – no one was much impressed if you knew that snapdragons belonged to the family *Scrophulariaceae*, though occasionally I could discover a more unusual plant family that the other students would not know existed and which contained perhaps only a single genus. Few know, for instance, that *Thesium humifusum*, the bastard toadflax, belongs to the family *Santalaceae*, or that the horned pondweed, *Zanichellia palustris*, is in its own family, *Zannichelliaceae*. Mind you, even fewer care.

There is, however, comeuppance for those who rest on their laurels. Botanists are forever changing plant names as their research reveals hitherto undiscovered relationships or species that have been previously described as something else. For all I know,

Zannichelliaceae has by now been lumped in with *Potamogetonaceae*. If you really want to know, go and look it up in a book. You won't, though, will you? You'll go straight to the internet.

Me? I'll stick with the Rev. W. Keble Martin. I know where I am with him.

Uprooted

And bold and hard adventures t'undertake,
Leaving his country for his country's sake.
'Sir Francis Drake', Charles Fitzgeffrey

The thing about aspirations is that they start small and grow out of all proportion. When I was fifteen I wanted nothing more than to garden day in and day out. It was my antidote to school, an escape from a world into which I did not fit comfortably. I liked plants, understood them, and wanted to work with them all day every day. So why then, after three years of working on the nursery, did I feel the need to follow Ken Wilson's advice and embark on that mapped-out career path – college, Kew, Wisley or Edinburgh Botanic Garden and that strange place called The Grotto? The answer is the same whatever the career – because it offered a challenge. There is always that little niggle, a kind of ache that is difficult to ignore. The 'what if?' in life that begs to be answered.

Oh, there were moments of great fear; more than one occasion when I could have stayed where I was, doing what I was doing. Why rock the boat when you are happy with the present voyage? Well, because you don't know if you will enjoy what is round the corner even more than where you are. Because you need to be stretched. And although we all make mistakes, the errors we generally regret are the errors of omission rather than commission. At least if you do something and it goes wrong there is no more 'what if?'. That was my reasoning. I think.

The horticultural college most local to me was Askham Bryan, near York. Like all horticultural colleges it majored in agriculture, and so the student clientele would be a colourful mixture of farmers and gardeners or, as I was now learning to say by way of giving myself respectability, horticulturists.

I applied, as instructed (so biddable I was, back then), and was called for interview at the age of eighteen. The main college building is an imposing, if not daunting, brick-built pile that stands at the top of a ridge on the main road to York. A dead straight drive runs up to its front door. I still find it intimidating, and whenever I pass it, ominous grey clouds seem to be looming behind it.

I turned up for my interview with the principal one blustery spring day in 1967, with a view to starting a one-year full-time residential course that autumn that would lead to the National Certificate in Horticulture. NCH were not initials quite of the standing of BA or BSc, neither did you put them after your name (unless you were desperate), but they did represent an intention, on the part of the holder, to take their career seriously. The first rung on the ladder.

My recollection of the day is hazy, but I do remember sitting in front of Lance Gilling – the tall, bespectacled principal who had the friendly but distinguished air of an agricultural patrician – and talking about bell ringing. He asked me nothing, as far as I can remember, about gardening, sorry, horticulture, just about ringing bells, which I had obviously put on my application form under 'hobbies'.

I thought our chat went rather well. But I didn't get in.

The letter informed me that impressive as my interview had been (I had obviously acquitted myself well on the campanology front), it was felt that older applicants should be given the opportunity to attend this year. The college would be prepared to take me the following autumn, when I had reached the age of nineteen.

I was a bit disappointed. And in order to make absolutely sure of a place in the last year of my teens, in 1968, I applied to another college, Oaklands in Hertfordshire, which also ran courses in both agriculture and horticulture and which specialised in glasshouse work.

I journeyed to St Albans, the nearest town to Oaklands, on the day prior to the interview. I travelled by train, in my best sports jacket and hipster trousers, with fresh brushed Hush Puppies, but my self-confidence was dented when it came to communicating with British Rail staff. I could not understand the guard's accent – and this from a lad who had spent one day a week for the last four years on the outskirts of Bradford, a city justly renowned for its variety of tongues. The guard was clearly a southerner. My mother would have called him a cockney (a term she regularly applied to anyone who lived south of Sheffield). When I asked about having dinner in the dining car (because that was, I assumed, what you did when you made monumental journeys of this kind – and I was determined to do it properly even on my meagre wage) he replied in one word: 'Dinrattertarpy'. I asked three times before, with an exasperated glance to the heavens, he repeated slowly: 'Dinner after Derby.'

In keeping with my intention of 'doing it well' I spent my first night away from home in the Peahen Hotel on the high street in St Albans. I ordered breakfast in my room. I remember the mahogany furniture quite vividly. I have absolutely no recollection of the interview, except that the subject of bellringing was not touched upon.

It can't have gone too badly. A few weeks later I received a letter explaining that I had been accepted by Oaklands and, if I chose, I could begin the course that autumn. I did choose. I accepted the place.

A month later, an offer arrived from Askham Bryan. At least they were true to their word. But I turned it down without, I hope, sounding as though I did so in a fit of pique, and left home on the last day of September 1968 to begin my new life at college.

There was no leaving 'do' at the nursery. Just mumbled good wishes and nods. Old Harry said, 'Aye, well, good luck to you' as he cycled slowly up the drive of the nursery and out of sight. Young Harry managed, 'Well done, lad. You'll come back and see us, won't you? No point in saying "good-bye" properly.'

There were similar muted salutations from most of the men. Dick Hudson, from the depths of his armchair in the mess room, managed a particularly splendid coughing fit. I could just make out the wave of his arm through the veil of smoke.

I like to think that it wasn't that they didn't care. I'd been the young lad on the nursery for the last four years and they must have worked up some kind of vague affection for me, not least on account of the man hours they had put in instructing me on the finer points of the art and craft of gardening.

Mickey shook my hand firmly, looked me in the eye and said, 'Good luck'. And the new propagator, the cocky Geordie lad who had taken over from Ron (newly promoted to the post of Parks Superintendent in Oswaldtwistle), said simply, 'You'll be back.' I wasn't sure whether it meant I was likely to fail and would come home with my tail between my legs, or that having done my stint down south the pull of my home country would be too strong to resist. I tried to put it out of my mind.

It was Albert who had the last word, as I pushed my bike up the rough gravel track that led from the nursery on to Little Lane.

'Bye Albert,' I offered, as I overtook his slowly plodding form.

'Oh, yes. You on your way?'

'Yes.'

'When do you start?'

'Next week.'

'Oh.' He looked wistful, and popped one of his stomach pills into his mouth.

'It's a good opportunity,' he said. Albert, the softly spoken man who looked as though life had offered him considerably fewer opportunities than he would have liked.

'Yes.'

'Education, you know. It's a good thing.'

'You think so?'

'I know so. I'd have got on better if I'd have had a good education.'

'Oh, Albert . . . you've not done badly,' I tried to cheer him up. He brightened a little and took hold of my arm, stopping me from walking any further.

'Well, take a word of advice from someone who's been on the globe a bit longer than you have . . .'

'What's that?'

'Don't let the buggers grind you down.' It was the first time I had ever heard him swear. He winked at me and sucked on his stomach tablet. I assured him that I would not, and I cycled home from the nursery for the last time.

Look and Learn

Cauliflower is nothing but cabbage with a college education.

Pudd'nhead Wilson, Mark Twain

I was worried, more than anything, about being homesick. For goodness' sake! I was nineteen! But the longest I had been away from home until then had been a weekend camping trip to Pateley Bridge with the Scouts when I was eleven, and that had not been significantly successful. As I carried my suitcase (still cardboard, but larger now, with expandable locks) up the curving tree-lined drive, past the green-painted gilt-lettered sign that proclaimed this Home Counties estate as 'The Hertfordshire College of Agriculture and Horticulture', I felt like a child dispossessed. I tried not to. I tried to remember that this was my great good fortune. And that I was a man, not a boy.

At least I would have a bit of space to myself. Every student – a hundred-odd of us, with only half a dozen of them women – had a room of their own. They lodged in the old house, with Matron, rather than in the two residential blocks called, imaginatively, East Block and West Block. These two modern brick-built hulks had lecture rooms beneath and bedsits on top, and each of the two accommodation floors had a shower-cum-bathroom at the end. Two thirds of the intake were agricultural students, most of them farmers' sons, a fair proportion with red hair. The rest of us were there to study horticulture – mainly commercial, although a few of us were enrolled on the attractively titled 'Amenity Horticulture' course. We were the arty lot who liked growing plants because we thought they looked pretty, rather than because selling them could make us money.

I hung up my suit in the wardrobe of my room. It was my first suit, charcoal grey and bought from Easby's of Ilkley (made to measure, mind). It was itemised on the list of required clothing sent through by the college once I had accepted the post, along with boots, wellingtons, jeans, donkey jacket and all the expected protective clothing, as well as 'sports jacket and flannels'. They didn't mention Hush Puppies but I took them all the same. I think I wore them under my suit for the college photo, which was one of those panoramic jobs that posh private schools have. I'd never been in one before, but I had heard stories that if you stood at the left-hand end of the group you could, when the camera started arcing from left to right, nip round the back and pop up at the right-hand end so that you appeared twice in the picture. Not that anybody dared. Not when Mr E.C. Pelham – known to lecturers and students alike as 'Chunky' – was principal. One glance at him told you how he had come by his name. He had the build of an all-in wrestler. When he entered the lecture room it was as if a cloud had crossed the sun. Fitting, really, since it was he who lectured us on meteorology. Once seen, his physical demonstration of the action of a katabatic wind was never to be forgotten. The choreography of his explanation of 'veering and backing' should have been committed to Laban notation. He made it look like something out of Walt Disney's *Fantasia*. I cannot see the hippos in tutus without thinking of him.

But there were two precursors to our education. One was the college group photo and the other the tetanus injection.

Picture, if you would, the line-up of burly farmers and growers, sports jackets over their arms and left sleeves rolled up, marching slowly towards Matron like the orphans in *Oliver Twist* advancing on Mr Bumble for their gruel. Matron stood at the head of the queue with her needle raised. She was not, as you might imagine, a grizzled old battle-axe, but a dishy brunette barely a year or so older than we were. There was not one of those beefy farmers or muscular growers who did not promise himself that he would get off with Matron by Christmas. But not one of them did. Not even by the end of the one-year course. She was as untouchable as the Holy Grail, and probably took great pleasure in remaining that way.

One by one the mighty sons of the soil advanced upon her as she wielded her hypodermic. The strongest of them paled at the sight of the bright spurt of fluid into the air, were momentarily pacified by the soft brush on the skin of the cotton-wool pad soaked in methylated spirits, and then rudely brought to earth by the insertion of the needle and the pumping in of its medication.

One macho farmer's son advanced upon Matron's slender form with something of a swagger. He was handsome, there was no doubt about it. Six foot three with a neat crop of curly ginger hair and a gaze that had melted many a milkmaid in its time. He looked down on her and smiled his most winning smile. It cut no ice. She dabbed, she stabbed and he keeled over backwards from the heels in a dead faint.

'Take him away, somebody,' was all she said, and the lifeless body was dragged into the student common room to be revived with tea and rude remarks.

It was my turn next. I looked away. I don't mind needles, but have found, since my childhood, that I am happier if I don't actually see the thing sinking into my flesh. There were mutterings and mumblings from Matron. She seemed to be trying to push me over. I stood my ground. More muttering and mumbling. I turned to look at her and she stared back at me with grave suspicion and said, with more than a little irritation, 'Skin like a rhinoceros.'

Eventually she managed to puncture my arm and pump in the serum, slapping a pad of cotton wool on to the wound and saying, 'Hold this for half an hour.' It was her way of getting her own back, I suppose.

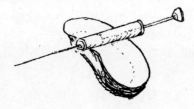

Holding my arm as instructed, I walked past the ginger-headed farmer, slumped on a chair. He had heard the battle of wills. I tried not to look smug.

Before the 1969 riots in Paris, which changed student life forever, so we are told, those of us in colleges this side of the Channel were ruled with a rod of iron. Not for us the freedom of university students. We were treated, to all intents and purposes, like pupils at a private boarding school. The college had responsibility for us and therefore made sure we were under control at all times.

The college grounds were basically a large farm – acres of cereals, cattle, pigs and the like, which were the province of the agricultural students – and then the glasshouses, orchards and ornamental grounds, which belonged to the 'hortics'. Here, in enormous 'aeroplane' glasshouses – the sort with span after span of glass ridges – were grown tomatoes and cucumbers, all-year-round chrysanthemums and carnations, pot plants and other 'protected' commercial crops. There was a smaller nursery area where a wide range of ornamental plants was grown and propagated. Apples and pears graced the sweeping grassy rides of the orchards, and the areas closest to the college buildings were laid out with beds and borders replete with everything from sub-tropical bedding to alpine plants, trees and shrubs to flowering bulbs.

There was little in the way of a gradual introduction to the rigours of college life. We were up at 6.30a.m to be ready for 'practical work' from 7 until 8. Here we undertook operations that varied in their monotony from washing leeks in cold, muddy water and packing them for market, to cutting and defoliating cauliflowers, packing tomatoes into trays, grading apples and pears or digging over vacant ground. There was nothing too taxing at this early hour, lest the half-asleep students should make a mess of it and cock up the reputation of the college in Covent Garden market where our crops were sold.

From 8.15 until 9a.m we breakfasted in the cavernous dining hall where Macedonian waitresses doled out cornflakes, bacon and eggs through wide hatches, shouting instructions to each other and hurling abuse at the students. Nothing actionable, just the sort of badinage guaranteed to achieve the same repellant results as Matron except by dint of volume rather than attitude.

By 9a.m we were on the move from the dining hall to the lecture rooms. Here we would be given the information that would arm us for a life in horticulture. We learned the Ministry of Agriculture's blueprint for growing tomatoes (doled out in deeply serious tones as though we were being schooled in breaking the Enigma code), and some weeks later, when that was completed, cucumbers.

There were lectures on botany from a lady who looked and carried herself rather like the Queen. For the college photo she wore a light-coloured tweed two-piece with fur-edged cuffs. So regal was her bearing, as she sat a few places to the left of the principal on the front row, that you half expected her to be holding an orb and sceptre. Her hair was always immaculately coiffed in the style of the monarch, and her vowels were rather strangulated, so that there was a strange yet sensual quality to her pronunciation of xylem and phloem, mitosis and meiosis. To listen to her explaining the behaviour of chromosomes was a bit like hearing the Queen talking about sex.

The mycology lecturer was at the other end of the spectrum – a bouncing academic, fresh from university, he had the air of a boyish Jonathan Miller and could make the driest facts about fungi seem as vital as the six o'clock news. Not that he always had a satisfactory answer to our questions. 'Why do some fungi have gills and others don't?' I asked. 'Why do you have five toes on each foot and not six?' came the rejoinder.

In 'crop protection' lectures we were apprised of the complex life cycles of the bugs, beasts and bacteria that would be likely to attack our charges, and of the full range of poisons with which we could assault them. Some of these had to be applied via spray lances with the operator wearing a space suit powered by a roaring machine that pumped air into it. This meant that you strutted about in the greenhouse or orchard like the Michelin man or Neil Armstrong on the surface of the moon. 'One small step for a man; one giant leap for the gardener.' There would be no stamping out of the flames on little piles of nicotine shreds here. Rachel Carson's *Silent Spring* was handed round by subversive students who had the courage of their convictions.

Along with lectures on top fruit, soft fruit, climate and soils, records and accounts (oh, how I yawned during those, the only bright spot being the red ink we used on the debit side of the page), glasshouse flower crops, ornamental horticulture, nursery practice and glasshouse construction, we were schooled in the use of machinery. The lecturer here was Mr Telford, a balding, middle-aged technocrat who loved nothing more than explaining the intricate workings of a Satchwell Duo-tronic Control for glasshouse temperature modulation. It is to his undying credit that I can remember what it was called. I fail him, alas, in forgetting quite how it worked.

Mr Telford was a softly spoken gent who always wore a white coat, even in his oily workshop. Deciding that we had quite enough pressure on us when it came to examinations, at the end of each of the three terms he would show us how to reverse a tractor with a trailer, or how to draw a diagram of a Vicon fertiliser spreader, and examine us on our efforts there and then while the operation was fresh in our minds. It seemed to me to be an eminently sensible way of proceeding. It also meant that hardly anybody failed. I have never used a Vicon fertiliser spreader since, but I can reverse my car with a trailer and I can also wire a three-pin plug, for which I owe Mr Telford a greater debt of thanks than I owe the lecturer who fed me the Ministry of Agriculture blueprint for growing tomatoes, which, forty years on, is now hopelessly out of date.

Once our lectures were completed, at 12.25p.m, and after a hearty lunch, we would have an afternoon of practical work in one of the various departments – the nursery, ornamental areas or fruit and market garden, where we were taught the practical skills of growing plants. True enough, I had learned a lot during my four years on the nursery, but there were always fresh techniques to acquire, from sharpening a knife properly, to whip and tongue grafting, budding roses and stratifying seeds. These terms, previously just words in a book, now took on real meaning.

I surprised myself by actually taking on board information at an astonishing rate. I had begun to do so at Shipley Tech, but now the learning was full-time it seemed easier to get the momentum going. The fog began to clear, and the mind I had thought incapable of proper reasoning or even of remembering facts seemed, like a muscle almost, to benefit from the exercise and increase its capacity.

I relished the chance to learn the life cycle of pests and diseases, and to bottle leatherjackets and wireworms in formaldehyde, the better to identify them. I won a prize for the best dried flower collection (my junior school training having given me a head start and the collecting bug coming to the fore) and spent night after night of private study (6 till 8p.m) in my tiny cell writing down botanical names and committing them, and the plants they described, to memory.

One afternoon a week was set aside for sport. Bearing in mind my scholastic sporting record, and my slightness of build, I was not a natural choice for games. I did try rugby once, but within half an hour I had my head crushed between the scrum half and the goalpost. The concussion sealed my fate – I settled instead for cross-country running. I enjoyed the solitude, if not the scenery, which I found flat and dull compared with the moorland runs of Yorkshire. But it got me out into the fresh air and cleared my head.

After high tea between 5.30 and 6p.m – when the rush for extra chips seemed to be the nightly athletic activity – and private study until 8, we were allowed out until 10.30p.m. This usually meant a walk of a mile or so to the nearest pub, the Bunch of Cherries. There began my introduction to the social life of the student; to beer and skittles, girls and the way to handle them.

Knave of Herts

Love is the irresistible desire to be irresistibly desired.

Robert Frost

Like most red-blooded men – alright then, boys – I'd been on the lookout since the age of about eleven. Not that I had enjoyed much success. Three months – with Rosemary – was my personal best, it wasn't for want of trying. There had been a couple of false starts at the operatic society in Ilkley, where I went for a bit of dramatic extra-mural activity, but nothing that amounted to more than a peck in the wings during *Oklahoma*. There were no girls at all on the City and Guilds Stage 1 Horticulture course at Shipley – gardening had yet to become 'cool'.

If I thought that college life would offer rich female pickings I was about to embark on a steep learning curve. There were 101 students in the 1968 intake at the Hertfordshire College of Agriculture and Horticulture. Just seven of them were female. But then one should always look close to home to start with, even if the competition is fierce. Not that the seven were exactly magnificent, though one of them did possess a brooding presence strangely reminiscent of Yul Brynner and James Coburn. She was one of the four farming girls (by far the most glamorous of the seven) but, alas, already attached to the hunkiest of the agrics – a blond adonis who would walk nonchalantly down the corridor of East Block after his early evening shower, with a towel wrapped round his waist, the better to show off his six-pack and a rippling physique clearly honed to perfection by teenage years spent hurling bales of hay. A body conditioned by four years of pricking out could not really compete. But then most of the students that year were more 'Party Seven' than six–pack.

The girl in question had shoulder-length fair hair and an hour-glass figure, together with a liking for wearing a black bra beneath a white blouse. Whether they had been together before they embarked on a college education I am not sure, but they were confident enough in each other's company for him not to mind when she pounced on a weedy agric in the dining hall and gave him a love-bite on his neck by way of a joke. We sat at the same table in the dining hall, but I managed to escape her vampire tendencies.

One down, six to go. But that makes the situation sound more hopeful than it really was. For a start, one of the six was at least thirty-five, and when you are nineteen, thirty-five seems as old as God. She looked it, too. Hair in a sort of marcel wave, glasses that went up at the sides like those of Dame Edna Everage, a sensible thick-knitted cardy and a Royal Stuart tartan kilt to mid calf. No point in going any further there. She had a way of speaking that made her sound as though she were just emerging from a deep sleep, and her eyes, under the soaring spectacle frames, were always half closed. If she was looking for a man she'd have had trouble seeing him.

Then there was the extrovert. Well spoken and exuberant, with the proportions of a cottage loaf and the bounciness of a beach ball, she seemed to have stepped straight from an Angela Brazil schoolgirl saga – 'Winnie, the terror of the fourth'. Pillow fights and midnight feasts that majored on iced buns were probably her speciality. A big girl. You could do a lot with her. One of our number did. He looked exhausted every morning.

The tiniest student of them all kept herself to herself. A

short, stocky girl with short, stocky hair, I hardly remember her speaking and she certainly evinced no interest in men.

There were two sandwich girls, students on the sandwich course, which involved one year in college, one year working outside in the industry and one year back at college. They were embarking on their final year now. One had been to Amsterdam and seemed incapable of beginning a sentence without the phrase 'When I was in Holland . . .'. I'm not sure where the other had been. They were both pleasant enough, but the confidence they had accrued by travelling the world (alright then, Holland) made them a touch intimidating. Fortunately one of them was hitched up to a fellow student and the other had met . . . a Dutchman.

One left. Quite a looker she was, fine featured with expressive hands. But emotionally fragile. You could be talking to her one minute, her face a picture of joy, and the next her features would crumple and she would burst into tears and dash from the room. No-one quite worked out why. She would reappear the following day as if nothing had happened and lull you into a false sense of security. Within a month the poor girl had disappeared due to some kind of mental breakdown. We were all very sympathetic. But lonely. There was nothing for it but to look further afield.

The nearest field was the local pub, the Bunch of Cherries. The landlord had two daughters whose thighs . . . well . . . whose thighs were memorable, maybe on account of being encased in white patent leather boots. Of the ninety-odd male students at Oaklands, not one claimed to have been successful with the landlord's daughters, but that may have been because the landlord was a tall, strapping man with sensitive hearing.

Anyway, there wasn't anything very exciting you could do of a weekday evening within sight of the landlord when you had to be back in college at 10.30pm. But on Saturday nights we could be back as late as 11pm – midnight if we had had the foresight to sign an exeat form (Roedean must have been easier to get in and out of than our college.) That meant we could make an expedition in the direction of Watford and two all-female colleges by the names of Wall Hall and Balls Park whose inmates would hopefully be grateful for the influx of a load of farmers and gardeners to brighten their Saturday night.

From 9 till 11 on a Saturday morning we had practical work to do in the orchard or the market garden, the glasshouses or the grounds, though our minds must have wandered with the prospect of freedom but a couple of hours away. Then there was a plant identification test – twenty plants to describe with the names of their family, genus, species and variety – before we would tackle a hearty lunch and set off into town. A new shirt maybe, or a pair of shoes, in preparation for the evening's entertainment – a film, or a night at the pub or, best of all, a bit of a bash at Wall Hall or Balls Park – the latter, on a poor night for talent, being rudely referred to as 'the knacker's yard.'

Within a few weeks of our arrival we had formed small groups of friends, with the hortics and agrics generally sticking together. Our worlds collided only at meal times, but the proximity provided by eight or nine hours of practical work and lectures meant that we got to know each other better and more speedily than could be managed over breakfast, lunch and dinner when the conversation was minimal and the appropriation of chips was of paramount importance.

And so, with Dick from Somerset, I would set out on a Saturday evening with high hopes and a drip-dry nylon shirt, hoping to meet the love of my life and live happily ever after. The back of Dick's van was equipped with a generous supply of cushions, a sort of den of iniquity on wheels. He wished. But then he did seem to have more success than I did, probably on account of his laid back technique.

His accent was pure Mummerset. He would have fitted

comfortably into the cast of the *Vicar of Dibley*. But then he did seem to be strangely attractive to women. Not that he was, to be honest, particularly choosy. If she had two legs, a pair of breasts and was capable of standing or – more importantly – lying down, then Dick was her man.

His relaxed attitude must have been what appealed to them. Having selected his quarry, he would chat her up in a refreshingly laconic style which involved rolling his 'r's more than usual and winking rather a lot. When it was clear that the two of them were going places he would lean forward into the snog, putting one arm round her, holding his fag and his pint in the other hand, and shifting his weight on to one leg as he raised the other off the ground. I onced asked him why. 'Turns 'em on' was all he said in reply. I couldn't work out how that could be possible, since the girl usually had her eyes closed. How could she have noticed that he was standing on one leg when she was leaning backwards? It only served to reinforce my belief that I knew nothing about women.

Until the night of the hospital dance. The flier had appeared on the college noticeboard, and those who were not attached or otherwise engaged made a mental note. There was no need to write it down in our diaries. None of us had one. Any impending social engagements were so thin on the ground that they were engraved on our hearts.

Freshly washed, shaved and reeking of Aramis, Dick and I set off an hour in advance of the scheduled time in order to partake of a stiffener before arriving at the appointed venue. It was winter, but it did not take long before our thick jackets came off in the heat of the dimly lit hall, where the sounds of The Hollies and the Dave Clark Five pulsated through the over-amplified sound system. Pints in hand, we scanned the sides of the hall for putative conquests. Dick's eye fell on an especially unprepossessing girl with a low-cut dress.

'Why her?' I asked.

'Because I'm knackered and she'll be grateful.'

'But . . .'

'Her face might not be up to much but she'll be good fer a grope.' And off he loped, with that rolling gait of his, in the direction of the unsuspecting nurse. I watched as he grinned at her and winked, and she melted into his arms in readiness for the one-legged lean.

I, on the other hand, had spotted the girl from the movies. Or so it seemed. One of my parents' favourite films was *South Pacific*. Liat, Bloody Mary's daughter, is a slender, dark-haired oriental girl with devastating good looks. She falls in love with the dashing Lieutenant Cable and he with her. In the face of the Chinese nurse with the long, shiny black hair and the limpid eyes, I saw the look of Liat. Summoning all my courage I walked across the floor and asked her to dance. She smiled, Liat's smile, and took my hand as I led her to the floor. We danced to the sound of the Moody Blues, and then to Procul Harem, 'A Whiter Shade of Pale'. She put her head on my shoulder and I wrapped my arms around her waist. Later we kissed. I kept both feet on the floor. We said goodbye at the gates and I took the telephone number of the nurses' hotel.

Dick was very chatty on the way back. I was silent.

'Come on then?'

'What?'

'What was her name?'

'Lyn.'

'What was she like . . . you know . . . down there?'

I looked at him quizzically. 'What do you mean?'

'You know. Was it . . . sideways?'

How could he reduce the romance of the evening to such a level. 'I don't know. I only kissed her.'

'Oh.' He seemed disappointed, let down that I could not help him in his research.

'How about you?' I asked, changing the subject.

'Alright. I got a good grope in the back of the van before you came out, but she was nothing to write home about.' Then he turned to me once more. 'You goin' to see 'er again then?'

'I don't know. I've got the number. Of the hostel . . .'

I agonised for days. But I never did call her. I had visions of my parents reaction to my taking home a Chinese girl. The music from *South Pacific* came flooding into my mind, 'You've got to be taught to be afraid, of people whose eyes are oddly made . . .'

I felt ashamed of myself. Ashamed of my reluctance to have the courage to call her. Sad that I would not see her again. She was simply beautiful, and one of the gentlest girls I had ever met. She had eyes I felt I could drown in. I had known her for just one evening, but I didn't wash the purple eye shadow off my cream drip-dry shirt for at least a month. It stayed in the laundry basket and I would take it out every now and then and stare at it, smelling the collar for the merest hint of her perfume. It diminished with each successive day. I kept, for several months, the piece of paper on which she had written her name and the telephone number. It lay on the windowsill in my room as a reminder. Eventually the name and number faded and the shirt went into the wash, but by then I had met Helen . . .

★   ★   ★

The point had come where I did wonder if I would ever meet anybody. It was possible, of course, and seemed increasingly likely, that I would go through life on my own. Or that I would have to adopt Dick's standards and settle for a good grope. But then he had a van filled with cushions and I didn't.

Then, one day, fate smiled and I noticed a tiny girl with a perfect figure and long blonde hair standing at the side of the dance floor with her dark-haired mate. Dick saw the direction in which I was looking. 'You go for her and I'll take the friend', he offered. His confidence astonished me, but it was never misplaced. He seemed to have a sixth sense where women were concerned. Maybe it was something to do with growing up on a farm in Somerset – a sort of basic agricultual know-how. He had brought that animal instinct to bear in horticulture, much to his father's chagrin.

It is the longest walk known to man – the walk of the adolescent male across the dance floor in the direction of his quarry. It is made all the more nerve-wracking by the fact that, should he be rebuffed, he will have to make the long journey back again with, he feels, all eyes on him and acutely aware of his failure. For this reason, a little geography homework is worth doing on arrival at any dance hall. First, locate both the bar and the gentleman's lavatory. That way, should your advance be rejected, you can adjust your subsequent movement so as to avoid retracing your steps. You can, instead, go straight to the bar or the lavatory. By the time you return, you will have plotted your next move or else your cover story. 'No; I was only asking her the way to the bar.' That way any embarrassment can be neatly circumvented.

Mentally I was walking towards the gents before I had even asked her, so it came as a bit of a surprise when she said that, yes, she would dance with me. Boy, was she a cracker. I could see the envious looks of the other students as I put my hands around her waist when we got to the slow, smoochy number, and she raised her arms and put them round my neck. She had on the shortest of mini-dresses and had the perfect pair of legs.

I got her phone number. Dick was silent in the van on the way home.

'You alright?' I asked.

'Waste of time that was. Right stuck up. Not interested.' I smiled to myself. A self-satisfied smile. A new sensation.

At lunch in the dining hall the following day the conversation turned, inevitably, to women. One of the ginger-headed farmers nodded in my direction. 'I like his', he said. It was a novel sensation. Not that one evening out proved that she was 'mine'. But I did have her phone number and I did ring it.

We went out several times. Happily, I thought. And she was devastatingly good-looking, with her long blonde hair held in place with a black velvet Alice band, the short skirts and the perfect legs.

Eventually she asked me to meet her at her home before we went out for the evening. I arrived at the Hertfordshire farmhouse – rather smarter than I had imagined – to find her deep in conversation with her parents. She seemed a bit petulant. Going on to her dad about her horse. I sat at one end of the chintz-covered sofa while the sun shone in through the French windows. Helen sat on the arm next to me. Her mini-dress allowed me a good view of her slender legs, but I tried to avoid looking at them in case her father noticed.

'I really didn't want to have him cut', she protested.

'Well, it's too late now,' he said, leaning on the mantelpiece with a glass of Scotch in his hand. 'He's been done and that's an end to it.' He drained his glass and left the room.

I felt slightly uncomfortable. Not least because I hadn't a clue what they were on about. Maybe she preferred her horse's mane long and her dad had cut it off. I was, for many years, unaware of the finer points of equine castration.

The conversation having ended, Helen got up from the sofa and said 'Come on.' I did as I was told, and we went out for a rather gloomy evening at the pictures. She didn't seem too keen on being kissed that night and I felt a bit short changed. She agreed, somewhat reluctantly, to meet again the following Saturday. We would go to the county show and she would show me the horses.

I met her at the appointed time, in the appointed place – at the end of the cowshed where bulls and heifers were pawing the ground. At first I did not recognise her. The mini-dress had gone, to be replaced with jeans and an army combat jacket. The Alice band had gone too, and with it the long blonde hair. It was the first inkling I had that it was not her own. She looked, if anything, a little dowdy, and her manner was that of a sulky child. Nothing I could say or do seemed to lift her mood, and we walked, in desultory fashion, past horses, cut and uncut (did I but know it), pens of sheep and suckling sows. By lunchtime she had clearly had enough and I asked her if she wanted to go home. 'Yes' she said. And made it clear that she would be travelling alone.

And that was it. My one real conquest evaporated into the agricultural light of day and I caught the bus back to college.

I didn't tell them it was all over for several weeks. They must have noticed that I wasn't going out very much, but if they did they were kind enough not to remark on it.

Eventually the ginger-haired farmer who had been so admiring asked 'How's that gorgeous bird of yours?'

'Not mine any more', I said softly.

'Oh. That's a shame', he said. 'I rather liked her.'

'So did I', I said. 'So did I.'

And then I plucked up the courage to ask him. 'Do you know anything about horses?'

Into the Smoke . . .

London, thou art the flower of cities all!
Anon

The Paris riots might well have changed everything for students there; it was of little consequence to me. I was about to become a student in a place where students were a part of the workforce and, in effect, civil servants, being employed by the Ministry of Agriculture, Fisheries and Food. There would be no mornings in bed and no skipping lectures. The world's premier botanic garden would be having none of that, not if you were one of the chosen few.

My college years finished, not so much with a bang as a whimper, at the end of July 1969. True enough, I had managed my first foreign trip while I was there – four of us went to Boskoop in Holland one half term to see how the Dutch grew shrubs. We stayed three nights and the only red lights we saw were holding up the traffic. Of the four of us, one in particular was a little tight with the funds. He would not agree to checking in to a guest house for bed and breakfast unless we had compared prices with at least three others, by which time the rest of us were weary and in desperate need of a beer. It was a trip pretty well devoid of fun.

It would be more fun to report that we left some lasting mark of our affection for the college on our departure, but even there

I have to disappoint. It was said that some students had once actually written a slogan on the lawn in weedkiller the night before they left. As the days wore on after their exit, the legend gradually became legible – 'BOLLOCKS TO CHUNKY', it said in straw-coloured grass among the verdure.

College, in the end, taught me lots of things besides horticulture. Self-discipline for one thing – evenings of private study leading to exams at the end of every term have that sort of effect. It also showed me that I might have greater reserves than I had imagined. Academic reserves? Well, a bit (and that was a surprise), but also inner reserves that up to now I hadn't been at all sure that I possessed. That year of self-reliance at the very end of my teens thickened my skin. I'm still too sensitive for my own good, but more resilient thanks to the years when I had to fend for myself.

If I'm honest I have to admit that I've always had a reluctance to grow up. I don't mean that I am unwilling to face up to my responsibilities. I can be sensible when I have to, and responsible, but I look, sometimes, at people in positions of power and think how far removed they are from their childhood. How joyless seems their way of life. How much they must have forgotten of their earlier selves and how much delight they must miss out on due to the weight of responsibility on their shoulders. I'm not talking about being child*ish*, but about being child*like*. There is a difference. If we subscribe to the theory that we are all born innocent, I think it's healthy to try to preserve *some* of that innocence in its purest form – it helps us to experience life more acutely.

I cherish Beatrix Potter's remark that it is important to keep the child in you alive. By doing so you will still be receptive to the simple pleasures of life – not just watching whirligig beetles spinning across the glassy surface of a pond, dabbling around with water-colour paints, making model theatres, walking over dew-laden grass with bare feet, opening a new book, watching an old movie in front of a log fire on a Sunday afternoon, feeling the coldness of a spire of delphinium flowers, even on the hottest day. It is more than that. It is trying to hang on to purity of feeling, to avoid being turned into a pessimist by the cynicism and world-weariness of those around you. To dare to be yourself, the self that you like best and that you want to hang on to. The self that doesn't exist to impress, but that can help to bring a faint glimmer of serenity to your soul in an often frenetic world. It is possible to be a realist without being a pessimist, even if it does take a supreme amount of effort. I think gardening and a love of nature have helped me a lot there.

John Fowles summed it up neatly in *The French Lieutenant's Woman*, when comparing Charles, the nineteenth-century 'hero' of the story with his counterpart in today's world: 'One of the commonest symptoms of wealth today is destructive neurosis; in his century it was tranquil boredom.'

Standing now on the threshold of my seventh decade (which is a fearsome and almost laughable admission for someone who has never felt completely grown-up), I like to think I've not become too bitter and twisted, too responsive to and coloured by the evil in the world at the expense of the good. Read the newspapers every day, or look at the television news – every hour, on the hour, if you like – and you will see real life. Or will you? Isn't the sunlight glinting on your garden pond and the sound of kids laughing in the street or the music of Handel's *Messiah* every bit as much a part of real life – *your* real life – as a tragic event several thousand miles away? I don't mean we shouldn't feel touched by such things, neither that we should be blind to them or not care about the welfare of others. Far from it. But we should keep a sense of perspective. It is not given to us, as human beings, to have the capacity to cope with every tragedy that happens every day in every part of the world. What is important – and it is something we can only do as individuals –

is to maintain a balanced outlook. It is a vital part of our survival instinct, and one we need to cultivate every bit as much as our responsibility for the world's woes. If we do not, we are changed; and not necessarily for our own or the world's good. So there we are. I think I've got that off my chest now . . .

When I left Hertfordshire to travel to Kew, did I imagine that it would change me from Yorkshire lad into some hard-bitten Londoner who forgot all about his roots? I don't think so. I knew that at my core that was what I was. What I still am, for better or worse. The rest – the stuff that happens subsequent to childhood and early youth – is nothing more than overlays. Additions. Adaptations. The 'nurture' that overlays the 'nature'. I know that now. I don't think I was quite so sure back in 1969 when I came to London for my interview at the Royal Botanic Gardens, Kew. The address was Richmond, Surrey, but it was – and is – to all intents and purposes London. The nice bit.

I didn't expect to get in. I don't think I really expected to get an interview. There were apparently several hundred applications for the twenty places that became vacant each year. But the letter calling me for interview arrived in the spring and I turned up at the appointed time to be faced with three serious-looking men in suits sitting behind a large mahogany table. The single chair that sat in front of them seemed like a lonely island in the middle of a darkly patterned carpet.

I'd worn the sports jacket and trousers. And the Hush Puppies (I should get another pair – they were clearly a lucky talisman). I looked at the men as earnestly as I could and made eye contact with all three, as well as with the stern faces who looked down at me from the gilded frames on the wall behind them – the likes of Sir Joseph Hooker, William Aiton and Sir William Thiselton-Dyer, past directors of Kew who had made their mark on the gardens that were founded in 1759 by Princess Augusta, the widow of Frederick, Prince of Wales.

Everything about the place was proper. Legitimate. I suppose that's why I had applied to Kew rather than to the other two establishments that Ken Wilson had recommended. Kew was the one I had heard the most about and so, I imagined, it was the best of the three. I might as well begin there.

'When would you prune *Caryopteris* x *clandonensis*?'

It was, I had to admit, not the first question I had expected. But it was the first question I got. I riffled through my mental card index. *Caryopteris* x *clandonensis* . . . a summer-flowering shrub. Fluffy blue flowers carried on new wood. You'd have to prune it late. After it had flowered, but probably not in winter lest its wood be damaged by frost. If it were pruned in spring it would then send out the new wood that would carry its late summer flowers.

'April.'

'I'd prefer March.'

'Oh.'

So far, so hopeless. But I persevered, and tried to appear personable. I suppose the fact that I had served four years of a five-year apprenticeship on the nursery, and then been to college and managed to get my National Certificate in Horticulture, plus my College Certificate with Credit, must have counted for something. Had I remembered to tell them that I had won first prize for my dried and pressed flower collection? Too late now.

More questions followed. About rock gardens. About Wisley. What did I think of the rock garden there? I tried to be diplomatic.

'Very nice. Very . . . well landscaped.'

Kew's curator, Dick Shaw, an Edinburgh-trained Scot, smiled indulgently. 'Don't you think it has a touch too much rock?'

'It does have a lot of rock, yes.'

He grinned and signalled to one of the two others that it was their turn. And so the gentle grilling continued until the moment I knew I could do no more:

'Thank you for coming. We'll let you know.' They rose from their chairs. I rose from mine, shook all three hands, smiled, I hoped winsomely, and left the room. Now came the agony of waiting.

Several weeks later the letter arrived saying I had been awarded a place on the September 1969 intake. My parents were over the moon. They bought me a transistor radio, and that autumn I took it with me on my journey down south to work and study in a botanical garden that had started up the rubber industry in Malaya, had been responsible for the breadfruit expedition that led to the mutiny on the *Bounty*, had benefited from the voyages of Captain Cook and whose first director had been Sir Joseph Banks. I was about to take my place in history – albeit a small and very insignificant one – as a student at the most famous botanical garden in the world.

Unlike the day-release system at Shipley, or Hertfordshire where we had lectures in the morning and practical work in the afternoon, the student's life at Kew was divided up into separate concentrated periods of theoretical and practical work. The lectures were grouped together in a three-month block, October to December for first-year students, January to March for second years and April to June for the third years. For the other nine months the students would work their way through all the gardens departments – tropical, temperate, herbaceous and alpine and arboretum, gaining, if they paid attention, experience from and knowledge of the greatest collection of plants in any garden on the globe. There were no lengthy summer holidays as at university, only three weeks' paid leave a year plus the odd bank holiday. At the end of the course, if you were successful in both exams and practical work, you would be awarded the Kew Diploma at Pass, Credit or Honours level. It all seemed so improbable from here, such a long way off.

The first problem was finding somewhere to live, a task not made any easier by the fact that the list of suggested accommodation was at least a year out of date. From late September, when I started, until late November, I lodged in a tiny room in a seedy house on the Mortlake Road, accompanied by the roar of traffic and an assortment of insect life with which I shared the bedding. The 8ft by 6ft room – one single bed, one chest of drawers, one wooden chair and one hook behind the door – was lit only by a 25-watt lightbulb hanging from the ceiling and an orange mercury-vapour lamp on the pavement outside my window.

Breakfast was usually a banana, lunch would be in the local cafe or the works canteen, and the evening meal, provided by my less than fastidious landlady, would be of massive boiled potatoes accompanied by watery fish or leathery and unidentifiable meat. I wondered, in all seriousness, if I was cut out for life in London, if all it could offer was bed bugs, boiled potatoes and bare light bulbs.

Then I had the great good fortune to take over a room in the end cottage of a little terrace that ran down to the river. It had been vacated by one of my fellow students who had decided to get married, and for the next five years, as it turned out, I lived in this stylishly decorated little house – mahogany furniture, scrubbed pine floors and assorted works of modern art – with Mr and Mrs Randall Bell. Randall was a rotund surveyor who played golf once or twice a week, for which he would wear voluminous plus-fours. Every morning, from nine o'clock until ten (he was not an early riser), he would sit in his easy chair and read *The Times*, clad in his plaid dressing gown with a rug over his knees and a pint pot of tea at his elbow. His wife, Eileen, was a painter, potter, admirer of the Bloomsbury Group and author of children's books. They took me under their wing, assumed responsibility for my cultural education – concerts at the Albert Hall and Festival Hall, visits to art galleries and museums – and generally brought me out of myself. He was known as Badger, and she as Cat. And that's what I called them for as long as I knew them. They died about a year ago now, both in their nineties, and both bemused and chuffed in equal measure at what had happened in the years that followed to 'Titch', the wiry Yorkshire youth who came to live with them.

You Can Take the Man
Out of Yorkshire . . .

Passions for one's country, yes, in the very bones and heart of
one, in one's writing, painting, poetry, the songs remembered
on a lovely walk, the pictures formed for comfort in ugly places,
the memory and tradition and love that makes a network to
bind one's heart to the same grey wind-swept upland . . . My
heart's in Yorkshire.

Winifred Holtby

'Never ask a man if he's from Yorkshire. If he is he'll tell
you anyway. If he's not you'll only embarrass him'. A
traditional saying that always makes me smile. I have lived outside
Yorkshire now for twice as long as I lived in it, and yet I still
count myself as a Yorkshireman. I was born there and my earliest
and most impressionable years were spent there and, by the time
he is twenty, a man is pretty well formed by the things that have
happened around him. You can, as they say, take the man out of
Yorkshire, but you can't take Yorkshire out of the man.

Of course, it irritates the pants off people from everywhere else.
I mean, what is it about the place that makes you feel you have to
go on about it so much? Folk don't witter on about Surrey and
Middlesex, do they? Er . . . no, they don't. I discovered that on
my arrival at Kew in 1969.

The thing about Yorkshire is that it is distinct and distinctive, like Cornwall or Scotland or the Isle of Wight. People from all those places are possessed of a particular kind of local patriotism that others find hard to understand. And yet I sympathise with them in being irritated by what you might call 'professional Yorkshiremen' – those who perpetuate the myth that all men from that county call a spade a bloody shovel, can't be doing with any foreign muck on their plate and think that a woman's place is in the home and preferably at the sink. There *are* still Yorkshiremen like that, alas, but they are, mercifully, a dying breed.

There are, I think, several reasons why Yorkshiremen rejoice in their birthright. The first is a geographical one – the distance from London. It is hard to feel connected to a place more than 200 miles away that, every day, assails you with news and views from Brixton and Dartford, Hampstead and Islington, places that have little real infl uence on Swaledale, Wensleydale or Wharfedale. I speak as a Dalesman, as opposed to a city dweller from Leeds or Bradford – not that they feel they have much in common with Hampstead and Chelsea, either.

Westminster makes its presence felt in the long run, in terms of the Dalesman's standard of living, but it is hard to believe that the Prime Minister spends much of his day worrying about livestock in Kettlewell or the depth of the snow on the top at Blubberhouses. When you are that far away, you become more conscious of your own particular identity and begin to build on it and rely on it.

Then there is the terrain of the place. Within 'Broad Acres', as Yorkshire – the largest county in England – used to be known, the Yorkshire Dales are unsurpassed for beauty. Rugged beauty, yes, especially in winter. There are rolling green dales with silver ribbons of river running through them, but there are wild moors, too, the backdrop for *Wuthering Heights*. They breed a certain toughness of character as well as constitution.

Which moves me neatly to literature and the arts. From Charlotte Brontë to Alan Bennett and David Hockney, the tradition continues. But I am beginning to sound like the Yorkshire Tourist Board, which is not the object of the exercise. So what is? Well, to explain the Yorkshire psyche I suppose, though that's something that has defeated finer intellects than mine.

It is sometimes thought of as a kind of philistinism. But Yorkshire poets and writers and artists abound. Neither is it a lack of sophistication. It is, perhaps, a deep-seated love of the place, characterised by a dryness of wit, a fiery self-reliance and a robust sense of proportion. The Yorkshireman is, they say, like the rivers of the dales – slow but deep. All these, of course, are generalisations, but they are often realised when I go back to my native Yorkshire, as I do three or four times a year.

I travelled up a few years ago and alighted from the train at Leeds station. The train to Ilkley had been cancelled, so I took a taxi. As we pulled away from the station on the road towards Ilkley the driver glanced in his rear-view mirror. 'You know who you look like?' he offered, giving me little time to reply. 'Titmarsh'.

'Titchmarsh,' I corrected.

'That's 'im. Titmarsh. Gardening man. You could be ''is brother.'

'Well, actually . . .'

'You even sound like 'im. It's uncanny. If 'e ever needs a stunt double you should put in for't job.'

The conversation carried on pretty much in this vein until we reached our destination. As I got out of the taxi the driver aimed one last sally – 'Titmarsh, that's 'im.'

'Well, I *am* him actually.'

The reply was swift and brief: 'Ha! I bet you wish you 'ad 'is money.'

I fared little better when I went, later that evening, to the King's Hall, scene of my earliest romantic episode with Rosemary Pickering, and where my dad used to dance with my mum when they were courting. It is inextricably entwined with Titchmarsh family history.

I was to entertain a mixed group with 'An Evening With Alan Titchmarsh'. The loos backstage were out of order so I nipped 'front of house' before I went on, slipping quietly into a cubicle so that no one would notice me. While I was there, two old men came in. They were about to take their seats in the audience and had come to relieve themselves, heeding the Yorkshire maxim that says always make sure you've been before you go.

' 'Ave yer been ter one of 'is do's before?' asked the first.

'Aye. Once,' confessed the second.

'What were it like?'

'It were alright. If yer like laffin'.'

So maybe it is that lugubrious humour that characterises a Yorkshireman. George Melly used to tell a story of trying to find his way through the nightmarish one-way systems of Leeds and Bradford on his way to a gig. He has my sympathy. What happened to him could so easily have happened to me and I confess that when I tell this story in my 'Evening With' I tell it in the first person. George, frustrated by the fact that he was totally lost, pulled up and asked a man who was walking his dog, 'Do you know the Bradford turn-off?'

'I should do,' replied the man. 'I married her.'

I am not getting very far in my analysis of what makes Yorkshire special, but the humour must be a part of it. And the candour. Asked by a friend what she thought of her newly decorated front room, my grandmother replied, 'I don't dislike the wallpaper.'

As for me, despite my love for Hampshire and the Isle of Wight – the two places where I have spent the last thirty years of my life – I am Yorkshire to the core. I am aware that when I go 'back home' my vowels flatten and I drop my aitches. But I feel comfortable there.

Of course, they all think I'm a traitor. That I have deserted the county of my birth. When asked what I am doing living down south I always say 'missionary work'. That seems to pacify them a little.

But then, there is also the reaction of southerners to contend with, who themselves think that if Yorkshire is so lovely, why have I come to live down here? I got my comeuppance when I gave a talk at the All England Lawn Tennis and Croquet Club at Wimbledon a few years ago. A rather smart woman in her early forties stood up to introduce me. She had been a Junior Champion at Wimbledon and was now an obstetrician. She cleared her throat. 'We are about to be addressed by Mr Alan Titchmarsh,' she said. 'Alan Titchmarsh is a Yorkshireman and, as you know, Yorkshiremen who come down south are a bit like haemorrhoids. If they come down and go back up they are no bother. But if they come down and stay down they are a pain in the arse.'

I think I'll leave it there.

Exceptional Botanical

Imperial Kew, by the Thames' glittering side.
The Botanic Garden, Erasmus Darwin

Not London proper, then. But Surrey. And on the banks of the Thames, with trees and lakes and glasshouses the likes of which I'd never seen before. If the greenhouses I'd inherited in the parks department were heaven, then Kew was paradise. The garden of Eden.

The Royal Botanic Gardens, Kew, to give them their full and proper title, are divided into three sections – the herbarium, home to several dozen botanists who busy themselves naming and classifying around seven million pressed and dried wild flowers, added to at the rate of 30,000 a year (I can't think they would have been impressed with my modest little prize-winning collection), the Jodrell Laboratory where the plant scientists work on research, and the gardens themselves, now referred to as the Living Collections Division (just in case you were in any doubt).

The students work in the Living Collections Division, in between their lecture blocks, and hope that it is still alive when they have finished. In 1969 we first-year students were thrown in at the deep end of academic work as soon as we arrived – day after day of lectures in the raked theatre of the Jodrell Laboratory, weekly plant identification tests (twenty plants at a time), and examination after examination at the end of each three-monthly session.

The plant identification tests are regarded as an important part of the course, since Kew aims to turn out *plantsmen* as distinct from mere *gardeners*. For this reason they were undertaken every week of the year, not just during the three-month lecture block, and with several hundred thousand plants to choose from, the ante was upped a bit from my college days when only a few hundred plants grew on the student campus. Plants were chosen, generally, because they were in flower or looking good at that particular time of year, so if you kept your eyes open as you walked round the gardens, you could probably narrow the field. But tests devoted to ferns or conifers could be real stinkers. Only those students who could identify pine trees by the number of needles in each cluster and their relative length – the nerds of the botanical world – would light up at the sight of twenty of these seemingly identical lumps of tree. With pines, I still struggle.

Over our three years of lectures we were instructed in the finer points of structural botany, plant anatomy, mycology, entomology, genetics, plant taxonomy and plant physiology. The botanical aspect was nothing if not thorough. In the third year we would graduate to landscape design and construction, and – least favourite of mine, since our lecturers were rather dreary men imported from some business college in Isleworth – management. So much of what they said seemed to me to be obvious. How could they compete with lectures on the structure and behaviour of plant cells or the life cycle of the potato cyst eelworm, which was, to me, a revelation?

We were still woefully short of women – there was only one in each year – and by the end of the first term's examinations, three or four students would have fallen by the wayside and been unable to cope, either with the new life away from home or the intensity of the lecture block. That whittled us down to a hard core of fifteen or so who then usually stayed the course for the full three years.

The thing about Kew's world reputation was it ensured that we had a ready supply of guest lecturers who would turn up on Monday evenings to talk to the archaically named 'Mutual Improvement Society'. I was the society's chairman during my time there, hosting the society's centenary celebrations. It's not quite on a par with being president of the Oxford Union – or even the Cambridge Footlights – but it was fun while it lasted, and while the likes of Graham Stuart Thomas, Christopher Lloyd and assorted eminent scientists came and talked to us about their pet subjects, or travellers and plant collectors came and shared their Boy's Own adventures with us as we sat enthralled by stories of derring do that far outranked *Swallows and Amazons* and the Famous Five – and all in the quest for plants. While they may not have had much physical resemblance to Harrison Ford, their exploits in far-flung corners of the globe, with primitive tribes and treacherous terrain, were the stuff dreams were made on and every bit as hair-raising as *Raiders of the Lost Ark*.

In spite of their passion and enthusiasm, the dazzling 'lantern slides' and the impressive display of artefacts and souvenirs that littered the podium, I decided that plant collecting was not for me. I was happier growing them once they had made it back to Blighty. I don't think it was the absence of a sense of adventure, more likely my lifelong affinity to hot and cold running water and personal hygiene, the legacy of having a plumber for a father.

Odd things stick with me from those lectures. The talk by a woman called Latimer who had rediscovered the coelacanth, the strange fish thought to be a link with land mammals and which was assumed to be extinct until she had found a specimen somewhere around Madagascar in 1938. It had been named *Latimeria chalumnae* in her honour. It looked a bit like her – pale and interesting.

A lecture on the flowers of the Drakensberg mountains – a 700-mile-long range in South Africa – was given by a Professor Killick who wore a pinstriped suit and looked like a bank manager. I wondered what he wore in the mountains. Maybe he slackened his tie.

There was another talk by a rather dour member of gardens staff on the flora of the Burren in southern Ireland, which is quite unique. The entire lecture was memorable for being mumbled through a thick grey beard. I only heard about one word in four, but it did make me want to visit the place. And nearly forty years later I did.

Each of these lectures would be preceded by 'Items of Interest' brought by students. It was a way of encouraging us to be more comfortable with public speaking. The idea was to find something unusual in the gardens (not too difficult considering it was about the largest plant collection in the world) and bring it along to fascinate your fellow inmates. Success was generally judged by the volume of the response – the more laughs you could get, the better.

The most memorable entry was *Lodoicea maldivica*, the double coconut or *coco de mer*, from the Seychelles. The tree itself is a tall palm, but it is the fruit that attracts the most interest. The museums at Kew are a treasure house of all kinds of oddities made from plants, and in one of them a student with a wry sense of humour had found a polished example of the double coconut. He held it out in front of him and got the desired reaction. When polished, the double coconut looks just like – there is no delicate way of putting this – a black bottom with two perfectly formed buttocks divided by a central niche. Beautiful, though. The image stays with me to this day.

Round and Round the Garden

Go down to Kew in lilac-time.
Alfred Noyes

In all walks of life there are choices to be made. One of the most important at Kew was whether to wear clogs or wellingtons. We were offered a pair of either during our first week there. It was simply a matter of going down to the stores in the Melon Yard – a range of long, low greenhouses or 'pits' where the exotic fruits used to be grown and where all manner of tender plants were now propagated – and asking Arthur, the grey-haired man with the moustache and the brown coat, for a pair of our chosen footwear in the appropriate size. Arthur was the dead spit of Ronnie Barker in *Open All Hours*, though without the stammer, and his voice had more of a Ken Livingstone whine than Arkwright's northern twang.

'Clogs or wellingtons?'

'Er . . . clogs please.'

'Size? And don't say sevens because I haven't any left.'

'Eights then.' Pause. 'Have you got any thick socks?'

'Don't do socks.'

The clogs were used competitively each autumn in the 'Clog and Apron Race', which took place on the Broad Walk that runs from Kew's Orangery to the Palm House Pond, a distance of perhaps a hundred and fifty yards. Clad in this traditional apparel (both still worn by Kew students in the late 1960s), those who were rash enough to enter would clatter their way down the wide Tarmac path, sparks flying from their footwear and their denim aprons billowing like kites. The prize was a crate of beer, which was shared round anyway, so it mattered not who won or lost, but how you clattered down . . .

Students of a romantic nature would plump for clogs as their daily footwear when working in the gardens. They had stiff black leather uppers, leather laces and wooden soles equipped with irons on sole and heel that resembled horseshoes. It was impossible to get around in them quietly. My romantic inclinations should have led me to request them, but on this occasion practicality outweighed any fanciful thoughts and I stuck with the wellies, being of the same disposition as Greta Garbo – unable to function properly unless my feet are both dry and comfortable. (She wore carpet slippers underneath that crinoline for *Queen Christina*. I just drop it in in case you're interested.)

Those who did opt for the clogs would generally capitulate to their discomfort after a couple of weeks and go grovelling to Arthur for a pair of wellies. He'd shrug and disappear into the dimly lit bowels of his store room – 'I haven't got any sevens, so don't ask' – before returning with a dusty pair of boots and handing them over with a resigned 'Sign here', pointing to the equally dusty Morocco-bound ledger on his wooden counter.

The lecture block over and exams behind us, we would now

The man who started it all – Grandad Hardisty with his one-year-old grandson on his allotment by the River Wharfe.

A young gardener's hero, Percy Thrower, host of *Gardening Club* in 1957.

Starting work – in the potting shed on the council nursery
in front of the 'Poisons cupboard'.

Out of the potting shed and into the flower bed – the fruits
of my labours on The Grove, Ilkley in the 1960s.

The Palm House shortly after it was built, and 100 years on with students Titchmarsh and Parkinson 30ft up among the fronds.

Year of '69 – the new students at Kew, I'm second from the right on the front row, Hush Puppies and hipsters to the fore.

In the greenhouse I built with Dad in Sunningdale, and Alison's first foray into photography on the back cover of my first hardback, *Gardening Under Cover*.

Into the studio – fake sky, fake shed but a genuine rugby shirt on *Nationwide* 1980.

Chelsea Flower Show 1985 – H.M. The Queen, a Gold Medal-winning garden and a blazer and bow tie that won no prizes.

On the cover of *Amateur Gardening* – what every celebrity gardener should have been wearing in 1983.

My first flower, Sweet Pea 'Alan Titchmarsh', raised in 1985 – still growing strong and smelling just as sweet.

Solving gardening problems for *Breakfast Time* viewers in 1985, with Nick Ross trying to get a word in edge-wise.

Introducing the new presenter of *Gardeners' World* to the nation, 1997.

Back to nature – exploring the River Wharfe at Bolton Abbey with Grace and Favour in 1993.

Barleywood, the television garden we lived in from 1981 to 2002.

The Last Night of the
Proms – microphone and
camera switched off so the
presenter can give voice to
'Land of Hope and Glory'.

The High Sheriff of the Isle
of Wight 2008–9, with hat,
sword and medals – a far cry
from pictorial knitwear.

be distributed throughout the gardens, to benefit the plants and more lowly members of staff with our new-found knowledge. The man in change of the 'Living Collections Division' was the Scot who had asked me about Wisley's rock garden at my interview, Dick Shaw. He was an earnest chain-smoker with a perpetually furrowed brow, usually clad in a bottle-green jacket, and who always had a smile and a word for you, if not much time. He did seem to have the weight of the world on his shoulders and – by all accounts – a fiery temper that would erupt like Vesuvius when his patience ran out. The running of the individual departments he left to five men, each with the archaic title of Assistant Curator.

The herbaceous and alpine department was presided over by George Preston, known, rather rudely, as 'Piggy'. He was a squat, bulky man in a tweed suit whose face, while not exactly Gloucester Old Spot, did have something of a meaty appearance. It was undeniable that he had the look of a pork butcher. Piggy Preston was an alpine specialist and ruled his rock garden and alpine house with a dibber of iron. He did not smile a lot, and expected total dedication from his students. He also had no neck – his head sat directly on his shoulders, which meant that if you said something to one side of him, he would swivel his entire body rather like Margot Fonteyn doing a half pirouette, fixing you with his gimlet eye as he came in to land. It was not without a certain degree of grace, and I always had to stop myself smirking when he did it. In later life I got to know him rather better when I served, briefly, on the Royal Horticultural Society's Rock and Alpine Group Committee, judging alpine exhibits at RHS shows. (Oh, I've lived.) By then he had become a gentle and rather avuncular figure and I wished I'd been better disposed to him – and he to me – during my time as a student. Like all the Assistant Curators he got round the 300 acres of gardens on a bike, his particular machine being identifiable by its wicker basket on the front. I never saw anything in it. Not a sausage.

The decorative department was responsible for the displays of bedding throughout the gardens – those large flower beds down either side of the Broad Walk, for instance, and the conservatory known as 'Number 4', which my landlady Mrs Bell always referred to as 'Bournemouth' on account of the fact that it reminded her of the winter gardens in that seaside resort, or what she *thought* it might look like. I can't ever imagine Mrs Bell in Bournemouth. She holidayed in Aldeburgh for the festival, and had a little cottage in Walberswick – much more her style. The decorative department came under Brian Halliwell, a plantsman of great knowledge who hailed from Halifax. Mercurial of temperament, he could go from laughter to anger quicker than anyone I have ever known. If he looked like having one of his black moods, the quickest way to divert him was to talk about theatre, which he was as passionate about as he was plants. I spent some time in his department working in the office, and learned as much about Noël Coward and Laurence Olivier as I did about nicotianas and lupins.

The temperate department came under the gum-chewing and inscrutable Ian Beyer. He was a sallow-skinned man who talked to you as though he knew quite a lot but did not want to let you in on the entire story. His eyes would dart this way and that, as if looking for the nearest exit, or for a tribe of Indians who were about to come over the hill with bows and arrows. His territory consisted of the Temperate House, the Palm House and the Australian House, perhaps the most pleasant climate in which to work – light and airy and not too hot, with no sign of any Indians.

The arboretum – Kew's magnificent collection of trees, many of them several hundred years old – was managed by George Brown, a Devonian with a rolling West Country burr and the most laid-back attitude of any of the Assistant Curators. What George Brown did not know about trees you could have written on a pinhead. He also had a balanced view of work. It was important and it was what he devoted himself to from 8 till 5, but he was also a family man, and a people person. George liked folk, and folk liked George. However much of a rush he might have been in, he always had enough time to talk to you – about trees, about the weather, or about what was in the news, though one always had the feeling that certain things about life baffled him: 'Oh, I don't know, Alan. Do you?' would come out in those soft, rolling tones, and then he would pedal his bike off in the direction of his office to tackle more of the paperwork that you felt he regarded as a complete waste of his time. George died tragically early after his retirement, a loss to trees and a loss to those who had enjoyed his company.

I spent the best part of a year working with him in his office and learnt as much about humanity as I did about arboriculture. I caught sight, one day, of a memo he had written, lying on his desk. I had the task, that day, of putting George's internal post into 'transit' envelopes, which were collected by uniformed messengers for distribution around the gardens. The memo was addressed to the curator and stated that although he (George) was grateful for the offer of more overtime, in that the funds were a bit short and extra was always useful, he would really have to decline, since he felt that money was not the only thing in life, and the one commodity he did not seem to have enough of was time. They were prophetic words. I've thought about them often since.

The joy of all these departments was to come, but the first one to which I was posted was the tropical department. This consisted of a range of nursery glasshouses – the Tropical Pits (sunk into the ground by the Victorians to help preserve heat, hence the name), the ferneries where Kew's tender ferns were grown, and the 'T-range', named after its shape, like a capital 'T'. This was a conglomeration of glasshouses that has since been replaced by the grand Princess of Wales conservatory. It sheltered, among other things, cacti and succulents in a couple of ordinary greenhouses, and one lean-to whose back wall was painted with a desert scene. Arizona came to Surrey courtesy of Mrs Sherman Hoyt, whose name the house bore. To go in there alone each morning was a weird experience, rather like being on the set of a John Wayne Western before the cast arrived.

Other greenhouses were devoted to orchids and to the giant waterlily *Victoria amazonica*, which grew in its own pool of warm water that was filled with a shoal of grey guppies. The atmosphere here was truly tropical – steamy and humid, with the pinging of 4-in diameter iron heating pipes all day long.

Stan Rawlings ARPS (he was a keen photographer) was in charge of the entire tropical department, though I seldom saw him without an overcoat. I suppose he felt the cold when he went out. A Londoner with the voice of a market trader, he brooked no nonsense from his students. In spite of the fact that I am pathologically punctual, I managed to sleep in twice during my first week in his department (I was purely and simply knackered from three months of intensive study). On the first occasion I was greeted with a raised eyebrow. I was only a quarter of an hour late.

On the second occasion – twenty minutes – it was suggested to me that on the next Saturday morning I go into Richmond and purchase a new alarm clock. 'Otherwise "Yarra-tervere."'

I got the message. I got the alarm clock. I was not late again.

Under each of the Assistant Curators were Gardens Supervisors, a rank equivalent to that of foreman, from which title it had been changed only a few months previously. In charge of cacti was E.W. Macdonald, known universally as 'Mac', an eccentric fag-smoking bachelor with sandy hair and a passion for Egyptology. Well into his fifties, he had the countenance of a smiling gnome and lived in a bedsit on the Mortlake Road. Like all the plantsmen at Kew, he had an unrivalled knowledge of his charges, but I did worry that one day all life might have to offer, when I became an expert in my chosen field, was an unrivalled knowledge of one group of plants and a bedsit on the Mortlake Road. It was Mac himself who warned me off. 'Specialisation leads to extinction,' he would say. It had a tragic confessional ring to it.

Bert Bruty was the fern expert, a round, swarthy, quietly spoken man with a flat cap, dark grey suit and – invariably – wellies. Ferns insist on high humidity. I did not work in his department, and as a result I never once heard him speak, though I imagined when he did that it would be the low rumbling whisper of a mole, the creature he most resembled. His ferns – not the most animated of plants – were happy with his silence. Perhaps gardeners, like people with dogs, also grow to resemble their charges.

Responsible for Kew's orchids, and my immediate boss, was George Nicholson, a shambling south-east Londoner whose off-white shirt with rolled-up sleeves seemed always to be escaping his trousers, and whose gap-toothed smile revealed a certain shyness. He spoke in a hesitating, stertorous manner, rather like a schoolboy who had just been reprimanded by a headmaster and who needed to explain that he hadn't really meant to do that but it had just sort of . . . happened. The orchid family is the largest in the plant kingdom, with 880 genera and around 22,000 accepted species – twice as many species as in the bird kingdom and four times more than the number of mammal species. While he might not have encountered all of them, George knew his subject inside out.

Taken together, the knowledge of all these experts was prodigious. What's more, it was available to any student who cared to ask for it. George, like Mac and Brian Halliwell, George Brown and George Preston (there were a lot of Georges) were always happy to pass on their experience, and it was that, as well as the breadth of the plant collection, that made Kew such a tremendous place to learn the craft of gardening.

At least during the winter we were warm in the T-range. Temperatures seldom fell below 70F in the warmer houses, though one or two of the cooler ones, where the cymbidiums lived, were allowed to drop to 60F. In summer life here was akin to the Caribbean and most of us wore shorts and T-shirts, though never George, whose grey flannels, off-white shirt and tie seemed never to change. Cockroaches loved the place. Turn on the light in the potting shed attached to the greenhouses after dark and you would see them scuttling away under our lockers and behind the potting bench. I never did grow to like them. When we rearranged boulders around the lily pool they would run out and we would squash them underfoot. They cracked, then squelched. Eugh! Even most of the insectivorous plants – grown in glass-fronted cases in their own corridor alongside the lily house – would turn up their noses at cockroaches. The Venus fly traps, sticky-leafed sundews and butterworts were happy with aphids and house flies – a cockroach would have given them severe indigestion. But the tropical pitcher plants, nepenthes, grown separately since they liked higher temperatures and greater humidity, were up to the job. Planted in slatted wooden baskets and suspended from the rafters of the greenhouse, they would dangle their urns of fluid from the tips of their leaves – surely the most sophisticated plant adaptation of all. Tip out the fluid and you would find cockroaches among the fermenting brew. Tough brutes, pitcher plants. And useful.

When it came to characters the little enclave of the T-range would have made a mini-soap opera in its own right. As well as George Nicholson it was peopled by Gregory, a camp Barbadian who wore Bermuda shorts, flip-flops and colourful shirts, but who changed out of his work clothes every evening to go home on the bus. He would put on a crisp white shirt and tie, a neatly pressed pair of trousers and a shortie raincoat, slip on his highly polished black shoes, splash on some highly fragrant floral aftershave, bid the boss 'Good evening, George' – ignoring the rest of us – and catch the No. 27. He liked to have his Sunday lunch at the Strand Palace Hotel and I wondered what he told his friends he did at Kew.

Cathy had been an art student in her youth and was a fine illustrator, but had taken to gardening, and orchids in particular, as a second career. She was a bit nervy, and good company for J.C., a tall, rather fey character who resembled Frederik of the pop duo Nina and Frederik, with a ginger beard. J.C. was never happier than when wandering among his charges wielding a hosepipe and eventually transferred to the laboratories, where he put on a white coat and grew orchids from seed under aseptic conditions.

Joy was the girl who could turn the head of all the male students at Kew. Slender as a pencil, she wore bell-bottomed jeans and a T-shirt and had her long, silky blonde hair held up behind her head with one of those leather-and-wooden-peg things from which it would perpetually try to escape. She wore hardly any make-up. She didn't need to. Naturally beautiful, with a ringing laugh, she was, alas, married to a third-year student and so beyond reach. The words of the hymn 'And with Joy we'll persevere' were a cruel reminder that there was little point. But I went to the occasional concert with her – she read a lot and thought she needed to extend her musical tastes. As Mrs Bell was facilitating the development of my own musical education by recommending suitable performances, Joy asked if she could come along once or twice. I basked in her reflected glory, especially at the bus stop when other students passed. I forget her opinion of Berlioz's *Harold In Italy*, but I remember wearing my new coat to impress her.

Jim Piper was the old man of the T-range. On the surface

gruff and dour, he had a wicked sense of humour and years of experience under his gnarled old belt. Stooped, with a rolling gait, a dome of a head and thick horn-rimmed glasses, he seemed to spend his life potting on orchids into a mixture of osmunda fibre and plastic string (we were experimenting with growing media) and without looking up would growl, 'It's no job for a grown man . . .'

Into this maelstrom of humanity came, each year, a fresh batch of students for them to get to grips with. It's a wonder anything grew at all.

We learned the difference between terrestrial orchids (those that grew in the ground) and epiphytes (those that clung to trees for support, as opposed to parasites, which extract nutrients from their host). I loathed the fat and blowsy cattleyas that always reminded me of the mink-coated ladies who would pin them in a corsage to their bosoms, and felt only slightly better disposed towards the cymbidiums whose long flower spikes, in the cooler of our orchid houses, could last for weeks on end.

I suppose, really, that I had never much liked orchids at all, except for our native species that are more modest and bashful than their tropical counterparts. But I swiftly learned that to say 'I don't like orchids' was akin to saying 'I don't like music', so varied are they in form, size and colour. If you can't find anything you like out of 22,000 species you are impossible to please.

I learned to love the slipper orchids – paphiopedilums and phragmipediums – the hot-house versions of our own lady's slipper orchid. I began to draw them, too, in pen and ink, relishing their strident markings that seemed to show up better in black and white. My drawing was never on a par with Cathy's, with her art college training, but she was kind enough to be encouraging and laughed that nervous laugh of hers when I said my drawings were rubbish.

Cultivation seemed to be a mixture of repotting, maintaining humidity by damping down the floor with a hosepipe three times daily, and raising and lowering the slatted wooden blinds, which were, at least, less labour-intensive than painting the green whitewash of 'Summer Cloud'.

The giant waterlily had a house all to itself. It was named *Victoria regia* by Sir Joseph Paxton in honour of Queen Victoria. Paxton was the first to flower the plant at Chatsworth in 1849, beating the Royal Botanic Gardens by several months, to Kew's lasting chagrin. I suppose Kew's revenge was to insist on the name change to *Victoria amazonica*, that being, the botanists claimed, the first correctly published description, so consigning Paxton's supreme grovel to botanical history.

We grew it in its own tank of warm water in a large glasshouse at the centre of the T-range. It was raised afresh from a seed the size of a dried pea every January, and grown on in a little water tank until it was ready to plant out in the centre of its final home. Over the course of the summer it would grow into a massive plant, with at any one time half a dozen leaves fully 6ft across, heavily ribbed and spined on the undersides, the better to make them float and to protect them from hungry predators. The leaves were said to be able to support the weight of a baby, and to prove the point we displayed an old photo of the feat by the side of the pool (no current member of staff being prepared to risk the life of their own infant). So hot was it in the Victoria house that the pool, with its 3-ft high stone sides, needed topping up once or twice a day to replace water lost by evaporation. It was all too easy to forget that the tap had been left on and to go about other duties, only to remember an hour later and run back to find guppies flapping their way across the path in the last gasp of life to the horror of passing members of the public. It was for this reason that we tried to do our topping up in the morning; the greenhouses opened at 1 o'clock in order to let us get our watering and general tidying done free of enquiring members of the public who might trip over a hosepipe if they were allowed to wander around willy nilly.

After six months of orchid and fish management it was time for another move, now that I knew all there was to know about orchids. Well, you could only learn a fraction in that time, really, but I knew more about them than I had when I arrived. Back in Ilkley Parks department, the nearest I had come to an orchid was schizanthus – the poor man's orchid. At least at Kew I was paid slightly more.

To the Palm House

I wish to build my fame upon this structure at Kew, which will
be unequalled as yet, by very far and not likely to be surpassed.

Richard Turner

Of all the structures at Kew – and there are many, from the
Pagoda, that eighteenth-century exemplar of the fashion
for chinoiserie, designed by Sir William Chambers for Princess
Augusta, to King William's Temple by Sir Jeffry Wyatville,
which was completed in 1837, the year of that king's death and
the first of Queen Victoria's reign – it is the Palm House, I think,
which is the most iconic. Its very shape says to most people 'Kew
Gardens'. The engineer of the structure, which was completed
in 1848, was the Irishman Richard Turner, but the architect
Decimus Burton is generally credited with the final design,
having simplified Turner's elaborate Gothic excesses. The result
is a building whose lines today are every bit as pleasing – and
modern – as they were a hundred and sixty years ago.

While most students were moved round the gardens every six
months, from temperate to arboretum, decorative to tropical, I
managed, for some reason, to spend a year of my time working
in the Palm House. It remains a period of my life that is dear to
my heart.

Thrills and responsibilities came in ever increasing increments
– the creation of my own little greenhouse in the back garden at

Nelson Road, followed by the three greenhouses of which I was given sole charge in the Parks Department nursery, and then the care of one end of the Palm House at Kew. It was a thrilling, if daunting, prospect.

If you look at the Palm House from the pond that lies in front of it you will see a high central domed area, flanked by two lower 'wings'. The left-hand wing houses Kew's collection of cycads – primitive plants that have survived 'since dinosaurs roamed the earth'. At least that's what I seem to remember reading in the guidebook. Cycads look like palm trees, except that their fronds are much tougher, harder and spinier. They are also much slower growing.

The gardens supervisor in charge of the Palm House was Ruth Storr, a pretty, elfin-faced woman whose slight physique belied her capacity for heavy manual work. She took a while to get to know, but once she felt she could trust you she opened up a little, sharing her knowledge of her charges and her sense of humour in equal measure.

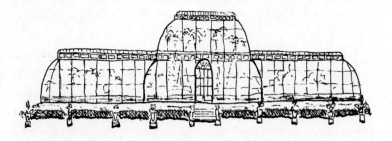

On that summer's morning in 1971 I pushed open the tall, heavy iron door in the central dome of the Palm House and walked in. I was nervous. Not of Ruth, but at the prospect of looking after plants in this horticultural equivalent of Westminster Abbey. Massive palms towered above me, their frothing heads almost out of sight up among the curving white-painted rafters and glazing bars. Two spiral staircases twisted through them, seemingly into infinity, and everywhere was the steady drip-drip-drip of water falling through ornate iron grilles that covered the floor into the dank depth below.

My feet echoed eerily in the silence as I made my way to the small wooden shed that sat, enveloped in foliage, at the centre of the house. Always dimly lit, this 'mess room' had a single 40-watt bulb illuminating its simple interior, with half a dozen chairs pushed against the walls, a sink, an electric kettle and a telephone – a link with the world outside this pocket-sized jungle. There was little else to see, apart from half a dozen tall, slender, grey-painted steel lockers for staff clothing, and a few old magazines stacked in a corner. And Ruth's copy of H.F. Macmillan's *Tropical Planting and Gardening with special reference to Ceylon* – a green cloth-covered book dating from 1946 that was still the bible of cultivation for all those of us working in either the tropical or temperate departments. It lay on a chair in this modest nerve centre from which the Palm House was run, and to which staff would return for their morning coffee and for lunch. It had the feel of a shack in the back of beyond, at the centre of the lost world.

There was no answer to my tentative 'hello', so I dumped my bag – holding my apron and a spare pair of shoes – on one of the chairs and went exploring. It really was like being on another continent. The interior of the glasshouse was so tall, so wide and so densely planted that only the formally arranged paths gave away the influence of civilisation. Those and the plant labels, of course. Every single plant at Kew has a rectangular black plastic label engraved in white showing its family, genus, species and date of introduction to the gardens, along with its indecipherable 'accession number' that allowed its history to be checked in central records.

I walked underneath the coconut and date palms, through tightly packed cocoa, tea and coffee bushes, past cotton plants laden with foaming balls of white wool. The light grew brighter now under the airy canopy of a grove of pawpaws, the whorls of leaves held aloft like parasols, each one fingered like a man's hand, but ten times the size, with fat green fruits clustered around the central stem like gigantic beads. Alongside them, banana plants pushed up their thicket of succulent sheaths, unfurling their scrolls of paddle-shaped leaves in dappled sunlight that turned each one of them into a stained-glass window. Their long, trailing flower stems were packed with hands of embryonic bananas and terminated in a purple pod-like flower that dangled beneath them like an elephant's willy. Such was the imagination of a student gardener.

I found Ruth eventually, hosepipe in hand, watering pot plants on the staging to one side of the house, and I heard then, too, the distant voices of other workers about their chores, their voices and whistling echoing around in the palm-filled heavens.

'Come with me,' she said, and led me to the section reserved for cycads. 'This is your end.'

It was a replay of that first day in the nursery, only now I was given a third of the most famous glasshouse in the world to look after. Not only that, but it did contain one or two rare and unusual plants.

Ruth thumped the side of a large wooden tub. It was taller than she was, and from it erupted a great knobbly stem, like the deformed leg of an elephant, topped by a massive fountain of spiny green leaves. 'They're a bit sensitive to overwatering, so be careful. And some of them are quite rare.'

'I see.'

'Stick your hand inside and feel the compost – if it's dry give them a really good soak.'

'And if it's damp?' I asked, knowing, in my heart, what the answer was.

'Leave them alone and try again the following day. Whatever you do, don't give them too much.'

'Right.'

She must have seen my expression.

'Don't worry, you'll soon get the hang of it.'

It didn't help that one of the plants had a label attached to it saying 'The rarest plant in the world' and that another bore the legend 'The oldest pot plant in the world.' Disbudding carnations wrongly was one thing, killing a plant that had been in Kew's possession since the time of Sir Joseph Banks and Captain Cook was quite another. But fate was kind, the plants both survived twelve months of my ministrations, and they are still there to this day, frightening the life out of students who are convinced that they will be responsible for their demise.

The cycads are not the only remarkable plants protected by the Palm House. The giant bamboo, which rejoices under the name of *Gigantochloa verticillata*, is one of the most astonishing. It can grow, in summer, at the rate of a foot every day. It is the plant everyone thinks of as having built the bridge over the River Kwai – though teak also played a part – and is frequently used for all manner of construction work in its native Burma thanks to its strength and durability. Even in the Palm House, a long way from its native home, its stems quickly reach the roof and have to be cut off before they punch a hole in the glass. But beware! The papery sheaths, glossy and parchment-like, that protect the growing point, and which eventually fall away as the plant grows, are covered in fine, silky hairs that look soft and delicate. They are not. They are capable of perforating human skin with the efficiency of a needle, but invisibly, leaving no trace of their entry. Make the mistake of picking up one of these attractive scrolls without wearing gloves, and the irritation persists for several days, and the hairs are so fine that they are impossible to extract.

We used to erect a scaffolding platform around the palm trees to remove faded leaves, but taking the top out of the giant bamboo required an even greater head for heights, a certain amount of agility, and nerves of steel. The way to get to them is via a curving ladder, affixed to the inside of the dome and about two feet away from it. To climb this you must face inwards. This is all very well on the lower part of the glasshouse, which is vertical, but once the structure starts to curve, you will find yourself climbing out across space, looking downwards. It is not a job for the faint-hearted. Added to which, you must make the journey carrying a long-handled saw with which to remove the offending stems.

Picture me then, on a hot July day, with the sun beating down through the glass, endeavouring to remove the top of a bamboo stem, lying on my stomach looking downwards 63 feet up in the air above the canopy of luxuriant palm fronds. It was a novel but effective way of staying slim. I mean, there cannot be many men 5ft 9in tall who weigh only eight stone. Forget your fancy diets – try a year in the Palm House at Kew. It worked for me.

The Emperor's Visit

The war situation has developed not necessarily to Japan's
advantage.

> Emperor Hirohito announcing Japan's surrender
> in a broadcast to his people after atom bombs
> had destroyed Hiroshima and Nagasaki

On a bright October day in 1971, just into my second year
of studentship, Kew was preparing itself to receive an
important visitor. The Emperor of Japan, known to the Japanese
as Emperor Showa, and to the rest of the world as Hirohito, was
on a state visit to Britain and, as well as going to see the pandas
in London Zoo and meeting the Queen, he would be coming to
Kew to plant a tree as a symbol of reconciliation.

I did not know very much about Hirohito, except that he had
been Emperor of Japan throughout the Second World War and
that he had escaped being tried for war crimes. The mood among
the gardens staff was confused. Those who had relatives who
had suffered at the hands of the Japanese thought the visit at best
inappropriate and at worst insulting. Others felt that it was time to
bury the hatchet. The Emperor was, after all, a respected marine
biologist; a man with many scientific papers to his credit. (It did
not escape the cynical that his specialist subject was jellyfish.)

Those anxious to find something good to say about him pointed
out that after his marriage to Empress Kojun – known outside

Japan as Empress Nagako – he had refused to take a concubine. One or two testoterone-charged students, previously unaware of this tradition, considered relocating to Japan.

The day dawned bright and sunny and at the appointed hour the smart burgundy Rolls-Royce drove through the gilded Main Gate of the gardens on Kew Green and drew to a graceful standstill only a few yards inside the gardens.

I was curious to see this man about whom so many had such strong feelings. Ken Wilson, my parks foreman, had been imprisoned by the Japanese and, unsurprisingly, had few good words to say about them. I felt uneasy on his behalf. Was it really such a good idea to open old wounds just twenty-six years after the war had ended?

Hirohito had become Emperor on the death of his father in 1926 at the age of 25. He had been 36 when his country had invaded China (to which he was said to have no objection), and when he was 40 his country had sided with the Germans in declaring war against the United States, Britain and the Netherlands. Experts argue over the amount of control Hirohito had over the Japanese army, but what seems clear is that he did little to discourage conflict. As Ken and his fellow prisoners would testify, the Japanese concentration camps were renowned for their brutality and inhumanity.

Hirohito had been created Knight Grand Cross of the Royal Victorian Order and Knight Grand Cross of the Order of the Bath in 1921, made a Knight of the Order of the Garter in 1929 and an Honorary Field Marshal in the British Army in 1930. All these honours were revoked in 1942.

After the war US General Douglas MacArthur was insistent that Hirohito should retain the throne of Japan in the interests of stability. The Emperor was never brought to trial.

The rear passenger door of the Rolls-Royce was opened by a security guard in a dark suit, and a small bespectacled man in a dark overcoat stepped out. From the other side of the car emerged an elderly Japanese lady in a pale blue coat and toque – the sort of turban-like hat that used to be worn by Queen Mary. Empress Nagako smiled in all directions, a kindly smile, not over effusive, not mocking. More than anything, it seemed to me a smile that radiated gratitude. The face of her husband bore no expression at all. Neither did I hear him utter a word. Slightly stooped, he walked across the grass in the autumn sunshine, which glinted on his round, rimless spectacles. He was accompanied by Kew's then director, Professor John Heslop-Harrison; at around 6ft 4in, the professor towered over the Emperor.

Encouraged by the director, the Emperor walked towards the 8ft Japanese cedar – *Cryptomeria japonica* – which had, as for all ceremonial tree-planting, already been committed to the earth. It was necessary for the Emperor to shovel on to it only a few token spadefuls of earth, which he duly did, still without expression.

The assembled company of locals, schoolchildren, gardens staff and students managed a polite round of applause. The Emperor made the slightest of bows and then walked off with the director in the direction of the herbarium.

Later I asked one of the botanists how the herbarium tour had gone. I was told that it had progressed according to plan. 'Did the Emperor say much?' I asked. 'Not really. But the funniest thing . . .'

'What?'

'We asked him if he would like anything from the gardens to take back to Japan. Do you know what he asked for?'

I could not guess.

'A packet of rose bay willowherb seeds.'

Rose bay willowherb you will know by sight. It is that tall, wand-like flower of rosy pink that grows wild on railway embankments and flowers in June and July. Many gardeners regard it as a weed – its silky-coated seeds float on every passing breeze and spread it like wildfire. It is sometimes called fireweed. And that was all the Emperor wanted. He was given a packet to take away with him. He smiled for the first time.

I hope it fared better than the Japanese cedar he planted. Within a few hours it had been cut down with an axe by those who objected to his behaviour during the war, and hydrochloric acid poured on its roots.

For several days the felled remains of the tree lay outside George Brown's office in the arboretum. I passed it every day, and eventually suggested, tactfully, that perhaps it should be disposed of, rather than be left lying there as a reminder of the bitter legacy of war. The following day it had gone, and by the end of the week so had the remaining stump. There was no sign that the Emperor of Japan had ever been to Kew Gardens, except that the herbarium was one packet of rose bay willowherb seed short.

I can still recall that day, almost forty years ago, with perfect clarity: the warm October sunshine, the shining Rolls-Royce, the expressionless Emperor towered over by our tall director, the fallen tree and the warmth of the Empress's smile.

Emperor Hirohito died on 7 January 1989. Empress Nagako died in 2000, aged 97 – the longest-lived Japanese Empress Consort in history, having fulfilled the role for 74 years. Look her up in a biographical dictionary, and you will discover her nickname. She was known as 'The Smiling Empress'.

Court and Social

There may be trouble ahead,
But while there's moonlight and music and love and romance,
Let's face the music and dance.

'Let's Face the Music and Dance', Irving Berlin

All this work – swotting for exams during the intensive term of lectures on botany, design, management and the like, and then knuckling down to the practical gardening, along with plant identification tests every week – would, you might think, make for a pretty restricted social life. You'd be wrong. No longer was I subject to the strictures of college life and the rules and regulations laid down by a dictatorial principal safely ensconced with his cup of cocoa in his ivory tower. I was now a working man with a wage packet at the end of every week – albeit a small one – and, aside from those three-month periods of intensive study, some free time in which to let off steam.

London in the early 1970s was, pretty much like today, exactly what you wanted it to be. There were drugs around in abundance if you mixed in 'that sort of company'. I think my parents worried about it. But then I didn't really mix in that sort of company. Drugs frightened the pants off me. Or rather the prospect of the effect they could have. I was quite happy drinking too much wine of an evening in terms of having a good time. At least the effect of alcohol was predictable: I would become happy; I would become more talkative (if that were possible); I would become good-naturedly argumentative, and then I would fall asleep and wake up with an almighty headache. Every single time.

As far as I am aware I was invited to only one party where I knew drugs would be a part of the scene. The invitation came from a swarthy Peruvian-born youth working in the tropical department. He called everybody 'man', regardless of gender, and had a hoarse voice that women apparently found irresistible. I did resist and found an excuse not to go, without, I hope, losing too much face – the main reason, I think, why so many kids succumb to drugs today. I was lucky and, as far as I'm aware, so were the rest of my student friends.

I was less fortunate where girls were concerned. 'Late starter' seemed to apply to most aspects of my life – not through choice, but through circumstances. One female student per intake pretty much reduced the chances of anything happening on that front. They tended to be snapped up within the first month by students quicker off the mark than I was. That tentative and hesitant walk across the floor to ask for a dance was now translated into the broader pattern of life. He who hesitates is well and truly lost. But I did have my moments, even if they were ill-starred. To list them is to risk describing a tragic catalogue of failures that make the years of my youth seem lonely and pathetic; but then solitude either sours or teaches self-dependence. I like to think that the latter is true in my case, and I relate the following in order to offer hope to those similarly unsuccessful in the quest for a suitable partner.

Heather was my first Kew love. A suitably horticultural girl by name at least. She worked in the alpine department – a far cry from her native Australia, which is not renowned for its snow-clad mountains. Maybe she enjoyed the change of scene. Heather was deliciously voluptuous with long blonde hair. Things seemed to be going rather well. I asked her out and she said 'yes', which was at least a 100% improvement on my previous track record in this postal area.

We went out once or twice a week for a couple of months. I even plucked up the courage to whisper 'I love you' in her ear, sitting on the window seat in the Roebuck at the top of Richmond Hill. I'd never whispered it to anybody before. She didn't whisper it back and I wondered if she had heard me properly. I thought it best not to check. The following Saturday we went to a party in one of the student's houses. I looked around after half an hour or so and couldn't see her. I went upstairs to the loo and happened to glance into one of the bedrooms. She was sitting on a bed kissing a Canadian. Perhaps she was just improving Commonwealth relations. It was the end of ours.

A few months later she returned to Australia, and some time after that a middle-aged couple came up to me while I was working in the gardens. They introduced themselves as Heather's parents. They were on holiday. I did my best to be nice to them and I enquired after her. She was very well, they said, and had asked them to find me, wherever I was, and pass on her best wishes. They did not ask if I knew where the Canadian was working. Maybe they'd found him already.

Next came Nita, who worked in the arboretum. She was small and petite, with long, *dark* hair (time to try a change of colour), tight jeans and wellies (always wellies) and dark brown eyes. We smiled at each other across wheelbarrows full of autumn leaves and finally managed to find ourselves in a corner at a student dance. She wore a long navy-blue velvet dress that hugged her neat figure. I was totally smitten. Again. We kissed, but I sensed – rightly – that I was the one making the running. Later in the week she slipped me a note saying, as nicely as she possibly could, that she was going back to her boyfriend. I had caught her on the rebound.

Pam was another brunette. She asked me back to her place for coffee and a snog on the bed. The trouble was, she couldn't stop talking. She did have a rather fetching pair of red velvet hot pants, but when you're trying to get to grips with the physical side of a relationship on a single bed, to find that your inamorata is intent on talking about Golgi bodies is a bit of a turn-off. Golgi bodies? Ah, Lowson's *Textbook of Botany* will tell you all:

'One specialist part of the reticulum which has been seen in plant and animal cells of many types constitutes the Golgi body, named after the Italian cytologist who first recorded its presence in nerve cells of animals. It frequently consists of a number of flattened cisternae lying close to and parallel with one another, and is never associated with ribosomes. Its function has been a subject of controversy over many years and is still obscure, though there is some evidence that it may be the region where new membranes are produced during development of the endoplasmic reticulum.'

My own endoplasmic reticulum was unimpressed. I gave up on her.

Maybe blondes were best after all. Especially when they were named after plants. Calluna was a laboratory technician who was *very* tall and *very* blonde. Natural, though, in so many ways. She towered over me at around 6ft, but I cared not a jot. She was a northern girl with flat vowels, but that was the only thing about her that was flat. One evening while we were engaged in a particularly intimate clinch she asked me what I saw in her. I told her . . .

You see, now it's becoming indelicate. Time for a veil to be drawn over the proceedings. Like the other relationships, this one petered out, though I think, again, at my own instigation. Perhaps scientists are, as a race, too prosaic in their outlook for me. Though she did look wonderful in that short and crisply laundered white coat . . .

It was time to look further afield than the gardens. I joined the local operatic society, met a girl who was a lovely dancer and eventually married her. She has never once, to her enduring credit, mentioned Golgi bodies.

On the Boards

All through the five acts ... he played the King as though
under momentary apprehension that someone else was about
to play the Ace.

Eugene Field reviewing
Creston Clarke's *King Lear, Denver Tribune*, 1880

I can trace the beginnings of my interest in 'play acting' to 1956,
when, aged 7, I was given the painted cardboard head of a
mallard drake and told to leap out of the way of Peter Crowther
who, by virtue of his Christian name, was given the title role in
the little dance we did at infants' school to Prokofiev's music
for *Peter and the Wolf*. My final leap (before I was eaten) was
particularly admired, so athletic did it seem for a small boy. As
sporting prowess goes, it remains the zenith of my achievements.
It is the only thing in life at which I have peaked early.

Like all those who take to the stage, at the core of the love of
drama is an instinctive if oft-denied desire to show off. And to escape.
To become someone else; to do things that one will otherwise be
unable to do; to be people that one will otherwise never be.

Maybe the combination of those two things was what appealed
to me back then (and probably still appeals to me now). After
Peter and the Wolf came the *Pace Egg Play* in the playground on
a summer's afternoon at junior school – a sort of moral pageant
about St George and the Dragon featuring such characters

as Beelzebub and the Bold Slasher (we were too young and innocent to find anything funny in him, 'slash' being a word we learned a few years later at secondary school). But we did snigger at the entrance of the patron saint of Ireland, whose opening line was, 'I am St Patrick from the bogs . . .' Especially since it seemed to have escaped the notice of Mrs Rishworth, the second-form teacher, who was given the role of director, that she had engineered his entrance from behind the boys' lavatory.

I played, to even greater acclaim than my drake, Little Devil Doubt, clad in yellow tights and tunic, with a yellow elasticated balaclava bearing tiny horns, and carrying a dustpan and brush. My moment came in the last part of the play when the mummers exact their dues from the audience of mums:

> Here I am, little Devil Doubt;
> If you don't give me money I'll sweep you all out.
> Money I want and money I crave,
> If you don't give me money I'll send you all to the grave.

I scrabbled around the floor and swept up the pennies hurled by proud mothers with my brush. My success – both histrionic and financial – emboldened me to continue.

There followed a series of plays at secondary school – everything from *Tom Sawyer* (schoolmaster) to an abridged version of *The Merchant of Venice* (I gave them my Shylock) to an adaptation of John Steinbeck's *The Pearl* (a snake) and the complete *A Midsummer Night's Dream*. Alas, I was permitted to give neither my 'Puck' nor my 'Bottom', though at the auditions I am told it was a close-run thing.

I played a monkey in Andre Roussin's *The Little Hut* for Ilkley Players (non-speaking, with a brief appearance only at the end of the play), but by the time I left school I thought my dramatic aspirations would probably have to be sacrificed now that I was going into gardening.

And so, for the first two years of my working life I did not have much of a social life. There is, after all, a world of difference between sowing wild oats and sowing begonias. Even my mother, happiest when she knew where I was, who I was with and what time I would be home, began to worry. 'It's time you got out a bit,' she said. It occurred to me that if she was saying it then it probably was. But where?

The solution presented itself courtesy of Joyce, our next-door-neighbour and mother of twins. She could be heard warbling gems from *The Count of Luxembourg* and *The Merry Widow* as she dashed away with her smoothing iron, producing clean clothes to be dirtied once more by her two energetic sons, Mark and Matthew. Quite how she persuaded the seventeen-year-old boy next door to go with her one evening to the King's Hall where Ilkley Amateur Operatic Society were rehearsing *Oklahoma!* I will never know. But I'm glad I went. In a funny sort of way it changed my life.

Not that I had a large part, and it was hard convincing my father that there was a good reason why I should, at one point, prance across the stage like a horse to the music of 'Surrey With The Fringe on Top'. It was not quite what he had in mind when he suggested that I broaden my horizons.

Rodgers and Hammerstein's *Oklahoma!* was followed by Lionel Monckton's *The Quaker Girl*, so in my first year 'on the boards' I had a taste of both American and Edwardian English musical comedy. And I loved them. I loved their air of romance and escapism. I loved the tunes, the magic of the footlights and the 'otherworldliness' of theatre. It took me out of myself to a place where I seemed to have confidence and a degree of ability. I had found similar qualities growing plants, but appearing on stage was more sociable.

It also allowed me to meet girls. Not that anything lasting came out of Ilkley Operatic or, as my mother liked to call them, 'your amateurs'. There was Marjorie – a strangely old-fashioned name even then – one of the dancers, who had the most wonderful smile and a graceful way of moving. She was a couple of years older though. Too old to look at me. There was another gorgeous girl I was making advances to until she turned up at a dance with a feller in tow – and a big, hulking rugby player at that. I smiled and went back to my half of Watney's Red Barrel.

I did borrow Dad's old Borgward one night and take out a girl from Guiseley who was in the chorus, but she went a bit faster than the car and scared me off. Pathetic really.

I managed only two seasons with Ilkley Operatic before I went to college, and then I was into five years of concentrated study with little time for anything other than a pint in the pub of a Saturday night and the odd visit to the theatre or the Albert Hall. Regular rehearsals would be out of the question.

But when my student course had ended and I was poised to stay on and work at the gardens, I reckoned it was time I had another crack at it. And at broadening my horizons socially. Clearly I was not destined to get it together with another gardener. Or even a laboratory technician, which was about as far as lateral thinking would get me at Kew.

Quite how I ended up at Ye White Hart in Barnes – a Thames-side pub on the last bend of the Oxford and Cambridge boat race course – I am not sure. I had sat in the audience of Kingston Operatic Society's productions at Richmond Theatre, and of Barnes and Richmond Operatic Society, who also performed there. I could have joined either. But the Barnes lot looked younger and livelier. More my own age and, I hoped, disposition.

None of my Kew mates was interested in dramatics, so I was well and truly on my own. It might not have been a long journey by train from Kew Bridge to Barnes Bridge in terms of miles, but it was in terms of confidence. I almost didn't bother. But I steeled myself, plucked up the courage and pushed open the door of the upstairs function room of a London pub where fifty folk were belting out 'Flash Bang Wallop'. I never looked back. That December I played the role of 'Buggins – a pessimist' in *Half a Sixpence*. Casting, I hope, against type.

I felt the same sort of camaraderie and friendliness of spirit during the rehearsals for that show as I had felt when I had gone along to the King's Hall for rehearsals of *Oklahoma!*. It seems rather facile now I come to set it down, but meeting a group of folk who laugh at the same things you laugh at, enjoy the same sort of music you do and share your own love of theatre is a potent and magical mixture. It is not about egos so much as companionship. There were folk there with whom I had little in common other than a vocal score. But there were others who became, and remain, my best friends.

Amateur theatre can, in some circumstances, be a hotbed of intrigue and a place of naked rivalry. It would be futile to deny it. But the half dozen true friends I made during the years I was a part of BROS were and are as interested in enjoying each other's company as they are in getting parts and showing off.

Mind you, I quite liked that bit, too. In my operatic career (1972–1981) I performed at Frank Matcham's masterpiece, Richmond Theatre, in such virtuoso roles as Ko-Ko in *The Mikado* and Sir Joseph Porter in *HMS Pinafore*, Simplicitas (sounds like sanitary-ware) in *The Arcadians* and Fyedka in *Fiddler on the Roof* – standing on a table to reach the top notes. I had a passable tenor, but sometimes it needed a helping hand. I played in *Cowardy Custard* and *Oh What A Lovely War!*, and even essayed the classics, playing Second Gravedigger in *Hamlet* for Richmond Shakespeare Society.

Every Saturday I would go to the Baldur Bookshop on Richmond Hill and, under the dyspeptic gaze of the grumpy fag-smoking proprietor, sift through the stacks of wooden drawers for signed postcards of Edwardian musical comedy stars – Lily Elsie and Joseph Coyne in *The Merry Widow*, Gertie Millar in *Our Miss Gibbs*, Gaby Deslys and Ellaline Terriss, Florence Smithson and George Graves, Carl Brisson and Seymour Hicks.

Along with the handful of gardening books I had brought with me from home, I also brought Mark Lubbock's *Complete Book of Light Opera*. It was an interest ignited by *The Quaker Girl* (in which I had played 'William – a waiter at The Chequers Inn' – very few lines, spoken in a rustic burr at the beginning of Act 1). The postcards – bought for only a pound or two, and sometimes as little as 50p – meant that I could put faces to the names of those original cast members of musicals by Franz Lehar and Carl Zeller, Lionel Monckton and Sigmund Romberg. I stuck them in a rather smart scrapbook and immersed myself in their music and that of Ivor Novello and Noel Coward. Odd? Well maybe a little, but I just loved the music, and the romance of it all. I still do. That wonderful world of melodic make-believe. An everyman's Arcadia.

But the operatic society was real. Aside from the music it meant meeting new mates of the same age but different backgrounds. A solicitor (Steve, with whom I would later go on holiday to the West Country), a baker, a bank manager, an accountant and a milkman.

But the best thing that came out of my brief but memorable dramatic career was meeting the woman who would become my missus. She was a dancer in *Half a Sixpence*. We went on our first date on New Year's Eve 1973 and her dad had to come out and get us in his Ford Cortina at one o'clock in the morning because there were no taxis to be had. It was foggy. He wore an overcoat over his pyjamas. He didn't look best pleased. But he looked happier when I married her a couple of years later.

Staying On

Stay for me there: I will not fail
To meet thee in that hollow vale
                    'An Exequy', Henry King

By the beginning of 1972 I had realised that I was going to have to make a decision about my future. The Kew diploma course would end in August and I would be ejected into the big wide world. If I consulted my mental checklist of Ken Wilson's mapped-out career, I had fulfilled three of his requirements – my apprenticeship, college and Kew. There was only The Grotto to go. But it did not appeal. Where was the thrill in going to a place of learning run by an organisation with the far from galvanising title of The Institute of Park and Recreation Administration? And did I really want an office job in local government, managing men around the town? What then? Where now?

It seemed that at least I was on course to achieve my diploma, so I would have a decent qualification, the Department of Education and Science having recently awarded the Kew diploma degree equivalent status. The thing was, where would I use it?

I quite liked it where I was. Could I stay on? Mind you, I was a bit wary of it. There were those who worked at Kew all their lives – botanists who had come here as callow youths and devoted themselves to a particular group of dried and pressed flowers until they ended up being dried and pressed themselves. At least one old plant taxonomist (not to be confused with a taxidermist – taxonomists classify things, taxidermists stuff them) had only been discovered slumped over his dried specimens several days after his death. Old taxonomists don't move much and seem to spend their lives hunched over pressed flowers with a hand lens to their eye, so it is easy to see how he could have been overlooked until he started to smell more strongly than usual. (The parallels between taxonomy and taxidermy now seem closer). But my real pleasure was in growing live plants rather than in classifying dead ones. Perhaps a post in the gardens themselves? I made enquiries.

It seemed that the post of Gardens Supervisor with responsibility for the Queen's Garden – the seventeenth century garden immediately behind Kew Palace – was coming up. Would I be interested in that? I said that I would. It was a garden I loved and, over the past few years, I'd been responsible for clipping the box hedges there as a way of earning a bit of overtime. I had, said Brian Halliwell, the Assistant Curator under whose charge the Queen's Garden came, a good eye and reasonable speed when it came to clipping. He probably only said that to keep me doing the job for a pittance, but I fell for his flattery, and night after night, in May and June, from six o'clock until it was too dark to see, I snipped away with hand shears (electric ones just did not achieve the same crisp line) at the long, low hedges that surrounded the formal parterre, and the great mound of box that was topped with the gilded iron rotunda, reached via a spiral path. Allowing for bad weather, it took me the best part of a month.

Of course, there was Betty to cope with. Betty was the chatelaine of the Queen's Garden; had been since its inception. She had shown the Queen around at its opening and asked: 'Your Majesty, what do you think of our laburnums?' rather in the way that one imagines Mrs Thatcher might have addressed our monarch in later years. Betty was a classic 'English pear' –

five feet nothing and invariably clad in a woolly cardy and black ski-pants. Her short, curly hair, which owed a lot to Boots the chemist, was as black as night, except for its snowy roots, and she had a Thora Hird way of adjusting her accent to suit the class of person to whom she was speaking. When irritated by members of the public intent on asking what she considered to be inane questions, she would pretend she was foreign and go off into a nonsensical babble that seemed to owe its origins to some obscure eastern European state. It was accompanied by ferocious arm waving and elaborate variations on rude gestures. At moments like this, the rest of us would stifle our laughter by clamping our hands over our mouths and diving into the shrubbery until the torrent of gobbledegook had subsided. When eventually the visitor departed, confused, we would emerge and Betty would continue the foreign conversation, complete with gesticulations, until the tears rolled down our cheeks and we begged her to stop.

The Queen's Garden was opened by Her Majesty (ably assisted by Betty) in May 1969, before I arrived at the gardens, and is what Kew's librarian of the time, Ray Desmond, called 'a kind of Stuart pastiche', using plants and garden styles appropriate to the reign of King George III, who lived in the adjacent Kew Palace – also known as the Dutch House – for about three months of each year. It is too intense, being crammed into an acre, to have ever been created on the site, but it does give a flavour of gardening styles of the time. The Palace itself is a small but beautifully proportioned red-brick, Dutch-gabled house, quite recently restored and refurnished to its former glory. The garden layout that was created behind it in 1969 comprises a sunk garden filled with herbs, a laburnum walk leading to a gazebo, a formal parterre with a rectangular pool in the centre of which a copy of Verrochio's *Boy with a Dolphin* spurts water. There is a curved yew hedge decorated with five 'terms' – carved busts atop pedestals (the sole survivors of the eight that were carved for Frederick, Prince of Wales) – a pleached allee of hornbeams and the box mound with its wrought iron 'treillage'. The Palace and garden ignited in me a passion for all things Georgian. Line, proportion, the importance of angles and the use of axial vistas I still regard as being vitally important, and Georgian houses are invariably filled with light. The thought of being in charge of this gem had tremendous appeal. Maybe one day I might make the post of Assistant Curator. When somebody retired. But all that was a long way off. No need to worry about the future yet.

I did pass my diploma, with credit, but fate intervened before I could take up the post in the Queen's Garden.

Dick Shaw, Kew's mercurial curator, had finally lost patience with the Sassenachs and taken up the post as curator of Edinburgh Botanic Garden. Perhaps they understood him better there. His deputy, John Simmons, had taken over and one day summoned me to his office. I was nervous. Maybe he'd decided I wasn't up to the job on offer and they'd have to let me go. I wiped my feet on the mat, cleared my throat (nervous habit) and knocked on the large mahogany door of his imposing office.

'Come in.'

At least the words were delivered brightly and with passion, but then John Simmons' words almost always were. Short and stocky with short, dark wiry hair and a goatee beard and moustache, he was the only member of the gardens staff to have a bike like my old one back in Ilkley – the one with the small wheels. Rather pathetically, I always felt something of an affinity with him over that. John spoke – and still speaks – very fast, his words running into one another, punctuated not with pauses, full stops and commas, but with chuckles and grins. If this was the brush-off, at least it would be delivered good naturedly.

'I gather you've been offered the Queen's Garden.'

'Yes.'

'Are you keen to take it?'

'Yes.'

He tugged at his beard – another habit – and sat on the edge of his desk. 'Only I've had an idea for a while and I wondered if you might like to be involved.'

It was a statement as much as a question, and one that seemed vague in outline. I could do little more than look interested and wait for him to continue. One thing John could always do was fill silence.

'Staff training. We don't do enough of it. And what we do is not very well put together. A bit ad hoc. I think we need some proper courses for members of staff – teaching them the basic gardening skills and some theory, too – how plants grow, that sort of thing. Pests and diseases, bit of botany, but mainly practical stuff. Give them a certificate at the end to show they've done it. I think that's important. What do you think?'

'Well, yes. I think it's very . . . interesting.' Interest seemed to be the key here.

'I'd like you to be Gardens Supervisor with responsibility for staff training – setting up the courses, running them and training the staff. What do you think?'

'What about the Queen's Garden?'

'Well, you couldn't do both. The staff training job will take up all your time.'

I was a bit overwhelmed; it was not the kind of thing that I could have seen coming. 'Could I think about it?'

'Course. Let me know by the end of the week.' He tugged his beard again, then chuckled and slid off the desk to shake my hand warmly. 'I think you'd enjoy it.'

I mumbled my thanks – I hoped effusively enough – and went back to work.

Why had he asked me? Well, that much, I suppose, was obvious. For the last six months, having worked my way through the other departments of the gardens, I had been seconded to the office of the Supervisor of Studies, working with Leo Pemberton, the lean, grey-haired organiser of the student course, to help with planning and running of the student course itself. Leo had obviously put a good word in.

What to do? I had just got my head round taking over the Queen's Garden, and now this bolt from the blue. But I had always toyed with the idea of teaching. I had even sent off for a prospectus for one of the teacher training colleges when I was at Oaklands, with the aim of teaching rural studies in secondary schools. But I think I had seen the writing on the wall. In my own secondary school, back in the early sixties, rural studies – taught by the redoubtable Ernest Wilberforce Heath, a sturdy man with a bristling black moustache, a bullet-shaped head and problematical adenoids – was only deemed suitable for the B, C, and D streams, and then only for the first couple of years of their school life. By the early seventies it had all but disappeared in schools across the country, and one of the most vital parts of the national curriculum – vital for the well being of the countryside as a whole, and vital in terms of opening children's eyes to the wonders of nature and their responsibility for it – had disappeared, shunted into oblivion by an increasingly metropolitanised society. I still feel passionately that children should be introduced to the world of plants and animals and allowed to connect with it. Those who are given the opportunity are usually entranced by it and may even discover that it is far more exciting than Play Stations and Xboxes (not that I'd recognise either if I fell over them).

Maybe this, then, was my way in to the world of teaching. Training the staff in the basic horticultural skills. By the end of the week I had made up my mind; the Queen's Garden – much as I loved it – would have to find another guardian and I would take up the challenge and set about organising a series of courses on practical gardening. It couldn't be that difficult, could it?

Please Sir . . .

For every person who wants to teach there are approximately thirty who don't want to learn – much.

And Now All This, W.C. Sellar and R.J. Yeatman

I still had to be interviewed for the post in the offices of the Ministry of Agriculture in Whitehall Place. All a bit scary and official, though with the Curator's weight behind my application I presumed that my chances were pretty good. The three mandarins didn't tell me whether anyone else was up for the job, and it was only a matter of days before the official letter arrived offering me the appointment. So that was that. A strange feeling. Not exactly elation, more a sort of acceptance. And relief. And more than a little apprehension.

They had to find me an office, of course. I ended up in the attic room of Descanso House, a dusky red-brick building in a corner of the gardens close to Kew Green. It had been built in 1760 as the residence for William Aiton, who worked for the founder of the gardens, Princess Augusta, and then as head gardener to King George III. It was Decimus Burton, designer of the Palm House, who recommended that the house eventually be turned into offices, so it is to him I owe my thanks for having to walk with a sideways lean, my room being in the very apex of the pan-tiled roof. The name Descanso is an odd one and was given to the house by George Willison, its tenant from 1888 to 1892. Willison had been a merchant in Brazil, and the word comes from the Portuguese name for 'a resting place'. I was to find it anything but.

I was sent to the stores to see Arthur. He smiled. I had gone up in the world now: no longer a student but a Gardens Supervisor – a rank that held certain entitlements. Arthur stroked his moustache and opened his ledger. I came away from his stores on that day in September, not with a pair of size eight wellingtons, or ill-fitting clogs, but with a bicycle, a black briefcase stamped with the gilded cipher EIIR and a large key on which was engraved the words 'Royal Gardens Kew'. The key to paradise. I was ridiculously proud. I even took it with me up to Yorkshire to show Mum and Dad. 'Get a trade,' Dad had said. I don't think he'd ever envisaged me becoming a civil servant, but then neither had I. Civil servants were boring grey men with bowler hats and brollies, I had a bike and a key to Kew Gardens. (I also had to sign the Official Secrets Act, and I'm still unsure as to how much of the gardening skills I learnt at Kew I should be imparting to others.)

The initial euphoria did eventually wear off, but I never tired of riding round the gardens on my bike (they even let students do it nowadays – standards have slipped), or of letting myself in through the side door with my key.

I was also entitled to a desk, two chairs, a telephone, a reading lamp and a filing cabinet, but not to a rectangle of grey carpet. That was reserved for the next grade up, so I made do with the brown lino.

I set to with a vengeance. The courses were to begin in October and would be set at two levels – one for beginners and one for those who had more experience. I needed magnetic charts and felt-tip pens, graph paper and a large diary, all helpfully supplied by the stationery department and delivered by an obliging uniformed messenger. This was pre-computer age and anything I needed printing had to be duplicated on a simple Roneo machine, reeking of methylated spirits and printed out in an attractive shade of purple. But there was a central typing pool where I could send my handwritten letters to be given a professional finish by the quietly spoken Mrs Brind – she of the pastel-coloured cardy draped over her shoulders – and her team of half a dozen girls. My correspondence would come back within a day or two, neatly ordered, with carbon copies paperclipped in place and envelopes addressed. I felt terribly important.

The classes I had to organise would be in the form of day release. Some of them would be lectures and others practical demonstrations, so at least I could still get my hands dirty, and I would still be among the plants.

Wellied and jacketed, I showed gardeners how to dig, how to hoe and the proper way to use a rake, with the words of my Shipley vegetable lecturer Lennie Best ringing in my ears: 'The rake is not for *breaking down* soil, it is a levelling tool'. With confidence I passed on his sage advice that a fork was the tool of choice to reduce clods to a fine tilth and that the rake be used simply to level the surface; over-rake – making the particles too fine – and the soil surface would turn into a crust in the first shower of rain. This handy hint, learned forty-five years ago now, has stayed with me. It might even have stuck with some of the gardeners I taught myself.

I organised plant identification tests, but steered clear of pines and ferns on humanitarian grounds.

My artistic prowess (O level in art) came to the fore in my lectures on pests and diseases. I made, from coloured felt, a picturesque explanation of the life cycle of the black bean aphid, showing its transition from egg to adult in four easy stages. I did sometimes see a look of incredulity in the eyes of my students, but I took this to be astonishment that I cared so much that I was prepared to spend my evenings crouched down with a pair of scissors cutting out felt shapes on my bedroom carpet. On reflection, they probably thought I was bonkers.

At the end of each term there were tests to organise. I had fought against them, thinking that they would be more than many of the gardens staff could cope with – they were manual workers who were not academically inclined – but John Simmons was insistent that they should have a piece of paper recording their achievements, and those achievements could only be measured by some form of assessment. I tried to make them as low key as possible, but with a dozen students to be tested individually on such tasks as potting on, pricking out and sowing seeds, the only way to do it was to enlist the help of two or three assessors from the gardens and from the nearby horticultural college, Norwood Hall, so that the tests could be got through in a day.

I organised an intricate timetable of who should be where and when – potting up at 10a.m, pricking out at 10.30a.m, seed sowing at 11a.m and so on – and arranged for the compost, the benches, the pots and suchlike to be in the right place at the right time. Doing my best to keep it low key, I made only one mistake. I was concerned, naturally, that each of the members of staff being assessed should be in the right place at the right time – it was a fairly intricate rota – and so when we all met up at 9.45a.m I briefed them, explained about the assessors, who were all very friendly, and then asked them to synchronise their watches so that they all showed the correct time.

I saw the look of horror on their faces. Suddenly it all seemed, to them, like a serious military operation. Something from the Battle of Britain: 'Synchronise watches, we're going in in fifteen minutes'. The very thought of it put the fear of God into them, and I spent the next quarter of an hour jollying them along and making light of it, riddled with guilt as I saw the beads of perspiration that spangled their brows, reality having bitten.

But at least nobody failed. They all managed to muddle through somehow, and when they looked confused or panicked I did my best to relax them.

Within a couple of weeks they'd all been up to my attic room individually to collect their certificates – stamped with the seal of the Royal Botanic Gardens and signed by yours truly – as an indication that they had undertaken their basic training. For some of them even that seemed an ordeal – a reminder, perhaps, of unhappier times at school, of being called into the headmaster's study. In spite of the fact that they knew me, and that most of them had known me as a student, one or two clearly found it an uncomfortable transition. Was I the same bloke as before? Could they treat me the same? As far as I was concerned, the answer was an emphatic 'yes', but I will never forget the acute discomfort that one or two of them clearly felt at the change of rank and, therefore, the perceived change of attitude. As a Gardens Supervisor I was still at the grade where they could call me by my Christian name (the next level up, Assistant Curators, were referred to as 'Mr'), but I was, like it or not, now a part of the hierarchy, and that undercurrent of mistrust was something I would have to live with. I experienced at first hand the difficulties that occur as a result of rising through the ranks.

But there was little time to brood. Soon it was all systems go for the next intake and a repeat of what had gone before, with lessons learned and, hopefully, improvements made.

I managed to stick it out for two years. I loved being a part of the place we fondly referred to as RBG Kew. I enjoyed the fact that I could cycle around the place, and that I worked with one of the greatest collections of plants in the world. And yet the repetition of the courses, year in, year out, was something that I found difficult. That and the unwillingness of some members of staff to take an interest in their job. When you are passionate about something it is hard to relate to others who are not – who will not give their working life 100%, who do not share your own level of enthusiasm.

I found myself, one day, standing up in my attic room with my hands in my pockets, gently banging my head on the sloping ceiling. It shook me when I realised what I was doing, and why I was doing it. I was bored. Simple as that. No longer challenged, no longer stimulated. I asked myself if it were not my own fault, if I had let the courses become stale. But I could not suddenly decide not to show folk how to dig, or how to sow seeds, though I supposed I could, at a pinch, ditch the felt black bean aphid. It was not enough.

There were several options: I could ask for another job in the gardens, but that seemed akin to admitting defeat. I could go into parks, but the thought of working in a local government office did not appeal one bit.

I decided that I would ask Leo Pemberton, the Supervisor of Studies, what he thought, when I had worked out how to broach the subject. Curiously, before I could pluck up the courage, fate took a hand once more.

Leo strode into my office one morning, waving in his hand a copy of the *Gardener's Chronicle*. 'Who do we know with a literary bent?' he asked.

I grinned up at him. 'Me.'

The Bookworm

If you have a garden and a library you have everything you need.

Marcus Tullius Cicero

It was a reflex reaction, and it did rather surprise my boss. It surprised me a bit. But at least I answered truthfully: I did have a literary bent or, at the very least, literary pretensions. No; literary interests. I had loved writing essays at school (even if Miss Weatherall did not think particularly highly of my literary contribution to her pile of weekly marking) and I was a keen reader. I won't say 'voracious' – it implies speed and lack of selectivity and, while not slow, I am no speed reader, neither do I read everything. But without books I would be lost.

From *Toby Twirl*, *Peter Rabbit*, *Squirrel Nutkin* and *Jemima Puddleduck* when I was little, through *The Wind in the Willows* and *The Secret Seven*, to youthful romanticism with Daphne du Maurier's *Rebecca* and the paperback Agatha Christies on holiday, I have been hooked. Later I came to devour biographies – everyone from Alan Bennett to Charlie Chaplin, Clementine Churchill to the Curzon sisters. Books on royalty, books on art, James Lees-Milne's diaries and the letters of Harold Nicolson, forays into Charles Dickens and Jane Austen, Anthony Trollope and the works of P.G. Wodehouse (I so want to be Lord Emsworth and lean over the sty scratching the back of my pig with a stick).

I went on a camping holiday with my mate Steve from Barnes Operatic, the year before I got married, and we toured the West Country in his Ford Anglia – the Harry Potter one with the sloping back window. In Dartmouth and Lyme Regis, Mevagissey and Fowey we would seek out old bookshops and feast on cod's roe, chips and Guinness. I came back with biographies of Caruso and Maurice Chevalier, books on theatre and music hall, vocal scores of Gilbert and Sullivan and a thumping headache. But it was worth it.

I have found books a nightly escape, a daily solace and, in my gardening books at least, a rich source of inspiration and information. Books on all subjects line the walls of my study these days, around a couple of thousand of them. Back in my Kew days I had a single shelf full, added to by the camping trip – Keble Martin's *The Concise British Flora in Colour*, Bean's *Trees and Shrubs Hardy in the British Isles* and the *RHS Dictionary of Gardening* among them, along with my original copy, bought at Broadbent's on The Grove at Ilkley, of *Percy Thrower's Encyclopaedia of Gardening*.

Leo dropped the magazine on to my desk and stabbed his finger at one of the adverts. 'You'd better apply for this job then.'

He'd seemed to get over his initial surprise quite quickly, and without the remotest sign of annoyance. Maybe after all those years of dealing with the caprices of students, nothing really threw him.

'You don't mind?' I felt guilty now. I'd not mentioned my restlessness at all.

Leo shrugged. He often shrugged. He put both hands in the air. He often did that, too. 'If it's what you want.'

He saw the sheepish look on my face.

'Look, you've been here two years – five if you count your studentship – perhaps it's time to move on.'

It was as if a weight had lifted. And a cloud.

The job was that of Assistant Editor, Gardening Books, with the Hamlyn Publishing Group. Not a particularly exciting address: Astronaut House, Feltham, Middlesex. Very 1960s. It couldn't really compare with Royal Botanic Gardens Kew, Richmond, Surrey. But then I had done the prestigious bit. I was looking for something that would stretch me, stimulate me and, perhaps, something a little less dependent on the moods of thirty other people.

I went for an interview with Hamlyn's Gardening Editor, Robert Pearson, a tall, white-haired, quietly spoken man in a dark suit, whose name I knew only through his column: he was gardening correspondent of the *Sunday Telegraph*. Bob was one of those men who seem permanently preoccupied, his thoughts elsewhere, as if composing his next column; but he was incredibly polite and seemed interested in my career so far, so much so that he almost gave me the job there and then, but said, in the interests of decorum, I suppose, that he would let me know.

A week later the letter informing me I had got the job arrived, and a few weeks after that I handed in my bike and my briefcase and my key to Kew Gardens. Funnily enough, handing over the key was the saddest part. It seemed like a talisman. I did even think of hanging on to it – not to use, just to keep – saying that I'd lost it. But my conscience got the better of me and so I slid it across the wooden counter where it disappeared into Arthur's vice-like grip. It had not been a new key. It did not have engraved on it 'Royal Botanic Gardens' as the later ones did, but simply 'Royal Gardens Kew'. It was probably a century or two old – it certainly looked and felt it – and I wondered who might have used it before me.

Too late now. I had decided to make the move and so I went by train, not bike, to Feltham, known for its young offenders institution rather than its botanic garden, wondering if I had made the biggest mistake of my life.

★   ★   ★

It did not take me long to work out why Bob Pearson had been keen to employ a man. Until my arrival he was the only male in the gardening department. He was probably looking for reinforcements.

The atmosphere was certainly different. The office itself was quiet for a start. I rather liked that. I've never been able to work with music blaring or endless chatter. When I'm not working – writing that is – I'm as noisy as the next man, but writing (or editing, come to that) is, for me, a silent occupation. I can concentrate better that way.

Susanne Mitchell was Bob's deputy. Able and kindly, she went on, some years later, to become the Royal Horticultural Society's editor. Alongside her worked Moyna Kitchin, the archetypal lady editor with a matchless grasp of English grammar and punctuation. Wiry and bird-like with a grey dome of hair and a passion for cats and orange lipstick (though never together), she was ever ready to give me an exposition on the correct use of the semi-colon or to stand up for the apostrophe. From her and from Susanne I would learn all I needed to know about caret marks and transpositions, metrication of measurements, the use of parentheses and italics, and the meaning of the marginal markings wf and np (wrong font and new paragraph). Oh, it was gripping stuff. Well, funnily enough, I enjoyed it.

In 1974 computerisation had still to arrive, so book proofs were still in the form of 'galleys' – sheets of paper around three feet long and nine inches wide, on which a column of text was printed. But the book would arrive from the author in manuscript form – typed out, double spaced with any luck, on sheets of A4. It was the editor's job to go through the copy and correct spelling, punctuation, grammar and general sense before the manuscript was sent off to the typestter. When it came back, the galley proofs had to be checked for 'literals' – spelling mistakes – and any other errors, since spell-check was a facility not possessed by 1970s typewriters.

Mistakes would, with any luck, be spotted, but the author, too, was sent a set of galley proofs to check, two pairs of eyes being better than one. I smile when folk say, 'Mistakes always leap out at me'. It's like saying, 'You always know when someone's wearing a wig.' Except, of course, when you don't.

The odd howler would occasionally creep through. I cherish the memory of the day when, proof reading a gardening book authored by a particularly prim lady, I spotted a 'literal' under the entry for lungwort – pulmonaria. In the manuscript it was described as having 'leaves spotted with white', but the galley proof read 'leaves spotted with shite.'

I have prevented readers from believing that African violets are 3ft tall (they are more likely to reach a height of 3in) and that the Latin name for the Scots pine is *Penis sylvestris* (it is *pinus*, though in German it is pronounced exactly the same).

Once the copy was sorted out, there were the illustrations to find, which involved letters to assorted garden photographers who would obligingly send in colour transparencies by the hundred. Finding good (and previously unused) illustrations was sometimes difficult, but necessary to prevent all gardening books from looking the same.

Illustrations and galley proofs would then be sent upstairs to the art department where they were crafted into pages by the book's designer, the galleys sliced up with a scalpel and stuck down on spread sheets with aromatic cow gum before being sent off to the typesetter once more. A few weeks later they would come back as page proofs. Oh, and there were captions to write for all the illustrations – in those days the province of the editor, rather than the author. (I bet nobody's listening.)

The book's jacket design (then as now a source of great angst and rivalry between the editorial and the marketing departments) would eventually be agreed upon and the whole kit and caboodle sent off to the printers, in those days frequently in Czechoslovakia or Italy for both economic and technical reasons. Well, that's what they told me.

A few more weeks would pass, and then we would have finished hardback books – shiny glossy jackets, crisp pages, illustrations that were, hopefully, the right colour, and a price tag on the front flap of something around a fiver.

It was all strangely interesting. And absorbing. I knuckled down to the editing of Will Ingwersen's *Classic Garden Plants* with the famous pipe-smoking alpine grower from East Grinstead taking a close interest in what I did. For this we commissioned line drawings and coloured illustrations from the artist Charles Stitt.

And I also got to work with a man whose name I had known since my apprenticeship days when his *Gardener's Golden Treasury* – as fat as *Who's Who* and every bit as informative – had been propped up by the side of the potting bench. His name was Arthur George Lee Hellyer and he was one of the nicest men I have ever met.

He lived in a house called Orchards, at Rowfant near Crawley in Sussex, a rambling pile with a sprawling garden that contained trees, shrubs and roses in abundance. In retirement he would amble through them in sloppy sweater, baggy trousers and white plimsolls, his grey, thinning hair being pulled this way and that by a low branch, and his military-style moustache bristling above a mouth from which a smile was rarely absent. He had a patrician air about him and was, for me, a link with the past – he had known the fabled Ellen Willmott of Warley Place, invariably clad in black bombazine and fond of her gin, and worked with A.J. Macself, his predecessor as editor of *Amateur Gardening* and something of a martinet.

Arthur's wife, Gay, was herself an author and specialised in house plants. Her accent was, as distinct from his well-spoken tones, that of east London, and she could be tricky to deal with. By the time I got to know her she was uncomfortable on her pins and walking with a stick, which might have explained her irascibility. When they both came into the office, Arthur would sidle out and chat to Bob when Gay would go on at me about some illustration she didn't like, or some page design that she could not understand. 'What have you done that for, silly boy? That's stupid.' I got used to her in the end and, I like to think, she to me.

But the author I had no trouble with at all was the man who, in childhood and early youth, had been my hero. They called him Britain's head gardener and he broadcast every Friday night on BBC TV, even in the days before it became BBC1 and BBC2. *Gardening Club* it was called at first, and then it became *Gardeners' World*. His name was Percy Thrower.

What I envied most about Percy was his delivery. It would now, I suppose, seem a bit old-fashioned, a bit measured – slow even – but in all the years I knew him it never changed. He had the ability to say almost anything and make it sound like the voice of God. He had been brought up in Buckinghamshire, then worked at Windsor Castle (where he married the head gardener's daughter) and Derby before becoming Shrewsbury's parks superintendent on New Year's Day in 1946 at the age of 32. His accent, overlaying those deep, rich vocal tones, was suitably rural and yet readily understandable. He would pronounce some words quite unusually – 'green-hewse' and 'com-poest', 'clee-may-tiss' and 'or-nith-o-gay-lum' – almost everything he said was shot through with rusticity. And he smoked a pipe.

His garden was redolent of the 1960s – a rock garden and a pool, island beds in the lawn, a greenhouse with a grapevine and another one for tomatoes. There were beds of heathers and specimen trees on the sloping ground that surrounded the modern chalet bungalow with its collection of Royal Worcester porcelain in specially built oak cabinets. It seemed to me to have all the trappings of a successful TV gardener's personal garden.

Originally he had broadcast in a three-piece suit, hanging up his jacket on the back of the greenhouse door in the TV studio, which had no glass. The later broadcasts would come from his garden, or from Clack's Farm, the home of Arthur Billitt, who became his co-presenter in the 1970s, and then he would wear an open-necked shirt. So great was his fame that he was immortalised in Madame Tussauds and appeared on the *Morecambe and Wise Show*. (I have followed him into the former but don't half envy him the latter).

I worked with Percy on his book *How to Grow Vegetables and Fruit*, travelling up to his house The Magnolias at Bomere Heath outside Shrewsbury (he was retired now as Shrewsbury's Parks Superintendent) and recording tape after tape with him, describing his cultivation techniques for everything from apples to strawberries, which I would then transcribe. Always he was affable, always there was a roast lunch – the joint cooked by his wife Connie and carved by Percy – and always the merest hint of friendly rivalry: the older, established gardener aware of the youngster snapping at his heels. I now know how he felt.

During my time at Hamlyn I edited several of his books, including his autobiography *My Lifetime of Gardening*. I learned a lot from Percy. I learned the importance of not being precious. I learned how to handle members of the public and leave them feeling happy and not short-changed. I learned a lot about broadcasting simply from watching him, and I began to understand even more the importance of words – their rhythm and music, how they could evoke mood and emotion, and how they were tools every bit as important as your spade and your fork, whether they were spoken or written down.

He was, in short, inspirational. And I had always told Mick Hudson that I wanted to be Percy Thrower when I grew up. I was not a Parks Superintendent, but I had my gardening knowledge and experience, and while at Kew I had taken my O level in English Language just to prove to myself that I could do it. I passed, and that, coupled with a little help from Moyna and Susanne, equipped me for the editing job. It even emboldened me to think that I might be able to write.

Waiting for the Muse

> I write when I'm inspired, and I see to it that I'm inspired at
> nine o'clock every morning.
>
> Peter De Vries

I cherish the remark made to me once by a photographer. 'I may not be good,' he said, 'but I'm quick.'

Unlike Oscar Wilde, who famously remarked: 'I was working on the proof of one of my poems all morning, and took out a comma. In the afternoon I put it back again', most writers cannot afford that luxury. Some may wait for the muse to strike, others (and I am one of them) just write. But then you probably guessed that. When one is not a Salman Rushdie or a Martin Amis, one just blasts away. That is not to say that I don't take trouble over my writing. I do. But I know that it is colloquial, unlikely to survive as an icon of twenty-first-century literature, and populist rather than esoteric or intellectual. Nevertheless I still have to do it. I still *have* to write every day and, at the risk of getting a third quote onto the same page, I do not subscribe to Dr Johnson's view that 'No man but a blockhead ever wrote, except for money.' Or do I? I have, to be honest, always been paid for my words. I suppose they were other people's words first of all, so then I was paid for punctuating them, correcting spelling and putting them in the right order. That is, in effect, what editing is all about. But it does embolden you to think 'I could do this', and so I waited for the opportunity.

It came in the form of a paperback book on house plants, written as a giveaway with a magazine called *Wedding Day and First Home*. Well, a chap has to start somewhere. I only landed the job because whoever it was that Bob Pearson had lined up to write it had let him down. I think he was wary of entrusting me with it, and when I turned in a reasonable job his relief was palpable. So was mine – it meant I earned a little more, and funds were not exactly in ample supply. Oh, and I was about to get married myself.

With the prospect of a mortgage on the horizon I needed all the help I could get, and so I sent a sample article to *Amateur Gardening* magazine, whose editor I had bumped into at Hamlyn when he had been visiting Bob Pearson. It was a piece I called 'Fur and Feather' – all about plants with furry and feathery foliage. (I did avoid over-alliteration in the article itself.) They took it, changed the title to 'Fur and Feathers' (oblivious to my witty allusion to a shooting periodical that features in the tales of Beatrix Potter) and sent me a few quid. Could I write for them every couple of weeks, they asked?

I was on my way, and Bob, having been happy enough with my booklet for newly married house plant investors, asked if I could write a proper book. About greenhouse gardening. I bit his hand off, and in 1976 *Gardening Under Cover* (a hardback illustrated with line drawings, price £2.99) hit the bookshops. I was now an author. Wot larks!

Alison and I were married in 1975 and moved into a tiny end-of-terrace house – three up, three down – in Sunningdale, Berkshire. At first I wrote in the spare bedroom – pine table, pale blue Laura Ashley sprigged wallpaper – but eventually (when Polly came along) I built a shed in the garden. It was a tiny garden, and so it was a tiny shed, more like a corridor, 4ft wide and 8ft long. It had a shelf down one side on which to put my typewriter, and bookshelves floor to ceiling on the other. (Already my collection was growing.) To reach it I had to cross a wooden plank bridge over a tiny pond that divided the garden in two. It was not a natural water feature; I had made it myself out of polythene (a proper butyl liner being beyond my means at that time). It made for hazardous journeys, especially on dark nights, and more than once I arrived at my place of work soaked to the knees and dripping on to the linoleum floor of my shed. I would have liked to have called it a study, or a studio, but there was no way it was anything other than a shed. I did not so much walk into it as slide between the shelves. But it worked, and we used a baby alarm from Mothercare as a walkie-talkie to summon me into the house for a phone call or a meal.

The garden itself was barely 15ft by 40ft but I didn't waste an inch of space. I planted old-fashioned roses – 'Cardinal Richelieu' and 'Belle de Crecy', 'Rosa Mundi' and 'Maidens' Blush', and those two disease-free rugosas, 'Fru Dagmar Hartopp' and 'Roseraie de l'Hay' – filling in around them with border perennials. A 'Doyenne du Comice' pear tree was already established, dropping its hefty fruits into the pond each autumn like depth charges. An old, gnarled wisteria wrapped itself round the front of the house, dripping with purple flower trails each April and scenting the entire house through the open bedroom window. The soil was Bagshot sand, fine as dust but easily cultivated, even after a thunderstorm. It simply swallowed up compost and manure.

At the bottom of the garden I planted a golden-leafed *Robinia* 'Frisia' and built an 8ft by 6ft cedarwood greenhouse with my dad – the second time we'd done that together. It was rather poignant. You can see it on the back of *Gardening Under Cover*. Alison took the photograph. I don't think she ever got paid.

I stayed with Hamlyn for two years, the same sort of time as I stayed at Kew after the student course. Maybe that was the length of my attention span. It was rather worrying. But I did feel that after two years I had achieved as much as I could as an assistant gardening books editor. And yet I did like the 'media' side of gardening. The chance to share one's passion through words, whether spoken or written. It's just that . . . well . . . in books it was a bit slow. I had enjoyed my calm spell, but perhaps now I needed a change. And then, with perfect timing, a job came up at *Amateur Gardening* magazine. It was a weekly publication on which life would, I reasoned, move a little faster; offer me a different sort of publishing experience. In 1976, a year after we were married, I took a job in London proper – on the umpteenth floor of King's Reach Tower in Stamford Street, as Assistant Editor of the magazine we all called *A.G.*

It was almost a year before I was rash enough to confess to another member of the magazine's staff that I hankered after a bit of broadcasting. You might have thought that by now any thoughts of being the next Percy Thrower would have evaporated in the cold light of day. Apparently they had not.

'That's funny,' said Graham Clarke, the magazine's sub-editor. 'We had a letter last year asking us if we knew anyone who could talk on Radio 4.'

'Well?'

'We said we didn't.'

'Oh.' My timing was obviously out.

'Hang on; I've got it here somewhere.' He fished around in his desk drawer among the rubber bands and paper clips, the old files and document wallets that might, one day, come in useful. 'Here you are.'

I smoothed out the creases and read the letter. In my lunch hour I set about drafting a letter of my own that I hoped might, somehow, get them to try me out on the radio. I thought it was long gone, but a few days ago, in a drawer of my own – clearly far more antiquarian in its contents than Graham's – I found the carbon copy that I had kept. This is what I wrote to a producer by the name of Denis Lower:

30 August 1977

Dear Mr Lower,

I believe that some time ago *You and Yours* were looking for someone to act as a kind of 'gardening correspondent' on the programme. If this is still the case might I express my interest?

A keen gardener since childhood, I have thirteen years experience in horticulture ranging from work in a small parks department, to full-time training and subsequent employment at Kew Gardens, and three years in journalism.

I am still only twenty-eight, still enjoy gardening, write frequently in *Amateur Gardening* and am keen to broadcast.

If there is an opportunity on your programme I would be very willing to discuss any contribution I might be able to make.

Yours sincerely,
Alan Titchmarsh
Assistant Editor

I love the 'still only twenty-eight'. I don't quite know what the significance of that was, but the letter did the trick.

On Air

Television is more interesting than people. If it were not, we should have people standing in the corners of our rooms.

Alan Coren, *The Times*

I waited anxiously for the post every day. I had written the letter on headed *Amateur Gardening* notepaper, so I knew it would not come to my home address. A month later, while I was in the middle of writing a column on the construction of the perfect compost heap, I got a phone call at work. From a lady at the BBC called Marlene Pease (nice name for gardening, I thought). She asked me a few questions. Well, more than a few actually. I wittered on, trying to sound interesting; concise without being monosyllabic. At least, that's what I hope I did. She listened to see if I could string a few words together without sending her to sleep. Then, after what I suppose would have been ten minutes or so – though it seemed like half an hour – she said, 'Can you do us a bit on laying turf?'

'When?' I asked.

'Tomorrow.'

Well, I did my homework. I had chapter and verse on the relative merits and costs of a lawn made from seed and from turf. But how to put it over? I thought of all my broadcasting heroes, from Percy Thrower to Peter Scott, and wondered how they would perform. Over the next few years I tried to be everyone from Phil Drabble to David Attenborough but decided, in the end, that I had really better be myself. And I suppose that's what came through in that first broadcast.

Like most people, I don't really like the sound of my own voice. I have become used to it. Learned to tolerate it. But it would not be one I would pick off the shelf. I'd rather it were deeper and richer in tone, like the man who interviewed me on that very first broadcast for *You and Yours* back in 1977 – Derek Cooper.

Derek looked like a retired colonel – he had a thick military moustache and peered at me, albeit with a kindly expression on his face, over the top of horn-rimmed half-moon glasses. He asked, in a voice that could have been minted by a gravy manufacturer, about the merits of both seed and turf, and the costs, and how one would go about making a new lawn. I tried to sound as personable as I could – chatty without being over-familiar.

The piece was recorded for the Sunday edition of *You and Yours*, now long gone, though the programme continues to air every weekday lunchtime on Radio 4. As a result, I had not heard Derek's introduction when I was with him in the studio – we just went straight into the interview. On that fateful Sunday Alison and I sat at home and listened, having turned the radio on at least an hour before transmission so we did not miss it.

And then the moment came. Derek set up the item and introduced me. As Alan Titchfield. I looked at Alison. She looked at me, sympathetically. 'Never mind,' she said. 'You sound fine.'

And then it was all over and Derek went into what is known as the 'back announcement': 'I must apologise to Alan Titchmarsh for calling him Alan Titchfield. Dynamic he may be, but no thunderbolt. I'm sure we'll be hearing more of him.'

It was a nice touch. Flattering even. And he was as good as his word. *You and Yours* continued to use me as their 'gardening expert' for the next few years. I learned to do everything – well almost everything – in four minutes, which seemed to be the magic length of time required for 'slots' on both radio and TV. I suppose it was regarded, after much research, as the average attention span of the audience. Today, thirty years on, it has probably been halved, and I would be expected to deliver all the finer points of making a lawn from seed or turf in two minutes flat. Odd isn't it? The programmes are not shorter, it's just that they cram more in and speak faster, fearful that people will not have the patience to stay with an item until it is finished, however interesting, if it lasts more than the twinkling of an eye. It's not just television and radio. It's films, too. I watched *The Prince and The Showgirl* recently. It starred Marilyn Monroe and Laurence Olivier, who also directed. Both pretty big names, you'd have to admit. It was made in 1957 and taken at a pace that would, by today's standards, be called leisurely. Even languorous. Fabulous costumes. Breathtaking sets. It ran at 111 minutes; today they'd make it in an hour. Ah, the pace of life . . .

You and Yours called me in every week or so to 'do a piece' on pruning roses or looking after house plants. I'd do seasonal and sometimes news-related items. I'd sit with the presenters of the day, Nancy Wise and Bill Breckon, often as not, and chat about the finer points of hybrid teas and floribundas, spider plants and weeping figs, gradually learning my craft, avoiding 'ums' and 'ers' and passing on information in what I hoped was an entertaining way. I've always felt quite strongly that entertainment – or, more accurately, engagement – was just as important as knowing your stuff. I had listened to enough lecturers over the years to know that being an expert in your chosen field was not enough. The ability to put it across in an accessible way was every bit as important as being 'an expert'. And I quite like making people smile, too.

The main current affairs programme on Radio 4 back then – as now – was the one that 'set the agenda' for the day: the *Today* programme. It had as its main presenters Brian Redhead and John Timpson, and that fleet of BBC newsreaders whose voices my mother regarded as being the voices of Truth – Peter Donaldson, Brian Perkins and Laurie Macmillan. When they read the news you knew you had heard it from the horse's mouth. With vocal tones like theirs, who could possibly doubt what they said? (Not like that man on ITV with the loud tie. Mum never trusted him. He looked too much like a used car salesman. He even winked at you.)

In the summer of 1979 Britain was invaded by a foreign army. It was an army of greenfly and it had come across the English Channel on a southeasterly current of air. This was no thinly scattered regiment, but a dense airborne squadron of aliens intent on making their mark on British soil. And they did. They plastered the rose bushes of southeast England in their millions. They stuck to emulsion and to gloss and ruined the handiwork of decorators from Margate to Dover. Deal, as I recall, was particularly badly hit, before the invaders dispersed to wreak havoc in the shires.

What could the nation do in the face of such an unexpected invasion? We'd had no way of knowing it was going to happen. There had been no intelligence. We should have been told about it. What was the government doing? The powers that be at the *Today* programme, ever willing to ask the questions the nation needs answered, got on the phone immediately to someone who would know. They rang me.

Could I come in the following morning and tell Britain's gardeners what to do in the face of an unprecedented invasion of aphids? Was it the end of gardens as we knew them? Would this epidemic ever end? Mercifully the terms 'global warming' and 'climate change' were unknown back then, and it was all put down to that comforting state of affairs we were once happy to accept: 'an act of God'. (Since fewer folk believe in him nowadays his powers are often overlooked.)

I assured the *Today* programme that, like Superman, I would leap to the rescue and pacify a British public whose 'Icebergs' and 'Ena Harknesses' were looking the worse for wear. *You and Yours* rang a little later, but declined to have me doing for them what I told them I would earlier have done for *Today*. I worried a little that I had turned into a media rent boy.

At 5.30a.m the following day a sleek black saloon pulled up outside our little cottage in Sunningdale and I was whisked off (rather like the father in *The Railway Children*), with my wife wondering if she would ever see me again.

Live radio this time. Not recorded. I sat down in the *Today* studio in Broadcasting House at the appointed hour, with the grizzly, bearded Brian Redhead and the florid-cheeked John Timpson quizzing me like a pair of secret service interrogators. I gave my informed opinion on the current state of the nation *vis-à-vis* greenfly. It must have made a pleasant change to switch to such a weighty subject, having had to spend a morning interviewing dreary politicians on inconsequential matters of state, interspersed with sports reports delivered by athletic young men in open-necked shirts and sports jackets.

I left the studio some time after the programme had ended, having declined all offers from its presenters of Scotch whisky, toast and marmalade. This was, after all, the end of their day, even if it was the beginning of mine. But they seemed pleased with my offering, and I will never forget the look on the face of the female newsreader – fresh from delivering her daily staple of terror and tragedy – when I spoke about the unusual and parthenogenetic sex life of the greenfly, which meant that the female of the species could give birth without any form of male involvement. The fire in her eyes was clear to see.

By the time I arrived at the offices of *Amateur Gardening*, the phone was already ringing. I took the call. It was from the early evening television current affairs programme *Nationwide*. 'We heard you on the *Today* programme,' said the voice at the other end of the line. 'Would you like to come in and advise our viewers on how to cope with the greenfly invasion?'

And so, at the other end of my working day, another black saloon car came to take me to the BBC's Lime Grove studios where *Nationwide* was beamed around the country. (It beat my usual second-class ticket on the 07.15 from Sunningdale to Waterloo.) In my smart blue-and-white-striped shirt and my navy blue tie with the white spots, I wove as best I could between rose bushes and sprayers, specific aphicides and syringes (organic gardening being but a twinkle in my eye back then) and told an anxious nation what I thought they could best do to rid themselves of these turbulent insects. Bob Wellings interviewed me, and scattered around the studio were the other *Nationwide* stalwarts Sue Lawley and Hugh Scully, Frank Bough and Sue Cook, perching on desks and standing in front of maps. Sofas had not yet been discovered, except on late-night chat shows.

'Wonderful,' they said at the end. 'You must come back and do some more.' I was over the moon. Live television was a great buzz. It sort of concentrated your energies, knowing that you only had one chance to get it right. A bit like theatre, I suppose.

I went home on a high. 'What was it like?' Alison asked. 'Well,' I said, 'it was a bit like tasting blood.'

Mum and Dad

> Children begin by loving their parents; after a time they
> judge them; rarely, if ever, do they forgive them.
>
> *A Woman of No Importance*, Oscar Wilde

I think my mum was pretty devastated when I left home. It also
coincided with the onset of rheumatoid arthritis, which was
to deform the most beautiful hands I have ever seen. She didn't
complain, of course, being the 'get up and get on' woman that
she was, or had been. In a way that made it even worse. She just
gritted her teeth and battled on, though she did become more
crotchety, more difficult to live with. On the bad days, when it
was cold or windy. You can't really blame her.

Dad remained his old self. 'Yes dear' was his most oft-used
line. But to assume that he was a hen-pecked husband in the
mode of those Bamforth Comic seaside postcards would be to
do him a disservice. He put his foot down when he needed to.

There was three months' difference in age – Mum was born
in January 1924, Dad in March of that year – and they lived just
a couple of streets away from one another in Ilkley, Mum in Ash
Grove on the north side of Leeds Road, Dad on the south side in
Dean Street. Both terrace houses. They never moved away from
the town they were born in, though when my sister and I were
little there was talk of emigrating to Canada that never came to
anything.

They went to the same school and then, when the war came, Dad was called up and sent to India – Bangalore, I think – as a craftsman sorting out tyres for lorries. A curious job for a plumber. But the war ended shortly afterwards – Dad told us that they had heard he was coming. Mum went to Lister's Mill in Addingham, wore clogs and worked on the looms. They met at a dance in the King's Hall in November 1946 (Mum had ditched the clogs that night). 'Was it love at first sight?' I once asked her. 'It must have been something,' was her reply. They courted for six months, were engaged for six months and got married on 3 December 1947.

The trouble was, they had little or no money saved, what with the war and their low wages, so they moved in with Dad's mum, Florrie, or Grandma Titch as my sister and I would later call her. Dad's spinster sister, Alice, was sent off to lodge with Mrs Heap, the lady she cleaned for at the top of the town, while Mum and Dad lived in the back bedroom and looked for a home they could call their own. It was a tricky couple of years – my mum and her mother-in-law did not always see eye to eye, and Grandma Titch had a habit of boasting to Mum about how wonderful her other son's wife was – Jenny, who had married my Uncle Jim. Mum would take it for so long and then snap. The atmosphere must have driven my dad up the wall.

Anyway, in the autumn of 1949 they found their own place – number 34 Nelson Road – which they bought, on a mortgage, for £400. I would have been six months old. My sister, Kathryn Victoria, arrived in 1954.

The great thing about having a plumber for a dad was that we were the first house in the street to get central heating – secondhand, mind; taken out of somebody else's house when they went for an upgrade. So much air was in our system that the radiators had to be bled with one of those little keys every evening. The hiss and bubble as the water dribbled into the plastic tooth mug became a regular bedtime ritual. I thought that's what you had to do with all central heating systems. It came as a pleasant surprise later in life that they could tick along quite happily without such nocturnal ministrations.

But as well as being a plumber, Dad was a great handyman – he made everything from wardrobes to toy forts, kitchen cabinets to vivariums where I could raise frogs from tadpoles.

Mum was handy too. Only our underwear was shop-bought. And our socks and shoes, of course. The rest was handknitted and handsewn – jumpers, shorts, long trousers, coats and the regulation winter balaclava. She also made her own dresses, pushing back the settee and chairs and pinning tissue-paper patterns to fabric on the floor in the front room. Some of her creations in the fifties almost qualified as ball gowns, though they were of the type that ended mid calf. I remember one gold lamé two-piece, a pair of lilac suede stiletto heels, and another brown and white dress in the shape of a tulip. She looked wonderful, coming upstairs to kiss us good-night as she and Dad went out to a dance at the King's Hall or to a fire-station social, leaving behind on my pillow the scent of Blue Grass perfume, to be replaced later in life, when funds were not quite so short, by the scent that reminds me of her to this day – Chanel No.5.

We lived in Nelson Road until 1965, when we moved to a pebble-dashed semi up the posher end of town in Victoria Close, the year after I had started work. £3,250, that cost. Harry's greenhouse came with us and, to my astonishment, when I left home my dad started growing tomatoes in it. It lasted a few years before age finally took its toll – on the greenhouse, not Dad – and it was replaced with an aluminium lean-to on the back of the house which, in turn, was superseded by a small conservatory.

Mum did not work while we were growing up. Well, not for money. She washed and ironed, cooked and baked and cleaned, shopped and looked after the garden, as well as two children, which seemed to fill the week to overflowing.

We had no car until my dad was given a firm's pick-up van in the early 1960s, in which we would journey up the dales for 'a run out' on Sunday afternoons. That was after we'd been to church, mind. Both Dad and I sang in the choir, and all three of us, Mum, Dad and I, rang the bells. Mum became 'enrolling member' of the Mother's Union and, later, Brown Owl of the church Brownie pack, all before the arthritis began to curb her activities.

Dad worked all day as a plumber, and his part-time job as a fireman saw him cleaning the shiny 'appliance' and checking hydrants on Tuesday nights. Then he'd go to the pub for a drink. Mum would go out one evening a week to her 'hens' – four friends who had known each other since their youth and childhood, and who would meet in each other's houses on rotation to chat and sew and knit and have a light supper together.

They'd go out to the pub together on a Friday night, with a couple of friends, and sometimes on Saturdays, too, often up the dale to Addingham where the pubs stayed open an extra half hour until 11p.m. Not that they over-indulged. Well, not often. Occasionally Dad would come back on Christmas Eve from having a lunchtime drink with the lads, after work had finished, and his cap would be a bit skew-wiff. Mum would go all silent until he'd slept it off in the armchair, with the newspaper spread over it to stop his overalls from dirtying the covers.

Having folk round to supper was just not something that would ever have occurred to them; instead they preferred to go out for their entertainment – it made it more special. And they did like it when the first Chinese restaurant opened in Ilkley, even if Dad did always have the mixed grill and that well-known Oriental pudding, pears Belle Helene.

Looking back I find it hard to imagine how on earth they managed on Dad's lowly wage. But, apart from the mortgage, they never owed anything. Mum put aside the money for the insurance man and the butcher and the grocer each week (she had tiny cash boxes from Woolworths especially for the purpose). She did not believe in the 'never-never'. When in later years American Express boasted that their credit card 'Frees you from pre-set spending limits,' my mother said, 'Doesn't that mean "allows you to live beyond your means?"'

We would have a one-week family holiday each year – usually to Bispham, which Mum considered the select end of Blackpool – and it was not until I was twenty and at Kew that we had our first foreign holiday, to Majorca. Mum loved the warmth, which eased the pain of her arthritis, but Dad never seemed comfortable with foreign food, which almost always disagreed with him. I disgraced myself by getting plastered on sangria and throwing up all over the bedroom floor. My sister moved out at midnight. When I woke up in the morning, Dad was asleep in the bed next to mine.

When my sister and I had both left home, their lives changed. Well, Mum's did. She went to work in her brother's grocer's shop on Skipton Road. Uncle Bert, and his wife Auntie Edie, ran an old-fashioned grocer's, the sort with sides of bacon hung above the counter, coffee beans and speciality teas, and a small post office in the corner. When Alison and I married, we would be sent home from our visits to Yorkshire with a wonderful food parcel of free range eggs and slices of ham, freshly ground coffee and assorted pickles – a real help in the early days of our marriage when our funds, like Mum and Dad's in their early days, were short.

Mum was the outwardly dominant of the two, but she depended entirely on my father for her stability. He was as solid as a rock – a small man, a little stooped and very slight – but he was straightforward, honest as the day is long, quiet about anything to do with emotion and with one or two surprising gifts. He had a fine tenor voice and sang in the church choir for years. He also had the neatest handwriting I have ever known. When he filled in a crossword it looked almost printed. Oh, and he could make a newspaper last almost all day. He was the only man I ever knew who read all the small ads. Maybe he just enjoyed the peace and quiet to be found behind the *Yorkshire Post*.

Dad was a man's man – it took him years to get over the fact that I bought an umbrella when I was sixteen, although in later years, when I had discarded it, he would not be separated from it. He did, though, have his occasional moments of self-indulgence. He would fill the bath to the brim and boast 'no links' – that is, no links of the plug chain left above the water – before going out reeking of Old Spice, to my and my sister's embarrassment.

He called me 'Algy' or 'Dig', after Digby, Dan Dare's sidekick in the *Eagle* comic, and my sister 'Kats'. He was not especially demonstrative in terms of physical affection, but when we watched television and I would sit on the floor with my back to his armchair, he would sometimes absently ruffle my hair with his hand. It was enough.

From this thumbnail sketch you would put him down as a typical Yorkshireman, from his flat 'at to the soles of his boots. And you would not be wrong. But he was, and remains, to me and to my sister the most special Yorkshireman who ever lived, bar none.

One seldom gets to know other people's view of one's own parents, so I was rather touched a couple of weeks ago when I met a man in Hampshire who told me that he knew my dad. He had lived in Ilkley for years and only just moved down south. He told me that dad had advised him on putting in his own central heating system. 'It was really good of him,' he said. 'And then when I'd done it he came to check it over and make sure I'd done it right.'

I smiled and nodded, and then the man said, 'That was the thing about your dad; he was a real gentleman.'

Mum was more gregarious than Dad by nature. A born flirt, she enjoyed the company of men more than women, whom she seemed to consider as rivals, though she was always steadfastly faithful to my father. The thought of going beyond making doe eyes at another man – which I think she just considered an engaging part of her femininity – would have frightened her to death.

Mum could be quite judgemental – women of whom she disapproved were always referred to as 'that dame' – and her prejudices were legion: everything from cream soda to Welshmen. The only thing I can say in her defence was that when tackled about it she could see herself how absurd were these assorted foibles.

As a couple they were totally devoted. Apart from Mum's hens and the fire service they did nothing without each other, so when my father died suddenly of a heart attack in 1986, the bottom fell out of her world. She was devastated.

I had been working in Stoke on Trent at the garden festival. There were no mobile phones back then. I drove back home to Hampshire, oblivious to what had happened, and only when I got there could Alison tell me the news. I walked up to the top of the garden and stood for a bit. Leaning on a tree. Then I came back to the house, packed a bag, got in the car and drove up to Yorkshire.

Mum never did get over it. The first year was the worst, as it always is, with all those anniversaries to be got out of the way. It did not help that I lived two hundred miles away and that Kath took the brunt of Mum's grief.

But we built her a granny flat above the garage and Kath and her family then moved into the house. Mum had a stairlift, and we always said that when she turned it on and it hummed into life, it was like hearing the approach of the ticking crocodile in *Peter Pan*.

But there were joys still to come. When I went back home – several times a year – Mum and I would go out to supper, just the two of us, to the bistro on The Grove that had once been Mr Moffat's florist's shop. There she would talk about old times, not in a maudlin, sentimental way, but brightly, with fire in her eyes. They were evenings that, at the time, I hoped would go on forever. On one occasion, her knee locked under the table, and I had to carry her over the threshold and out of the bistro. She told me that now I would have to marry her.

As the arthritis intensified, and the steroids and assorted drugs that she needed to cope with it grew stronger, her mobility was reduced in direct proportion to the increase in her irascibility. Not all the time, but more and more frequently, she led my sister a merry dance.

It is a common predicament, and one that is universally acknowledged, that absent sons are often thought of more highly than the ever-present daughters who do all the work. I owe my sister more than I can say for hanging on in there while I juggled radio, television, writing, a family and, to a lesser extent, the wellbeing of my mother.

The nicest thing is that my mum, and my dad to a lesser degree, saw me 'getting on'. I say this, not from an egotistical point of view, but simply to prove to them that their early confidence, thought by some to be foolhardy, was not misplaced.

It was impossible to realise, until they were gone, just how much of my life revolved around them. Whether or not it is healthy or normal I cannot say, but since their passing I have realised just how much I did to impress them. I know in my heart that it is the natural order of things for children to outlive their parents – and the reverse option is intolerable – but when they go they leave a massive hole in your life.

Mum soldiered on without her man for sixteen years, but then in December 2002 she had a stroke and was taken into hospital. Another one followed and it was clear that she was unlikely to pull through. The last time my sister and I were with her she made some silly joke about my not hearing what she said. 'He needs a blow through,' she said, and made a blowing motion with pursed lips. Silly the things that stick in your mind.

I went back one last time on my own before I had to return to Hampshire, where we were moving house. It seems so dreadful now that I did not stay with her, but I could not leave the family to up sticks without me, and it was unclear how long Mum could carry on. I'd be able to return as soon as we were settled in. I sat with her and held her hand. She drifted in and out of consciousness and smiled at me from time to time. From above the sheets only her head and her right hand were visible. Her hair was still dark, even at 78, though she had never in her life coloured it. Hair dye would be for 'that dame'.

After an hour or so I got up to go and she opened her eyes. 'You going?'

'Yes. Will you be alright?'

She nodded.

We had never, as a family, been especially outspoken in our sentiments. We kissed and hugged every time we met, but we never *said* anything. You just didn't do that in Yorkshire. Not back in the 50s and 60s. But now it didn't seem to matter any more. I squeezed her hand and told her that I loved her very much.

She squeezed it back, with as much strength as she had. 'Not as much as I love you,' she said.

I kissed her forehead and got up to go. At the end of the hospital ward I turned round and looked back at her. She slowly waved her fingers above the sheets, and winked at me. It was the last time I saw her. Two days later she died peacefully in her sleep.

With money she left me I bought a little hexagonal summerhouse. Pale blue it is. Sitting in the sunshine across from where I write. Mum wasn't mad about my writing – not about the novels, anyway. She had heard they were a bit saucy, and found any excuse not to read them – in the normal hardbacks the print was too small for her; in the large-print version the book became too heavy. It was a neat way out. But what she did always love was the gardening – the books and the television programmes. That and the fresh air. She would never be in the house without a window, and preferably the back door as well, wide open. She did not like, as she put it, 'being fast', meaning stuck or unable to get out.

I had a plaque made for the back wall of the summerhouse, which is open on three sides, just as she would have wanted. I didn't want to put anything too maudlin on it, but I did want it to be a reminder of her. It's not flashy, just a simple oval of slate:

In happy memory of
Bessie Titchmarsh
1924–2002
who loved being outside.

I think she would have liked that.

Going it Alone

What no wife of a writer can ever understand is that a writer is working when he is staring out of the window.

Burton Rascoe

It was, of all the decisions I have ever had to make, the most difficult. Apart from asking somebody to marry me. The year was 1979, we lived in the tiny house in Sunningdale, with a mortgage, and we had a baby on the way. It was, on paper at least, the very worst time in my life to throw up a steady job and go freelance.

I had now reached the heady heights of Deputy Editor on *Amateur Gardening* magazine. Not bad at the age of 30. Secure. Pensionable. Not unhappy with my lot, seeing that I was able to write columns for the magazine during the day and books in my spare time. Except that meant I did not *have* any spare time. And as Deputy Editor I did seem to spend a fair proportion of my day sorting out other people's problems rather than getting on with my own job. It was beginning to dawn on me that I was an independent soul, rather than a company man. I like people, very much, but I do wish they would get on with life rather than finding problems. Or expecting me to sort them out. (Not a natural social worker then.)

But then a timely spanner was thrown in the works. The magazine, it was decided, would move to Poole in Dorset, one of

IPC's country outposts where, not unreasonably, it was thought that a gardening magazine might be suitably stabled. Except that neither Alison nor I wanted, at that time, to move to Dorset. Well, not to be tied to a job that I did not intend to keep for life. And what about our friends? They all lived in and around London.

We had already had the family discussion about my workload. It had become a bit weighty. I would journey up to London by train early in the morning, work all day in Stamford Street (not my idea of Shangri-la), come home for about 7p.m, watch television, chat and eat until 8p.m – a whole hour to ourselves – and then go up into the spare bedroom to write until bedtime at 11p.m. This was the Monday to Friday routine, which would explain why the young married couple became rather tetchy with one another in the laundrette on a Saturday morning. We did eventually get our own machine, but that and the spin drier only partially solved the problem.

Mrs T, with her usual capacity for common sense, suggested that something had to go, and that she would rather it was not her.

And so I gave up the day job. Just like that. And went to work each morning in my shed, the spare bedroom now having been decorated for the imminent arrival of our first child.

Well, not exactly just like that. There was a lot of soul searching. Lots of sums. I worked out that with the amount of freelance work I now had we would be able to survive – just. But it would mean a drop in salary. Still, *Amateur Gardening* had said they would keep commissioning columns every week and now I would be paid for them. And there was the radio work, and the occasional TV. *Nationwide* had now started using me every Friday, so that was something. It was, we decided, worth the risk, and I did hate commuting. What could be better than writing about gardening in a shed halfway down the garden?

The answer to this rhetorical question came six months later with the arrival of Polly. I thought I liked being a gardener, but being a dad, at the risk of becoming far too sentimental, was and is just the best thing of all. Bar none. I worry, of course. Dads do. About all kinds of things. Not least the amount of space children take up, which was why, in 1981, we moved down to Hampshire so there would be more room. Camilla arrived in August 1982. Since then I have shared my life with three women. Even our three dogs have been bitches. There are the cats, of course. They were boys, yes, but cut out for a bachelor life. It is, I maintain, good to be the undisputed master of one's own household. And if you believe that . . .

After trying me out a little, and discovering no discernible reduction in viewing figures, *Nationwide* created a Friday slot for me. 'Down to Earth' it was called, with refreshing candour. I had a potting shed and a lawn, situated up on the roof of Lime Grove during the summer months, and in the studio during autumn and winter. At least that way the sun always shone. Having been interviewed for my first few appearances, I was now allowed to go solo and do 'pieces to camera', since they clearly had no difficulty in getting me to talk.

But what to wear? I discounted Percy's three-piece suit. And country tweeds. I plumped instead for rugby shirts. Suitably casual and appropriately rugged, I reasoned. Quite why I was persuaded a year or two later to go into hand-knitted picture-fronted sweaters I cannot imagine. It was my first fashion *faux pas* and one of which I am regularly reminded when some well-meaning soul brings an old copy of *Woman's Own* or *Amateur Gardening* for me to sign. There I am, with my gap-toothed grin (I have always resisted the lure of orthodontistry, believing it to be the thin end of the cosmetic-surgery wedge) proudly sporting a pullover decorated with a prize marrow, complete with 1st prize rosette, or a desert island with palm trees, or a country scene with sheep. Why, oh, why, oh why ... ? They even had a competition in *Woman's Own* to design me one. How I envy Daniel Craig his Brioni suits and his association with *GQ* magazine.

I followed this with a predilection, during the mid 1980s, for striped blazers and bow ties. I even showed Her Majesty the Queen round my garden at Chelsea Flower Show wearing one such combination – white flannels, white shirt, a pale lemon bow tie and a maroon and black striped blazer that I picked up from Oxfam. I ask you ... Anyway, it didn't stop *Nationwide* from employing me. Neither did it put off *Breakfast Time*.

By now, *Nationwide* had transformed into something called *60 Minutes* (BBC producers do occasionally go through particularly lean phases when it comes to creative titling). From time to time they also live by the motto 'If it ain't broken, break it', but I'll stop there on the grounds that I have not yet retired. And so *Nationwide*, which had once brought us the skateboarding duck, but which, more importantly, gave Britain a sense of identity, with correspondents in all the regions chipping into the network every evening, began its rather inglorious descent into broadcasting oblivion.

Breakfast Time was the first successful early-morning TV programme, surprisingly trouncing the much-heralded *TV AM* with its bevy of stars: Angela Rippon, Michael Parkinson, Anna Ford, David Frost and Robert Kee. It was anchored by Frank Bough (with whom I had worked on *Nationwide*) and Selina Scott. They had launched the programme in 1982 with a West Country gardening expert by the name of Don Hoyle, who had died suddenly and unexpectedly before the first twelve months was up. Considerately they had not replaced him, but on the programme's first anniversary they had decided to fill the hole Don had left, and they asked if I would like to take the job.

Instead of one live spot a week on the regulation Friday night (gardening being something that people only do at weekends), I was offered two – a Tuesday phone-in and a 'straight piece' on the Friday. I leapt at the chance, and for the next four years I rose at 4.30a.m two days a week in time to get to the studio for 5.30a.m and be on air an hour later.

For the first time in my life I felt completely at ease with what I was doing – writing and broadcasting about something I am passionate about, and being allowed to do so from home.

'How do you discipline yourself?' People ask it all the time. My reply is always the same. There is no need to discipline yourself to do something you love. It takes far more discipline to stand on a station platform every morning and wait for the 7.25a.m train to London. I don't feel as if I *work*, really. I just *do* things.

And then there is the other question. If you had to give up writing, or broadcasting or gardening, which would it be? That's like asking someone which is their favourite child. Luckily, I don't have to give up any of them. Well, not until they give *me* up. Which they probably will. Eventually. Telly will be the first to disappear. When bits of me start to fall off. Or I lose my marbles. Until then I'll keep on trying to get away with it.

The thing is, like most folk, and a lot of plants, I'm a bit of a hybrid. I'm a sociable soul who enjoys company and is genuinely interested in people. But I also need solitude. Gardeners are often happy and content in their own company, and I am a gardener. I write in solitary confinement here in the loft above the barn that runs alongside our house. I used to write in a shed. There is no music playing. The silence, apart from the birdsong through the open skylight, is something I enjoy. The church clock across the lane strikes every quarter, but that's comforting, rather than distracting.

I talk to myself every now and then. Nothing wrong in that, unless I start an argument. And when I've written for about five hours – as much as I can usually manage – I'll go out into the garden and potter. I don't double dig (only prize parsnip growers do that) but I prune and plant things, pull things out and replace them. The creation of a garden is ongoing. It is not like decorating a house: 'That's it love; I've done.' It keeps on changing; views that were once pleasing become less so. Borders that were once in their prime go over the hill and need to be replanted. I wouldn't have it any other way. It is an opportunity for renewal and that is, perhaps, its greatest appeal.

Gardening was, and always will be, a challenge, but if you learn how to do it and what sort of attitude to approach it with it becomes rewarding rather than frustrating. Most of the time. Above all, there is nothing better than sharing your successes and your failures, and that's what writing and broadcasting about plants and gardens allows me to do.

Breakfast Time gave me an opportunity to enthuse about my passion to a wider public. Several million of them, rather than the few hundred thousand that the gardening magazines could offer. Practical gardening has always been my forte – just growing plants, and putting them together in a pleasing way. It all stems back to that enjoyment of art, and my only O level!

As well as demonstrating the craft of taking cuttings on live early-morning television (try not to perforate the skin with a sharp knife – the resultant gore might put people off their bacon and eggs), I also undertook country walks, proving, I hope, that gardening and a love of nature are inextricably entwined.

The walks were not live. We would record them a week or so in advance and I would usually take Lulu, our yellow Labrador, with me. She was a TV natural. No matter how many times I had to re-do a walk through a patch of woodland, due to my own or the cameraman's ineptitude, Lulu was able to repeat it flawlessly. We walked past spring lambs and she would be perfectly behaved; we would stroll along country lanes and the noisiest tractor would not phase her; children would be allowed to crawl all over her with nary a growl. But show her a patch of water and she was in, and would not emerge until her appetite for a swim had been assuaged.

Time and again Alison and I would stand on the banks of the River Wharfe in Yorkshire, while Lulu doggy-paddled midstream, convincing other passers-by that she was drowning in spite of our protestations to the contrary.

She would roll in fox poo and eat absolutely anything, after which her breath could fell Muhammad Ali. When she was well into double figures we took on two Labrador pups, Grace and Favour (their grandfather came from Sandringham so we thought it appropriate). The *One Man and his Dog* presenter Phil Drabble suggested that a youngster or two for company might give her a new lease of life. He was not wrong. Lulu, with dogged determination (sorry), lasted several more years and remained the grand old lady of the family. She is buried in our old garden at Barleywood, underneath a dogwood.

We are dogless now, Grace and Favour having departed several years ago, but I would not like to think that we will be without one for much longer. Spud, the black and white cat who, in *Gardeners' World* programmes, liked nothing more than jumping on my shoulders while I was planting potatoes, has outlasted his brother Hector who died a few years ago. He rules the roost and has, to my relief, stopped catching much in the way of wildlife. I tell you this only because people enquire after him. The old saw about not appearing with children and animals is as true now as when it was fresh minted. Try as I might to make the technique involved in planting potatoes stick in people's minds, they need to be reminded every year. But they have never forgotten the cat.

The Naming of Names

They talk of avarice, lust, ambition, as great passions. It is a mistake; they are little passions. Vanity is the great commanding passion of all.

Richard Brinsley Sheridan

To have one plant named after you may be regarded as good fortune. To have six looks like boastfulness. That's what Lady Bracknell would have said. It is, truth to tell, a bit embarrassing. I suppose I should have a flower bed in which they all grow, but I can't bring myself to do it, lest some garden visitor should enquire what one of them is called, and then another and another. They would think the needle had got stuck in the groove.

The sweet pea was the first, back in 1985 when I was gardening on *Breakfast Time*. I had a letter from Robert Bolton, a famed grower of the flower. Could he, he asked, name a variety after me? I did have the presence of mind to ask if I could see it first. He sent me a bunch. In a box. I unwrapped them and discovered they had no scent. I rang him up. How to put it tactfully? I talked around the subject until he eventually said, 'Of course, you won't smell, having been in the post for a day or two.'

'I do have a decent perfume then?'

'Good heavens yes! Wonderfully delicate but quite marked.'

So I thanked him and graciously accepted, and 'Alan Titchmarsh' the sweet pea has survived now for twenty-four years. He can be a bit tricky. Sometimes he gets bud drop. But in a good year he is cream, flushed pink with frilly edges and a delicate scent. And he has won medals, probably thanks to a good, stiff stalk.

After twenty years or so, when Robert Bolton had died, it looked as if 'A.T. sweet pea' was on his way out, to be superseded by other newer varieties (it is in nature as it is on the screen), but he was rescued by an old Kew student, Dave Matthewman, and is now firmly planted on his seed list. I'd like to think Dave resurrected me because I'm worth growing, rather than just for old times' sake. I keep meaning to have me growing on one side of the front door and 'Percy Thrower' (he's lavender blue) the other. I'd rather like that.

The garden pink came next, a good fifteen years ago now, raised by Steven Bailey. I do have stamina. I was a special offer in the *Daily Telegraph* a couple of weeks ago. You could have three of me for around a tenner. Very reasonably priced. I'm white with a green eye that is slightly bloodshot. (A stickler for accuracy is Steven Bailey.) Try me next to 'Doris' if you like, though to be honest I'm more comfortable with 'Mrs Sinkins', in spite of her split calyx.

The lupin was launched a few years ago now, tall and yellow and bred by the Woodfield brothers of Stratford-upon-Avon. I've never grown 'me' the lupin. Well, I'm on chalk, and they don't much like it. Their leaves become yellow and chlorotic. But I'm flattered that a plant as tall, stately and elegant as a lupin bears my name. It's all very well being squat (the pink) and a good climber (the sweet pea) but both tendencies are open to criticism.

The 'Alan Titchmarsh' fuchsia, raised by Carol Gubler, is what they call a 'good doer', and the 'Alan Titchmarsh' hosta from Park Green Nurseries has wonderfully bright leaves – soft green with a butter-yellow streak right down the centre. (I don't think they were being funny.)

But it was in 2005 that my dream came true and I finally became a rose, thanks to David Austin. David is famous for his 'English Roses' – shrub roses that are repeat flowering, unlike a lot of the older varieties that have but a single flush of bloom in late June and early July.

The English rose 'Alan Titchmarsh' is . . . well, modesty forbids that I should describe myself. I will simply repeat the poetic description of me from David Austin's book *The English Roses*:

'This variety bears quite large, deeply cupped, full-petalled, slightly incurved flowers that are well filled with petals. The outer petals are pale pink, the centre petals of a much stronger, glowing warm pink. The side flowers nod nicely on the branch and are held in small groups of three or four, while the main branches from the base may consist of much larger sprays with the flowers well apart, making an almost candelabra effect. They have a warm Old Rose fragrance with a hint of citrus. 'Alan Titchmarsh' forms a quite large shrub of elegant, arching growth, providing a most satisfactory overall picture. The leaves are red at the bud stage, soon turning to glossy, dark green with seven to nine leaflets. This rose has very good disease resistance.'

So there you are. I have a border of me just outside the house. Do I have any faults? Well, my neck is perhaps a little weak – the flowers nod gracefully – but I am, as David says, very disease resistant and after a year or two I make a splendid and statuesque plant. In short, I like to think that, in spite of one or two minor faults, I am worth persisting with. It is in the garden as it is in life . . .

Showtime

When passéd was almost the month of May,
And I had roméd all the summer's day . . .
The Legend of Good Women, Geoffrey Chaucer

My first taste of Chelsea Flower Show came when I was at college in May 1969. I'd like to claim that it blew me away. It would make a better story. The truth is that I have little recollection of it except the flapping canvas of the Great Marquee, show gardens that were staid and restrained by today's standards – rectangles of lawn and formal pools – and in the Great Marquee the floral seasons strangely mixed together – daffodils with roses, strawberries with chrysanthemums, delphiniums with tulips. Odd.

I went there every year after that and got to know it rather better, but it was not until 1983 that it became a part of my life and a permanent fixture in my diary. For the last twenty-six years the third week in May has had a line drawn through it – everything else revolves around it.

By 1983 I was writing a gardening column for *Woman's Own*. They decided, at one of those meetings they have every hour on the hour in magazine offices, that it would be a great idea to have a garden at Chelsea Flower Show and raise the horticultural profile of the magazine. At least, I imagine that's what they thought. They asked me what I could come up with. What I came up with was a family garden. It was not at all elaborate, or large – about 20ft by 40ft with a stretch of lawn, a swing, a sandpit, a bright pink parasol and a millstone water feature, which was then quite a novelty.

Three weeks we had to build it, me and Mike Chewter and his mate Ray. Mike was a Chelsea veteran who had been recommended to me and in whom I found a trustworthy and hardworking project manager. We were rather pleased with the result. We won a Silver Gilt Medal, and I won a place on the BBC television presentation team.

By this time, Peter Seabrook had been presenting the Chelsea Flower Show coverage since 1976, with a different 'floating' presenter every year – either a broadcaster (usually a woman) or someone who was involved with the show in a professional capacity – a garden designer or an exhibitor in the Floral Marquee.

I had been on the box for about three years by this time so thought I knew the ropes, but putting together an hour's worth of television at an outside broadcast is a world away from four minutes in a studio, as I was to discover.

I had always watched Peter enviously in previous years, as he perched among the begonias and the bonsai on his shooting stick, crafting his next piece to camera and checking his facts in the little shorthand pad he always carried with him.

Not that I was simply invited to participate. I was asked to come in for a chat with Neil Eccles, the executive producer, in his office in Shepherd's Bush. Peter Seabrook was there, too, and took part in the light grilling that followed. At the end of this flexing of presentational muscles – the old hand making sure that the new boy was up to the job – I was asked if I'd like to be a part of the team. I said that I would, and went home with barely suppressed glee and the usual helping of apprehensiveness.

Back then the Chelsea coverage amounted to two hour-long programmes, one that Peter did on his own – *Growing For Gold* – about the build-up, which transmitted on the Sunday night before the show opened, and one evening programme on the Tuesday of show week. The latter would be where I was involved. We filmed from the Sunday right through until Tuesday afternoon, working twelve-hour days and often laying down the voice over as late as ten minutes before transmission.

This is hard enough work on its own, but when you are also building a show garden it is totally exhausting. I'll be grateful to the old man until my dying day for his generosity with facts and information, which he shared unstintingly with the young presenter wished upon him. He was an absolute brick.

This sort of presentation is a steep learning curve. With cameras in position, a young assistant producer will come and find you and ask you to talk for two or three minutes on anything from cacti to orchids, cauliflowers to flower arranging. You'll be taken to the stand, introduced to the exhibitor (if you're lucky) and have a couple of minutes to pump them for information before you have to stand in front of the camera and speak as though you are an expert on everything that meets your eye. Well you are, to some extent, but it's the nitty gritty bits that often catch you out. What year was this plant raised? Who bred it? What sort of growing conditions does it like? You will probably have to walk and talk at the same time, so this is no job for the Gerald Fords of the television world – those who cannot walk and chew gum simultaneously.

Anyway, I can't have done too badly, since they asked me back the following year. The year after that, 1985, I made another garden for *Woman's Own* (the editorial staff must have had another meeting) and this time landed the Holy Grail – a Gold Medal. It was a country kitchen garden with fruit and vegetables, flower borders and daisy-studded grass, a brick and flint wall with a little gate in it, two Chinese Chippendale benches from Chatsworth Carpenters, a little rill – oh, it did look lovely.

What's more, the Queen came to look at it. Along with

other members of the royal family, she pays a private visit on the Monday afternoon before the show opens to members of the RHS on Tuesday. She seemed impressed. She said, 'I like your onions. They're nice and small.' Then, seeing that I looked a little crestfallen, she added, 'When they're big they taste of nothing at all.'

The garden was, by today's standards, very modest in aspiration. I charged *Woman's Own* £11,000 for making it, which included all my time as well as the plants and the building costs. The garden that was awarded Best in Show in 2009, by comparison, cost £350,000.

In the intervening years the show coverage has changed dramatically. The contract was awarded to Channel 4 for a couple of years at the turn of the millennium, and then came back to the BBC and so, with just a couple of years off, I have been presenting the coverage for 27 years. Best be quiet about that or they'll start to think it's time for a change.

For the last twenty years I've been the main anchor of the television coverage, which now stretches over seven days, with a half hour at lunchtime and at least an hour most evenings. Where once we offered an hour's coverage, we now supply around twelve hours over the week.

My own Chelsea week begins on the Saturday night before the show, when I move into a local hotel with a week's worth of clothes. 'Don't you have a London flat?' I get asked. My answer is that it's rather nice to have someone else cook supper when you get back in the evening, so I prefer a hotel. It is, I reckon, a necessary perk. I'll rise at 5.30a.m and be in the grounds of the Royal Hospital at around 6.30a.m on Sunday, filming right through until 6 or 7p.m. That sort of regime will continue for the rest of the week, ending on Saturday at around 6p.m when those who have been stalwart enough to stay for the sell-off will stagger home with towering delphiniums, hanging baskets dripping with fuchsias, monstrous tree ferns and whatever else they can lay their hands on.

I get ribbed about the clothes. Sunday will be relatively informal – a jacket and an open-necked shirt – but Chelsea is still a part of that uniquely British phenomenon called 'The Season' so I like to do it the honour of smartening up. On Monday – Press Day and the day of the royal visit – I'll wear a suit and tie, and keep the tie and a jacket for the two members' days that follow. Then, when the show opens to the public for Thursday, Friday and Saturday, it's back to a jacket and open-necked shirt. Does it really matter? Does anyone really care? Well, I like to think we don't get enough 'special' in our lives, so I try to keep Chelsea special. I reckon it's worth more than a T-shirt and jeans. Must be my age . . .

Then there's the badge. It gets a lot of comments, mainly because it glints in the sun. I wear it on my left lapel. It's the Victoria Medal of Honour – the Royal Horticultural Society's highest award, limited to no more than 63 horticulturists at any one time, the same number of years as Queen Victoria's reign. They gave me it in 2004 and it came as a bit of a shock. This year they made me a Vice President, at the same time as Lord Heseltine. I'm hoping for a seat in government very shortly.

The organisation of the television coverage of the show is

now finely tuned. It has to be. You can't turn out twelve hours of watchable television without getting your act together. Of course, there are always the complaints – the music is too loud, there are not enough flowers, why is there so much stone and concrete? – but we aim to reflect the style of the show and its breadth. We have to give the show gardens the lion's share of the coverage on the Sunday in particular because the displays in the Great Pavilion (which replaced the marquee) are not ready by then. But after that we do try to major on flowers and plants. That said, twelve hours of dense plant coverage does need leavening with light relief – not silliness, but good humour. I like to think that gardeners want to smile as well as be informed. This one certainly does.

I still get a thrill out of being at the show, even after all these years. It does have its own special atmosphere. Spread out in front of Sir Christopher Wren's Royal Hospital like a brightly patterned carpet, it is a showcase of international horticulture, a gathering of the finest botanical minds and a place to meet old friends. It is a place to shop, a place to spot scarlet-coated Chelsea Pensioners who remind you where you really are, and a place that fosters new talent in garden design and growing plants. It is not overstating the case to say that no plants, anywhere in the world, will have been grown more skilfully than those you see here.

As for the style of the show itself, it changes each year. Some things remain constant, of course – the height of the delphiniums, the succulence of the National Farmers' Union vegetables, the outrageousness of the National Association of Flower Arrangement Societies' stand – but the prominence of a particular group of plants, sometimes cottage garden flowers, sometimes orchids, is often a reflection of plant fads and fashions and the way our gardens are going.

The show gardens, in particular, reflect current trends. The use of energy-saving devices and the importance of drainage, for example may seem prosaic, but even they have come to be important in recent years when so many front gardens are being lost to parking spaces.

Chelsea, more than ever, offers a wake-up call each spring to anyone who thinks that gardening is unimportant or stagnating. I don't mind if it sometimes irritates, provided that the irritation results in a positive outcome and makes people think about their surroundings. It can also put them off, of course, since it is a counsel of perfection and in its way quite unreal. How can anybody hope to achieve a garden that looks like a Chelsea garden? They can't, of course. Chelsea gardens are designed to look perfect for one week in May. They would look pretty dreary in September or February. But what I hope the show does do, more than anything else, is inspire people to at least have a go. With any luck, having watched the television coverage, or turned up at the show, they will go home fired up with enthusiasm for their own patch. They may never turn it into anything remotely resembling those gardens that are built within three weeks and then dismantled in a few days, but I hope their determination lasts rather longer than that. For a year at least, until we can give them another boost next May.

I sit in our outdoor studio eyrie – the spot where we link the entire programme together at the end of each afternoon – and I look down over the thousands of people who have turned up to what is justifiably described as the greatest flower show on earth. If you consider that each one of them is there because they care about their surroundings, because they like growing things, and because they think it's important that plants and flowers and vegetables and fruits are a part of their lives, then it reminds you that all is not lost. The more people we can interest in growing things, the more people we can get raising their own food or beautifying their surroundings, the better this world of ours will be. It may sound like a grandiose claim, and one that is out of touch with reality. But there is nothing more real than growing things. It gives you a sense of perspective, a sense of continuity. It calms the spirit, soothes the soul and fosters patience, creativity and an understanding of nature. If you know anyone who thinks that those things are not important, then bid them a fond farewell. They are not worth knowing.

Horticultural Heroes

Andrea: Unhappy the land that has no heroes! . . .
Galileo: No. Unhappy the land that needs heroes.
The Life of Galileo, Bertolt Brecht

Galileo's view seems to pertain nowadays, but I'm with Andrea. I've always felt sad that we can't, as a nation, decide on who should occupy the fourth plinth in Trafalgar Square. It seems to me a sign of mean-spiritedness rather than egalitarianism that we can't agree on one mortal who deserves this country's approbation. Maybe when the Queen has gone we'll solve the problem. In the meantime we'll have to content ourselves with members of the public standing up there for an hour at a time and letting off helium balloons and having their bit of fame, which is, of course, every bit as important as remembering General Sir Charles James Napier, Commander-in-Chief India, Major General Sir Henry Havelock, hero of the Indian Mutiny, and King George IV. Perhaps today we are more comfortable with Landseer's lions at the foot of Nelson's column, and the dolphins cavorting in the fountains.

Anyway, in my case there is no disagreement whatsoever on who my own heroes are. The people who chivvied and encouraged and who could spot latent talent. Well, what they *thought* was talent. Or something.

It started with Grandad Hardisty, of course, on his allotment.

The one with the blackberries on the bedsteads and the sunken tank of soot water. It's the stuff of heroes, is soot water. But outside the family, Harry Rhodes must count as my first real hero. He taught me for only a year when I was nine, but his influence was profound and long-lasting. He was, for a sensitive and unconfident boy, a kind of Jiminy Cricket character. Not that he resembled the insect. He actually looked a bit like a Roman emperor, if the drawings in my school textbook were anything to go by. His nose was Roman, certainly, and he had a high forehead and rimless glasses.

His enthusiasm was boundless and in evidence both in the classroom and at Sunday school. I don't remember him ever being rabidly evangelical – that was not his style, and anyway Ilkley All Saints was low church, understated rather than happy clappy. He taught us Religious Knowledge in the same way that he taught us English and sums, matter of factly but always brightly.

But the reason that he is a hero is twofold. First, because he was always pleasant and encouraging, realising that such an approach was more effective than the reverse, a concept strangely incomprehensible to many teachers back then. Second because he was a keen gardener. Each autumn, at the church bazaar in the King's Hall, he sold cacti and succulents that he had grown in his greenhouse at home. I bought them for sixpence apiece and grew them first on the lavatory windowsill and then – when that overflowed – in my little polythene greenhouse. Mr Rhodes taught me my first botanical Latin. *Bryophyllum pinnatum*, a succulent that produced tiny plantlets along the serrations of its leaves and gave a young gardener the easiest possible introduction to plant propagation.

It is difficult not to make Harry Rhodes sound holier than thou. He wasn't. He just had a fresh and wholehearted approach to life. I never once saw him look bored, and only very occasionally did he ever get angry, at repeated misdemeanours, or when he felt his good nature was being taken advantage of.

I saw him occasionally in later life. Aside from my parents, there is no-one whose opinion mattered more to me, and he never hid his happiness at my achievements. Harry died seventeen years ago now, but I'm still in touch with his widow, Barbara, who lets me know when she likes what I do on the telly. And when she doesn't. When the gardening club of which Harry had been a member sadly disbanded, and returned all cups and trophies to their donors, she gave me the silver-plated salver that she had presented to them after his death:

Commemorative:

Harry Rhodes

1926–1992

'He loved roses'

If I were to grab one possession on leaving my blazing house, I would have to choose between the budding knife given to me on my first day at work, my grandfather's spade and Harry's silver salver.

I've probably said enough about Percy Thrower, who was my second hero. If meeting him for the first time was a thrill, then getting to know him a little better over the space of thirteen years was just as rewarding. I still aspire to his level of professionalism, the smoothness of his delivery and his relaxed style of broadcasting. He, more than anyone, influenced my television career, and I can only hope for a fraction of his charisma and watchability.

Percy was in his mid-seventies when he died. I was working in Birmingham when I heard he was in hospital in Wolverhampton. I almost put off going to see him; I was tired after a week of broadcasting and thought I could call in to see him early the following week when I wasn't so shattered. I had one more programme to do the following day, and tonight I really ought to rest up and prepare for it. But something made me go.

I almost walked past the hospital bed in which he lay, until a voice stopped me in my tracks. 'Look who's here,' said Connie, Percy's wife, who was sitting beside the bed of a pale, thin man I hardly recognised. I sat down on a chair on the other side of the bed and chatted for as long as I thought was advisable, bearing in mind Percy's weak state. He didn't say much, but Connie seemed pleased to see me. Pleased to have reinforcements. After half an hour I got up to go. I leaned over the bed to shake his hand. Whatever else Percy was, he was not overly demonstrative, but on this occasion he held on to my hand for around half a minute before letting go. I had to lean forward to hear the words he whispered: 'Thank you for coming'.

I did my work the following day and then got in the car and drove home. Half an hour into the journey I turned on the car radio. The third item on the news was the announcement of his death. I pulled in to the side of the road for a while. Quite a long while.

Not all my heroes have hopped the twig. Beth Chatto is very much alive, and she is a heroine to countless gardeners. I have known Beth for almost as long as I have known my wife – around thirty years – and we swap regular letters and the occasional phone call. There will be periods when we are out of touch for a while, sometimes for a year or more, but then we take up where we left off with hardly a pause for breath. She is, I suppose, a soulmate, simple as that. We have the same interests and, just as important, the same sense of values. Why is she a heroine? Well, not just because of her astonishing gardening expertise and skill with plants, but because she is such good company and still curious, still learning. We all know folk who know their subjects so well that they feel they never need to ask questions of anyone else. Beth is not like that. She will ask you for your opinion on almost anything – from plants to music to painting – and listen, and evaluate, and reason and then come back with her take on it. She is stimulating, in the same way that Christopher Lloyd – another hero – was stimulating.

Christo's garden at Great Dixter in East Sussex was, and is, a Mecca for keen gardeners, but he was a tricky old stick to deal with. The secret was to stand up to him and give as good as you got, politely but firmly, and never to bluster or pretend you knew something you did not. Oh, he would have a go at you – 'Fancy you not knowing that Alan; well you do surprise me!' – but always with a twinkle in his eye.

His plant knowledge was prodigious and practical; he knew what grew well with what, but took great delight in shocking people, planting clashing colours to make visitors raise their eyebrows. And he was no respecter of tradition, ripping out the rose beds at Dixter to make a tropical garden. Sometimes his schemes worked and sometimes they didn't, but it was trying them out that gave him such pleasure. In Fergus Garrett he found a helpmate, amanuensis and friend who allowed him to exercise his originality when his own muscle power was in decline, and the garden continues to inspire thanks to Fergus's extensive knowledge and passionate commitment.

Like Beth, Christo enjoyed mixing with younger people who were stimulating company. When people he knew complained, 'All my old friends are dying,' Christo would snap back 'Well, get some young ones then. I have.' And he did. Dozens of friends – of all ages in fact – were invited down for weekends at Dixter, where the conversation would revolve around everything from opera to sculpture, with gardening and plantsmanship being the common, leavening factor. He loved music – he apparently played the oboe well, though I never heard him – and was a regular at Glyndebourne. He took Alison and me there once and we provided the picnic, which was in itself daunting, since he was a great cook – his sorrel soup was the best I have ever tasted. We saw Richard Strauss's *Arabella*. Not my favourite opera, but the evening was memorable on account of the company if not so much the performance.

Like Beth, Christo's enthusiasm was infectious and challenging. He could be exhausting company, demanding and sometimes a touch moody, but I never found him anything less than exhilarating. You just needed lots of energy when you were with him . . .

I'd put any one of these four on the remaining plinth in Trafalgar Square. Many people would not have a clue who they were, but then the fame of Havelock and Napier – even, arguably, George IV – have been lost in the mists of time. How fitting it would be to have among the warriors and kings someone who had made their mark through the peaceful occupation of growing things.

There is, of course, an alternative hero who fits the bill on two counts. Firstly he is royal, and secondly he is as good a champion as the natural world has ever had. The Prince of Wales takes more flak than most, for doing a job he did not choose to do and doing it with every ounce of energy he possesses. I have never known a harder worker. He takes on architects and he takes on governments. There are those who think he should pipe down, but I reckon he's the best royal voice the people have ever had. You might quarrel with some of his opinions, but public opinion seems to be coming round to more and more of them. And when he rattles those in high places who think they are beyond criticism and that he has no right to interfere in their exclusive provinces of architecture and medicine, science and sustainability, I feel a sense of satisfaction at their discomfort. He is a keen and knowledgeable gardener, a passionate environmentalist and a born countryman who deserves to be judged on things other than an unfortunate marriage. The achievements of the Prince's Trust alone – unmatched by any government initiative – qualify him for heroic status. Yes; he'll fit the fourth plinth very nicely.

Making Gardens

A garden-seat stood on one side of the door, and on the other a roller; for the Mole, who was a tidy animal when at home, could not stand having his ground kicked up by other animals into little runs that ended in earth-heaps.

The Wind in the Willows, Kenneth Grahame

'Design', as such, really only entered my consciousness at college. Up until then I knew the things that I wanted in a garden, and it was simply a matter of arranging them like the pieces of a jigsaw so that they fitted together properly – greenhouse in the best-lit spot, vegetables down the far end so that when they looked horrible in winter you wouldn't see them, and a nice big lawn in the middle. Neat. Tidy. I like orderliness. I am a naturally tidy person. Like the Mole.

At Kew the process of designing was taken much further in Landscape Construction and Landscape Design lectures, the latter with John Brookes, whose taste very much influenced that of all his students. He wasn't a bad role model. John had designed many gardens for 'important clients' as well as those at Chelsea Flower Show for the *Financial Times*. He had also worked with the legendary Brenda Colvin and we treated him with the respect he deserved.

But it was with Mrs Bell, my landlady at Willow Cottages in Kew, that I first felt the exhilaration that comes from a well-designed garden. In a way that's perverse, because her garden was anything but 'designed'; it just seemed to happen. And it was tiny. But she used a range of plants that I had hitherto been unaware of – shrub roses in particular – to create an arty-yet-artless mix that was full of atmosphere and the most wonderful place to relax at the end of a long day. Underneath boughs of 'Buff Beauty', 'Nevada', 'Vanity' and 'Madame Caroline Testout', with the perfume of roses drifting down and the aroma of *Geranium macrorrhizum* wafting upwards, we would sit on wooden benches strewn with plump cushions, drink home-made wine and talk about art and music. Since then I have always felt that my ideal garden would look something like the landscape in Fragonard's *The Swing*, minus the threatening sky.

My first garden of my own – if you don't count the ones I commandeered from my parents – was the 15ft by 40ft patch in Sunningdale where I built the greenhouse, the shed and the pond that cut the garden in two. But my scope there was limited. It was not until we moved to Barleywood in Hampshire that I really had a chance to flex my muscles.

It was a foolish place to try to make a garden. That's what *The Times* gardening editor, Roy Hay, told me. To be honest he put it rather more strongly. His actual words were: 'You're mad.'

The garden was on a north-west facing slope, 80ft wide and an eighth of a mile long. It had a gradient of 1 in 4 on the steepest part, and the soil was chalk, clay and flint. I think Roy was probably right. Why make a garden there? Well, because we loved the spot, we could afford it – it was far enough away from London to be reasonably priced – and the house sort of felt right. And at the back of my mind I knew people could not say, 'Well it's easy for you', because it wasn't – they could hear the flints clanking on my spade whenever I planted anything.

The house was at the bottom of the hill and the garden rose up from it. Friends asked if I was going to terrace it and were surprised when I said 'No'. But if you terrace a garden when the house is at the bottom of the slope, all you see is a series of risers – it's like standing at the foot of the stairs. When the house is at the top of a slope terracing makes great sense, for then the garden is presented to the house. But in my situation, the garden was already presented to the house, all I had to do was sculpt it.

Making a garden is a combination of things – art, obviously, by which I mean sculpting as well as painting the picture, but also craft – a skill that needs to be learned and then adjusted depending on the site in question.

Too many 'garden designers' inflict their designs on plots of earth with little thought for, or knowledge of, the place itself or the people who will inhabit it. They proceed rather as if they were wallpapering a room for their own pleasure and amusement. I don't mean that they do not choose 'the right plants for the right place', which is of paramount importance when making a garden (otherwise the plants will die), but that they don't get to know the feel or 'the genius of the place'. Now you could argue that I am being posey. What is 'the genius of the place' in a back garden on a housing estate, surrounded by interwoven fencing and measuring 20ft by 30ft? Point taken. But even in these situations the style of the house – brick or stone, pebbledash or clapboard – and the lifestyle of the occupants – childless couple or young family, for example – should suggest the style of garden.

The garden should complement the house, or at least resonate with it in some way, rather than seeming to be tacked on. There is no reason why it should not contrast with the house, provided that the contrast is either pleasing or exhilarating, or preferably both.

Barleywood was in a Hampshire village. It was nothing flashy. It had originally been one of a series of corrugated iron shacks, each built on an acre of land to accommodate men returning from the Boer War. It had been built around and added to in the 1970s (and we added to it even further in the 1980s) but it was basically a chalet bungalow – a house with bedrooms in the roof, illuminated by dormer windows.

My taste in gardens has altered over the years. These days I am as formal as I have ever been (though not necessarily in my mode of dress), but Barleywood was a country garden that needed to be treated as such. Nevertheless I have always liked good lines, and so I made a zig-zag path up the garden, which was part lawn and part gravel or cobbles set in cement, and filled in between it with billowing banks of flowers. Good, strong lines softened by planting have always appealed to me.

I had a veg patch, too. I've always had a veg patch. We had an allotment in Sunningdale when I could not squeeze any fruit and veg into the garden itself, but I have always been a fan of *small* kitchen gardens. Manageable ones. Make them too big and they will overface you and become weed-ridden eyesores in a matter of weeks. Stagger your sowings, too, to avoid gluts and that all-too-familiar sight of long rows of lettuces running to seed. Only grow what you like eating (obvious, perhaps, but often overlooked) and site the kitchen garden as near to the kitchen as possible to avoid long, soggy journeys in wet weather. If the kitchen garden is too far from the kitchen you'll find any excuse not to go there. End of lecture.

Barleywood came with an acre and a third of land. The third of an acre was the steep slope immediately behind the house, and above this was an acre of paddock where the ground flattened slightly. It was not until I started presenting *Gardeners' World* that I took the paddock into cultivation and created a sweeping series of borders that could be home to different styles of planting. The challenge was to make the garden work as a cohesive whole, as well as accommodating a series of features that would provide inspiration for viewers with less space. It also gave me room to have a large greenhouse divided into three sections and surrounded by a formal Mediterranean garden.

It was fun making the garden at Barleywood, though it took me twenty years to do so. We'd been there for fifteen years before I started presenting *Gardeners' World*, so the lower portion was well established by then. The extra acre gave me the opportunity to try things I had not tried before – a tropical garden and a woodland garden – and to grow plants that I loved but had no space for lower down, tree ferns particularly.

We were lucky enough, over the years, to be able to buy additional land at the top, where we planted trees by cajoling friends to turn up one Sunday and 'Plant a wood in a day'. We managed to get in over 1,000 trees – oak, ash, beech, birch, wild cherry and the like – between dawn and dusk. They were little 6-in high whips that were protected from deer and rabbits by tree shelters. I gave demonstrations on how to do it and Alison provided soup and bacon sandwiches. It was a real achievement and is now, seventeen years on, a fully grown wood that we used to visit every now and then on *Gardeners' World* to show tree planting or, in the patch of older woodland we bought, the glory of bluebells.

In the last few years, other presenters came and joined in – Chris Beardshaw and Rachel de Thame, Pippa Greenwood and Joe Swift, who designed the border at the back of the greenhouse. Much as I enjoy their company – and they all four rank as friends – it is tricky having other people digging your soil. They tease me about the fact that I used to hand them a fork after they had done a piece to camera standing in one of my beds or borders, but they all got used to having to fork out their footprints. I told you I was tidy minded.

Why is it hard to let others loose in your garden? Well, because we all do things differently. The gardens I like best are those that reflect the heart and the soul and the personality of their owner – something you never find in a garden that has been designed by committee or run by an institution. Kew and Wisley are superb gardens, but they are impersonal in a way that Great Dixter (Christopher Lloyd) or White Barn House (Beth Chatto) are not. Sissinghurst (Vita Sackville-West) and Hidcote (Lawrence Johnston) were designed and planted by individuals and then taken over by an institution (the National Trust). They have become hybrid gardens where the personality and spirit of the founders can still be felt. If planting and restoration are handled sensitively, this will continue to be true. But there is an ever-present danger that the gardens' original character and atmosphere will be lost. It is inevitable since no two gardeners are alike in their approach – good gardeners, anyway.

But then that's the problem with gardens. Unlike buildings, they don't and won't stand still. Go to Chartwell and you can walk round Churchill's house knowing that it is exactly as he left it. You can even feel his presence. But his garden? To use a phrase employed by Samuel Pepys when referring to the portraits of ladies of the court painted by Sir Peter Lely, they are 'good but not like'. It is not a criticism of those who take gardens on, just an observation on the ways of nature.

It was Sir Frederick Gibberd, the architect of Harlow New Town, who confessed that he found gardening the most difficult art form of all in that as well as dealing with shape, size, form, texture and colour, he was also dealing with time. Not only in terms of the seasons and the fact that gardens change in spring, summer, autumn and winter, but also because of the march of the years. A bed or border – or even an entire garden – that looks good one year may well have gone over the hill a few years later when the scale of it has changed and some plants have either died or overpowered their neighbours. So a garden can never be perfect, and neither is it ever finished. It is an ongoing job – and hopefully an ongoing joy.

After twenty-one years we moved from Barleywood to an old Georgian farmhouse a couple of miles down the road. It was a wrench after twenty-odd years – and we did hang on to Barleywood's woodland – but I felt that I had one more garden in me, and I had always wanted to make one around a Georgian house. It's not grand, more like a small doll's house, really, with a door in the middle and two windows on either side on two floors. The new extension, the kitchen, was built in 1777 – the date is scratched on a brick. It is a friendly sort of house and has about an acre of garden, plus three acres of wildflower meadow and a pond behind the long, low barn that sits alongside it. The barn is where I write.

The garden, Roy Hay would have been pleased to note, is flatter than that at Barleywood, and the soil not nearly so flinty, having been enriched by farmyard manure for hundreds of years. Thanks to the assiduous work of a local historian we now know the name of every owner and lessee of the house dating back to 1066. In the early 1800s it was owned by Sir Thomas Miller, although it was not grand enough for him to live in. Jane Austen, who lived a mile away, wrote to her sister Cassandra recording his demise: 'I treat you with a dead baronet in almost every letter'. So that's nice – not his death, but the fact that Jane Austen knew the owner of our house.

Because the house sits squarely in the centre of the acre, and is (hurrah!) surrounded by a brick and flint wall, I designed the garden on more formal lines than Barleywood. There's a York stone terrace running right round the house, formal beds and borders close to, and an informal winding path beyond them that snakes through tree ferns (I'll never give them up!) and woodland plantings. I tried curves nearer the house when we first moved in, but they simply did not work. In the end I went for the obvious, which is often a guide as to what is most natural, and used straight lines that complemented those of the house.

I like intersecting vistas and axes with focal points at the end (not original, I know, but pleasing), and plotting these and getting them to interlink is a great challenge. I also have a circular, raised, formal pool with, at its centre, a cheap copy of Verrochio's *Boy with a Dolphin*. I never did get the Queen's Garden at Kew, but at least I have the statue to remind me of it.

There is lots of topiary – clipped cones and balls of yew and box. I worry, sometimes, that the place looks like Trumpton, but evergreens offer form and solidity in winter when deciduous trees are bare, and when they are formally clipped they look much less like the planting in a cemetery.

Behind the barn the land is not so much a garden as a

conservation area. We made a large wildlife pond and planted a mixture of British native broad-leaved trees as well as three cedars and a lot of country hedging. Two years ago we acquired another couple of acres, to take us up to four, and I sowed these with a wildflower mixture. It took me half a day, using a bucket when my old seed fiddle broke. Now, in its second summer, the meadow is a delight. First came marguerites, then vetches, then wild carrot and knapweed and scabious. Crested dog's tail mingles with cocksfoot and sterile brome, and I scattered some yellow rattle to help weaken the grass on what was previously rich farmland – it is a parasitic plant that saps the strength of competing grasses that might otherwise overpower weaker wild flowers.

The birds and the butterflies love this haven – painted ladies and commas, ringlets and meadow browns, and the occasional blue, flit among the flowers and lay their eggs on the grasses and in the hedgerow. Last week I went round with the Reverend Keble Martin's book under my arm. I totted up 75 different species of wildflower, and those were the ones that I knew and that I could see, which probably means there are around 100 different species growing there.

Of all the things I have ever done, I think sowing a wildflower meadow and planting a wood are the most satisfying. I'm lucky to have been able to do it, I know, but on the other hand it means I will be leaving behind a piece of ground that is in better heart than it was when I took it on. In that way I feel I've paid my rent.

Branching Out

You wonder how they do it and you
    look to see the knack,
You watch the foot in action, or the
    shoulder, or the back.
But when you spot the answer where the
    higher glamours lurk,
You'll find in moving higher up the
    laurel covered spire,
That the most of it is practice and the
    rest of it is work.

               'How to be a Champion,' Grantland Rice

I seemed somehow to have found myself a niche, and one that suited me, pardon the pun, down to the ground. I would sit in my shed and write columns for magazines – *Woman's Own*, *Homes and Gardens*, *Amateur Gardening* and, later, *BBC Gardeners' World Magazine* – and for newspapers – first the *Daily Mail* and now the *Daily Express* and *Sunday Express*. Plus maybe two books a year. It is embarrassing how you can clock them up when you do it for a living: *Knave of Spades* will be my 56th, but then I have been at it for thirty-odd years.

Radio and television got me out of the shed, from *You and Yours* and the *Today* programme to *Nationwide* and *Breakfast Time*.

But it was in 1986 that I had an offer I almost refused and which was to change the direction of my life altogether.

Between breakfast time and lunchtime the BBC showed either schools' programmes or the test card. By the mid-eighties it became clear that an opportunity existed to fill more of the airwaves, and daytime television was born. I was asked by a man called Roger Laughton, who was given charge of the hours between 9a.m and 6p.m, if I had ever considered doing any television other than gardening. I told him I had not.

'Do you fancy auditioning for a new programme we're planning to run late morning? A viewers' feedback programme. Like *Points of View* but longer and with more teeth. It will be called *Open Air*.'

I hummed and hawed. But it did sound like a challenge, so I went up to Manchester and auditioned along with a pleasant, fresh-faced chap called Peter Bazalgette. It was a baptism by fire – sitting in a studio fielding phone calls and conducting interviews for an hour and a half, when previously, apart from the Chelsea Flower Show, I had presented nothing longer than four minutes. Anyway, I got the job. Peter didn't. Instead he went on to found Bazal Productions, which became part of Endemol, which came up with the ideas for *Changing Rooms* and *Ground Force*. He's now a powerful media mogul. Funny how life works out, isn't it? And it says a lot about Peter that he never bore me a grudge.

I was offered the anchorman's job, five days a week. I turned it down, explaining that I was a gardener first and foremost, with writing commitments on top and that I would be prepared to do just one day a week – Fridays.

Looking back I am astonished that a) I had the nerve to be so picky and that b) they agreed to take me on under those terms. So who did they get to do the other four days? An Irish lad called Eamonn Holmes.

Along with Eamonn and Patti Caldwell I presented *Open Air* for a year, and was then offered the chance of having a crack at a lunchtime show to be transmitted from BBC Pebble Mill. By now I had the bit between my teeth. I simply loved live television – I still do – and the chance to front a magazine programme for an hour every lunchtime, rather than simply talk about last night's TV, was too good an invitation to turn down. I took the job and along with Pamela Armstrong (for the first year), Sue Cook, Judi Spiers and Floella Benjamin, presented *Daytime Live*, which eventually morphed into a chat show called, simply, *Pebble Mill*.

I still kept the gardening going – I have never stopped writing about it, in books, magazines and newspapers – and I had a gardening slot in the programme every Friday until its last few years, when *Pebble Mill* majored on celebrity interviews and music.

The programme ran for ten years between 1987 and 1996, and during that time I had a chance to talk to a wide range of heroes, from Alan Bennett (who had a fresh pear and cold tongue for lunch in the canteen) to Dirk Bogarde, who chatted amiably about his life as we sat in the stalls at the National Theatre. I leaned on Sir Georg Solti's piano in his home in St John's Wood while he played Mozart, and sat next to Placido Domingo as he took Evelyn Glennie's hand in his and sang 'Your Tiny Hand is Frozen'. I can still see the rapt expression of incredulity on her face.

I met other musical legends, too, from George Shearing –
'Have you always been blind?'
'So far.'
– to Ivor Novello's leading lady Mary Ellis, who was simply enchanting and signed my copy of *The Dancing Years*. Evelyn Laye brought tears to my eyes singing 'When I Grow Too Old to Dream', and there were 'one-hour specials' with Laurie Lee and Charlton Heston, Shirley Bassey, Barry Manilow and Dudley Moore.

There were trips to Los Angeles to interview Jerry Herman and Mel Torme, Tony Bennett and Artie Shaw, and to New York for chats with Al Pacino and Jack Lemmon, Cindy Crawford and Donald Trump. Forgive the name-dropping; I only do this to explain why I allowed myself to be diverted a little from the gardening. The family feel of the production team and the high quality of guests combined to make the *Pebble Mill* years some of the most memorable of my life, and I look back on them with great fondness.

There are those who are sniffy about daytime television. To me it doesn't matter what time a programme is transmitted; what matters is that production standards remain high regardless of the hour. They don't always, of course, but I like to think I've done my bit to help. There is, I reckon, a world of difference between popularising and dumbing down. Sadly not all critics see it that way.

It was while I was billeted at Pebble Mill that I was asked to present *Songs of Praise*. It was the shortest job interview I've ever had. I bumped into the series producer Roger Hutchings in the corridor. 'You go to church, don't you?' he asked. 'Sometimes,' I said. 'Fancy presenting *Songs of Praise*?'

I was very wary at first, not wanting to be seen as holier than thou or a 'God botherer'. My faith is at the heart of my life but I do shudder when someone comes up to me and says, 'You're a Christian, aren't you?' as if to imply that I am somehow different from the common herd, have three heads, am a member of some secret society or about to effect a conversion job on everyone I meet. My beliefs are private; my business and nobody else's. If folk think I've 'got religion' they might steer clear of me. That's what 'low church C of E' does for you. It is a suitable faith for a Yorkshireman – deep maybe, but understated and tacitly accepted, rather than something to make a song and dance about. But I reasoned that there are moments in everyone's life when they need to stand up for their beliefs, however tentatively, and I do think it is important that *Songs of Praise* remains on television on a Sunday evening, shunted from pillar to post though it might be, to accommodate more 'mainstream' programmes. (I wonder what God makes of the fact that he is not considered 'mainstream'?)

So I overcame my reservations, telling myself that in the interviews that are a part of the programme I would be taking the standpoint of 'everyman' rather than an evangelist. In the five years that I presented the programme, alternating for the most part with the delightfully cheerful Pam Rhodes, I visited Jerusalem and Bosnia, Romania and New York, and towns, villages and cities the length and breadth of the British Isles. I saw more of the world and the UK with *Songs of Praise* than with any other programme I've been involved with before or since, and it gave me a heartening view of humanity – I met people who had overcome the most fearsome obstacles and tragedies in life with stoicism and good humour, backed up by a faith that might sometimes be shaky but which had, in the end, seen them through. One or two of them might even have given Richard Dawkins pause for thought.

Of all the things I saw, the images that stay with me the most strongly are those of refugees queuing in Bosnia – doctors and businessmen carrying their lives in a plastic bag, lining up with the long-term poor – and the abandoned babies in serried ranks of cots in a Romanian orphanage. I stop and think, every now and then, what might have become of the dark-eyed infant called

Cosmina I held in my arms twelve years ago, and who wrapped her fingers around mine. Where is she now? Is she being looked after?

Could I have done something about it? Or was I just a television presenter doing a job, who had no option but to put her back in her cot and give her the teddy bear I had brought for her before stepping out of her life as quickly as I had stepped into it? There are some questions in life that can never be answered. And some images that always return to haunt you.

Back Into The Garden

We are stardust,
We are golden,
And we got to get ourselves
Back to the garden.
             'Woodstock', Joni Mitchell

You will have gathered, by now, that I do not make plans but rather allow myself to be nudged this way and that by fate. I like to think I give it a helping hand every now and again or, at the very least, tackle what it throws up with every ounce of energy I possess. I don't really do half-hearted. But I've never had a proper career plan, not since the one that Ken Wilson mapped out for me when I was fifteen, which has obviously gone seriously awry. If I'd followed it to the letter, of course, I would just have retired as the Parks Superintendent of some large town or city. The very thought makes me shudder – well, they both do, the Parks Superintendent bit, and the retirement bit. I tell the missus that I know I should do a bit less – and I will, I really will – but she just looks at me and raises an eyebrow. Well, the trouble is that it's all so enjoyable. As Noël Coward once said, 'Work is more fun than fun.'

But, here's fate for you. *Pebble Mill* came to an end in 1996. 'It has run its natural course,' they said. I was about to find myself without a job, on television at least, though the writing seemed set to continue unabated. And then they asked if I would like to take over *Gardeners' World* when Geoff Hamilton stepped down. Like most other things in my life, it came out of the blue.

The funny thing about fate is that while you can help it along, you can't force its hand. I had auditioned for *Gardeners' World* back in the early eighties – when Geoff had ended up landing the job. They said that Geoff's garden was more relevant to the majority of their viewers because Barnsdale was in the Midlands, rather than mine which was in the south. They were probably just being kind. Geoff was a more experienced broadcaster than I was back then. But by 1996 he was ready to leave, having presented the programme for 17 years.

He and I had known each other for a long time; I had even written for him in the 1970s when he was editor of *Practical Gardening* magazine. I wrote under what he called a 'pew-sod-o-nym', Tom Derwent (it sounded suitably rural to me, with overtones of the Lake District). We chatted about when he wanted to step down from *GW* and when I would take over, and agreed that Easter 1997 would be a good time. But fate stepped in again, this time in the saddest of ways. Geoff died of a heart attack in the summer of 1996 and I was rushed back from leading a garden tour of South Africa and thrown in at the deep end to complete the series.

It was probably the toughest job I had tackled up until then. The sadness of his premature death infused the first few episodes and I found it hard to make *Gardeners' World* my own. I soldiered on under the spotlight as brightly as I could, but the mood was not helped by some concocted scandal about peat.

Geoff was a committed organic gardener, as am I. So when I mentioned in the second or third programme that I was using ericaceous compost to pot up some rhododendrons, I thought nothing of it. But ericaceous compost was assumed, by one or two journalists and the charity Plant Life, of which Geoff had been a great supporter, to mean compost containing peat, which is a non-renewable resource that must be conserved at all costs. 'How could he?' came the tirade. 'After all Geoff had done to discourage the use of peat.'

Well, as most people know, the word 'ericaceous' does not in fact mean 'containing peat'. It means 'lime free'. The compost I was using was based on bark but was free of lime. But by then, of course, the damage was done and nothing I said was of any consequence. I just kept my head down and battled on until the end of the series as best I could, reflecting ruefully that my old mate Geoff now seemed to have become St Geoff while I was a mere mortal.

It was only when the programme returned in the spring of 1997 that I felt I could really start to make it my own. I was not Geoff, I told myself, I was me. I could only be myself, and those who tuned in would have to take it or leave it. So from then on I did my own thing. I cherish the remark made by one correspondent whose letter began unpromisingly:

'When you took over *Gardeners' World* from Geoff Hamilton my heart sank.
I have been watching you closely over the past few months. You'll do.'

It was, for me, a turning point, and I shall forever be grateful to the viewer who took the trouble to write and let me know.

It was in that first 'proper' year of *Gardeners' World*, 1997, that *Ground Force* came along, and that the names of Charlie Dimmock and Tommy Walsh became part of the nation's vocabulary, along with 'water feature' and 'decking'.

Nobody expected much at all of *Ground Force*. I certainly didn't. I very nearly turned it down. I mean, gardens evolve, you can't make them in two days. The very idea was unrealistic. But John Thornicroft, the producer/director who Peter Bazalgette had charged with persuading me to have a crack at it, was like a dog with a bone. He knew that the way to get me to agree was to suggest that I could *not* make a difference to a patch of ground in two days. 'Of course I could,' I replied. He had me where he wanted me.

With Tommy to take charge of the hard landscaping, along with builder's mate Willy, and Charlie to help me with the gardening, we tackled our first challenge in West Wickham, near Croydon. The rest is history.

The programme was so successful that we were moved from BBC2 to BBC1, and the repeat of that very first programme pulled in 12 million viewers – second only to *EastEnders*. You've got to smile. Twelve million folk watching a gardening programme. Wonderful! Of course, some said that it wasn't a gardening programme at all, it was entertainment. The very idea! That gardening should be entertaining. Whatever next?

It does rattle me, you know, when people are snooty about gardening, and about *Ground Force*. It was described by one notable garden designer as having taken garden design 'to an immeasurable low'. He completely missed the point. It was a programme that aimed to appeal to and inspire those who would never dream of watching *Gardeners' World* and to whom the garden was a foreign country whose language and customs were beyond comprehension. It did not set out to be the last word in contemporary landscape design, but just to take people by the hand and show them that they could create a pleasant environment outside their back door. With luck, some of those 12 million viewers might go on to watch *Gardeners' World*, and maybe even really get the gardening bug and become members of the RHS.

I do have one or two regrets. I know that I will forever be associated with decking, which is perhaps not as classic as York stone paving but it is cheaper and easier to lay. I know that I had a predilection for blue-painted fences. Cuprinol even brought out a timber preservative called 'Barleywood Blue'. But then we used to wear bell-bottomed trousers and kipper ties. Fashions change. At least the programme got people talking about gardening and, hopefully, doing it as well.

I stayed with the programme for six years and designed a total of 67 gardens, by which time I realised I was in danger of running out of steam and ought to quit while I was – marginally – ahead.

The high spots? There were many. We made gardens for people whose plots of earth had been inaccessible because they were wheelchair bound; now they could get round them and potter away to their heart's content. We made a garden in the courtyard of the hospital in Port Stanley, in the Falkland Islands. (It's probably been blown away by the wind by now.) We built a child-friendly garden for an orphanage at Palna in India, and a garden for the vicar of Rome in Umbria.

But the highlight has to be the garden we made for Nelson Mandela in the Transkei. I wrote about it in detail in *Trowel and Error*, so will not repeat it here, but the memory lingers, and grows more fond with the years. He really is an extraordinary man, with the quietest and most powerful charisma of anyone I have ever met, and that human quality I prize above all others – generosity of spirit. When we met, I asked him why he was not bitter. His reply: 'There is no time for bitterness. There is too much to be done.' There are other world leaders who would do well to remember that.

To sit down and talk with Nelson Mandela is a rare privilege. Like many great people, he has that knack of making you feel that you are the only person in the room – or the garden, in my case. And he does love plants. The story he tells in *Long Walk To Freedom* about the tomato plant he grew while he was imprisoned on Robben Island and which, in spite of his ministrations, withered away, is heart-rending. It was, he says, the only thing in his life over which he had any control. When it died, he buried it with some ceremony in a corner of the exercise yard.

I have a copy of *Long Walk to Freedom* that he signed for me. It is inscribed: 'To Alan, Best wishes to a competent and caring journalist. N. Mandela.'

And so, when others accuse me of incompetence, I can say that Nelson Mandela thinks otherwise. I'm grateful for that.

Words . . .

Every author really wants to have letters printed in the papers.

Unable to make the grade, he drops down a rung of the ladder and writes novels.

P.G. Wodehouse

I would not want you to think – and you could all too easily think, from what I have written so far – that all I have ever done is to wait for opportunities to present themselves, and gone where others suggested I might go. Well, I have a bit, but then I've also taken a few risks. And done things which, really, it would have been wiser to have avoided. Like writing novels.

I mean, there I am, plodding along nicely with *Gardeners' World* and *Ground Force* and writing gardening books. Why rock the boat by having a bash at fiction? Never mind putting your head above the parapet, writing a novel is like jumping stark naked from the battlements. And yet . . .

At school, I loved writing stories. I loved writing them rather more than Miss Weatherall liked reading them, but that's by the by. And then I grew up. A bit. And I realised, when I grew up, that unless you are an artist, or a composer, or a novelist, you never get to use the one thing that gives so much pleasure as a child – your imagination.

Quite how I found the time, not to mention the nerve, to

write a synopsis and a couple of chapters and send them off to three publishers I will never know.

They always say, 'Write about what you know', so I wrote (or started to write) the story of a young TV gardener, Rob MacGregor, and his love life. I had in mind a sort of romantic adventure story, believing myself to be both romantic and adventurous. I received one rejection slip, one request to see more and one invitation to lunch. Having always taken rejection badly, and never wanting to do more than I have to, and because I can never resist a hearty meal, I went to lunch with a man by the name of Luigi Bonomi. It is not made up. He really does exist and, as far as I am aware, in spite of the sound of his name, he is not a fully paid up member of the Mafia. Rather he's a good egg. A very good egg.

Luigi found a publisher. The book came out. It sold well. I have now written seven novels, all of which have made it into *The Sunday Times* top ten. (That's the second boast in only a few pages and I apologise for the lapse. It will not happen again.)

But the great joy is that I have found a method of self-expression that I had hitherto only dreamed of. It's also another string to my bow and one that I hope I can carry on employing for a few years yet.

Writing fiction is agony and ecstasy in equal measure, depending on how the day is going. I do not write groundbreaking literature. Neither am I of the deeply cerebral or highly esoteric school. I write what I hope are well-crafted stories that will take you out of yourself. They tell stories of ordinary people in often extraordinary circumstances. They do, in their simple way, reflect human nature. There are smiles. A few tears. But above all I hope they just take the reader off into another world in the company of characters who they may like or loathe, but at the very least about whom they care. The novels I least enjoy reading are those whose characters are so deeply unattractive that every moment in their company is an ordeal. I don't mean that I don't like villains – they are vital to any story – but I want my villains to be compelling as well as repulsive.

The world of fiction writing is, I've discovered, a world of ferocious snobbery and intellectual elitism. At its heart is (or should be) a love of telling stories, and yet 'popular fiction' is used by many in the world of publishing as a derogatory term. J.K. Rowling was lauded when the first Harry Potter book hit the shops back in 1997 and hailed as the successor to Roald Dahl. And yet when the later books broke all publishing records, it seemed that she had overstepped the mark and the critics began to sharpen their quills and dip them in the vitriol that is reserved for those who are hugely successful. One eavesdropping I treasure was overheard at the British Book Awards a few years ago. As prize-winning authors stepped up to collect their 'Nibbies' (the awards are shaped like golden pen nibs), Jeffrey Archer leaned across to Jilly Cooper and whispered, 'What wouldn't we give for one of those?'. Jilly whispered back, 'And what wouldn't they give for sales like ours?'

It is up to all authors to plough their own furrow – whether it be light fiction or prose laden with scholarly substance – and to write well, within their genre. The reader will read what he or she wants to read, and it is not up to anyone to tell them what that should be.

As for my own modest contribution, the sense of place is always important to me. *Mr MacGregor* was set in Yorkshire; *The Last Lighthouse Keeper* in Cornwall, *Rosie* on the Isle of Wight and *Love and Dr Devon* in Hampshire. I set novels in places I know, and base them on subjects that interest me or about which I want to learn more. Rest assured I will never write a story about a computer software salesman who is a wizard at information technology. As far as I am concerned, IT is not it.

The seventh novel, *Folly*, is set in Bath (I'm still a sucker for Georgian architecture) and tells the story of two families over three generations, something I have not attempted before, but it's always good to raise the bar a little. It revolves around the art world and features Sir Alfred Munnings, making it the first novel in which I've included a person who actually existed. Munnings was the finest equestrian artist since Stubbs, and weaving him in and out of a story about warring families, forgery and intrigue was a satisfying contrast to the more bucolic aspects of my world, gardens and gardening.

When I started writing fiction, I had no concept of the process. How did one begin? Had the whole plot to be written down on a chapter-by-chapter basis and then adhered to slavishly? I didn't think that would be much fun, so I thought a lot about characters and had only the vaguest idea about plot. Both Rosamund Pilcher and Jilly Cooper were hugely encouraging and, like Harry Rhodes all those years ago, said 'Yes, you can' when all I could think of was 'No, I can't'. Jilly even sent back the first few chapters with red ink all over them and an encouraging note. Few authors display such generosity of spirit.

So with a vague idea of where I was going, but not how to get there – or, as Ros Pilcher says, 'I knew where the train was starting and what *might* be its final destination, but I didn't know the stations in between' – I started.

Having written about forty books up to this point, I began *Mr MacGregor* in the winter of 1997/98, in the shed at the top of the garden at Barleywood. I have always written best in the morning – I'm a lark, not an owl – and so I would sit down at around 8.30a.m and write solidly until 1p.m or 2p.m, then collapse, exhausted. My usual rate is around 3,000 words at a sitting. Sometime more, sometimes less. One really good day is usually followed by a poor one, so the numbers even out.

After a light lunch I'll potter around in the garden and think about where I am going. But even then, things don't always work out as one imagines. I learnt that within days of starting on

Mr MacGregor. I had planned for our hero and his girlfriend to go up the Dales for supper that evening. He suggests the idea to her. I tapped away at the laptop and discovered that his girlfriend had other ideas. She was going out that evening with her boss.

I actually sat back from the keyboard and wondered what had happened. I had it in my mind that they were going out that night, and yet she had contradicted me and said they were not. Maybe this was what it was like when you were writing fiction. Maybe the characters *did* take over. I had a choice: either I could *make* them go up the Dales that evening, or I could hand over the plot and let them decide. I plumped for the latter, and that's what I've done ever since.

Not all writers can proceed in this way. Whenever I read a P.D. James murder mystery and the story begins 'On the day of the third killing . . .' I know that one of our finest authors has plotted her tale so intricately that she knows exactly where she is going. But then her stories are different to mine and rely on labyrinthine construction as much as emotion.

I feel a touch pretentious setting all this down; as if what I write has some kind of literary merit, when I really just tell stories. But folk are often curious as to where such stories come from. How they get a life of their own. The truth of the matter is that I wish I knew, but I do enjoy helping them to unfold. Acting as a 'medium' in a funny kind of way, for the characters who exist only in my imagination and, hopefully, come to life on the page.

I worried that I did not know all of them as well as perhaps I should, until I talked to the thriller writer Val McDermid. 'Just as in life,' she said. 'You know some people better than others.' Then it all made sense.

The storytellers I admire the most are those who have lightness of touch and who can weave a spell. P.G. Wodehouse is a favourite and I escape to Blandings Castle whenever I can. His writing simply reeks of enjoyment – his own as well as that of his reader, which seems to me how it should be. *The Wind in the Willows* remains a favourite from my childhood, and Daphne du Maurier, though dated now, is the mistress of atmosphere and suspense.

My shelves groan under the weight of everything from Arthur Ransome to Patrick O'Brian, Oscar Wilde to Winston Churchill. Some I dip into, others I read from cover to cover. But Churchill himself summed up my feelings for them:

> . . . if you cannot read them, at any rate handle them and, as it were, fondle them. Peer into them. Let them fall open where they will. Read on from the first sentence that arrests the eye. Then turn to another. Make a voyage of discovery, taking soundings of uncharted seas. Set them back on your shelves with your own hands. Arrange them on your own plan, so that if you do not know what is in them, at least you know where they are. If they cannot be your friends, let them at any rate be your acquaintances. If they cannot enter the circle of your life, do not deny them at least a nod of recognition.

His remarks apply more to non-fiction than to novels, I think. It is the hope of every novelist that their work will be taken up and discovered to be 'unputdownable', wherever the reader may be. I do not care whether my novels are bought in hardback or paperback, taken out of the library or snapped up for 50p from a charity shop. They can be read on the bus or the train, in a book-lined study or on a lilo, by butcher, baker, computer-maker or housewife. They can be denounced as of little consequence and ignored by the classier literary supplements. It matters not. Provided that they can give the reader a day or two of escapism, and a fraction of the pleasure that they give me to write, I ask no more.

. . . and Music

The English may not like music, but they absolutely love the noise it makes.

A Mingled Chime, Sir Thomas Beecham

When I was a boy there was one night above all others when my family would watch television together. *The Last Night of the Proms* was a must, and Mum and Dad, while resisting the temptation to wave Union Jacks in the air, would sit in their armchairs happily singing along to 'Land of Hope and Glory' with the rest of the audience more than 200 miles away in the Royal Albert Hall.

Cookie next door would be brought in to join in the fun; beef and onion sandwiches and a glass or two of Double Diamond would help the evening go with a swing, and then we would all go to bed, having reminded ourselves that we were British and proud of it, and that we really did have some wonderful tunes.

It never seemed insular, prejudiced or – a word we never heard back then – jingoistic. It was just a part of our lives, and pride – not the sort that goes before a fall – was very much a part of it.

Nearly fifty years later I was to be given the best seat in the house at the BBC Proms – the box at the centre of the Grand Tier. Except that I had to sit with my back to the audience and keep talking when they had fallen quiet.

The Proms is a remarkable institution, which has mercifully

weathered the vicissitudes of life and the slings and arrows of prejudice and political correctness to endure almost unscathed for more than a century. Founded by Sir Henry Wood, the Proms have ensured that each summer we have a platform for the best in classical music performed by orchestras and artists from all over the world.

I had presented the occasional Promenade Concert on television, having been involved with music programmes on BBC Radio 2 since the 1980s. Now I present a programme on Radio 2 every Sunday evening and get a chance to play an hour and a half of my kind of music, everything from music hall to opera, musicals to classical fare. It really is a great treat. But of all my musical presenting, the four years I spent as anchor man of the Last Night of the Proms from 2004–2007 are the highlight.

It is an evening of tremendous atmosphere, with 'promenaders' queuing up overnight to make sure of seats for the grand finale of the season. The hall is never less than packed to the rafters, and tickets are at a premium. The orchestra rehearses in the morning, and the presenter for the television coverage arrives at about midday to begin the technical run-through, sitting in the Grand Tier box and being kept in touch with what is going on via an earpiece through which the producer and director in the massive scanner parked behind the Albert Hall offer advice and timings.

The concert itself starts at 7.30p.m and ends around 10p.m. and these are the hairiest two and a half hours of live television any broadcaster is ever likely to encounter. The evening is introduced with the presenter on screen, and the artists and the conductor are introduced off screen as they make their way on to the stage. There is the laurel wreath placed on the bust of Sir Henry Wood by two promenaders, and all sorts of other comings and goings, to be described, or accompanied by a thoughtful silence, or generally marshalled. In the presenter's hand is a 4-in thick pile of cards containing not only the script (in case the autoscript on the camera fails) but also details of everyone performing. These are handy if gaps need to be filled and information passed on to the viewer.

It is all very well when things go according to plan, but if a conductor or a performer takes the law into their own hands and comes on or goes off when they are not supposed to then it is up to the presenter to smooth things over, paddling madly beneath the water but remaining calm and serene on the surface, slinging cards away when they are not needed, and scrabbling around for facts when no one appears on cue.

Then there are the names. Joshua Bell and Sir Roger Norrington offer little in the way of a challenge, but Jiri Belohlavek and Dmitri Hvorostovsky take a little practice. But it is all part of the fun.

There are in-vision interviews to conduct in the intervals between the music, and with any luck you will get a musician who can string a sentence or two together, and a musicologist who has the ability to speak in a style understandable by the common herd as well as the cognoscenti.

Once the second half is underway and the broadcast has switched from BBC2 to BBC1 (the first half of the concert is generally considered too highbrow for the more popular channel) the presenter kicks off part two and is then out of vision for the last section of the programme. But by now the adrenaline is flowing, and before you know where you are, 'Land of Hope and Glory' is ringing out through the Hall and you can glance at your family sitting in the box next door (a perk of the job) and join in with them, singing at the top of your voice, waving your Union Jack and hoping that both the camera and the microphone are switched off.

There is little to compare with the satisfaction of getting to the end of the evening and signing off on time, having glued together those bits that seemed in danger of falling apart, and having endeavoured not to talk too much, or in the wrong places, but just to act as an unobtrusive link to one of the most famous musical occasions in the world.

Apart from a bomb scare on one occasion, which meant that we had no rehearsal time at all for the television links and came on air ten minutes late into the bargain, the Last Night usually went according to plan. Mostly. But there were other concerts when things went slightly awry. Tchaikovsky's 1812 overture was scheduled for one performance. I sat in on the rehearsal. When the moment came for the cannon and mortar fire to begin, the roof of the Albert Hall was almost lifted off and the orchestra ground to a halt. The special effects team had mistakenly installed stadium-sized mortars, rather than those suitable for the Albert Hall arena. It was half an hour before our ears stopped ringing and the new, smaller, mortars were brought in to replace them. I don't know who swept up the fallen plaster.

But the Prom concert I will never forget is the one that was performed for the Queen's 80th birthday. I cannot remember now what music was played. I was simply aware that when the audience fell quiet after the applause for each musical item, I had to carry on talking in a normal voice as usual. The Queen was in the next box but one to mine and, out of the corner of my eye, I could see her leaning forwards and looking in my direction to see why I was still wittering on.

Added to this, I was sitting on two stacked chairs, rather than one, with the object of raising my head above the brass rail in front of the box, which would otherwise appear to run through my head. It is rather a perilous position, but provided I sit still it is unlikely that I will topple over the edge.

After the concert all the performers – and me – were instructed to make their way to the room at the top of the hall to be presented to Her Majesty. Bryn Terfel had been presented with the Queen's Medal that evening, in recognition of his unique contribution to British music, and I found myself standing next to him when the Queen approached. She chatted to Bryn, who is a delightful and unassuming man whose basso profundo can rattle windows, about the medal itself, and his singing. Then she turned to me. I apologised for continuing to talk during the quiet bits and said that I hoped the Queen did not mind. 'No,' she said. 'Not at all. It was just your chair. We were worried that you might fall off.'

Back to Nature

Nature, Mr Allnutt, is what we are put into this world to rise above.

Katharine Hepburn in *The African Queen*

They always say, 'Be careful what you wish for', the implication being that when it happens it might not turn out quite as you imagined. As a child I had always wanted to be Percy Thrower; that dream came true, in a manner of speaking, and it lived up to expectations. But before the gardening bug bit, it was 'nature study' that captivated me. I wouldn't say that I wanted to be Peter Scott or David Attenborough (I remember them from the days before they were ennobled) but I did admire them. They were the sort of people who spoke my kind of language (albeit with longer words) and liked the kind of things I liked – animals and birds and, to a lesser extent, plants and flowers.

I had been presenting *Gardeners' World* for six years when an approach came from the BBC's Natural History Unit. It put me in a bit of a quandary.

In the eighties and nineties, and the early part of the twenty-first century, *Gardeners' World* was a kind of 'club sandwich' in terms of its format. I would introduce and 'pay off' or close the programme, presenting three items during the half hour that were interspersed with features and reports from other 'experts'. These stalwarts included Stephen Lacey (the high-class plantsman),

Sarah Raven (the high-class plantswoman), Joe Swift (every man's garden designer), Rachel de Thame (every man's dream), Chris Beardshaw (every woman's dream), and Pippa Greenwood (the garden doctor with the pleasant flowerbed-side manner).

The programme was filmed in my garden at Barleywood in Hampshire every Friday and transmitted the following Friday, so that we were only a week behind the weather. My five items – opener, closer and three middle bits – had all to be prepared in advance and any plant material ordered and ground prepared. The programme ran from February to October and we did anything from 30 to 36 episodes, which means around 180 items per year. I stayed with the programme for seven years, so during the course of my tenure I put together and presented 1,260 different items. It's only when you look at it like that that you realise what a fearsome commitment is *Gardeners' World*, especially when you're presenting it from your own garden. Since I left, the programme has been presented from Berryfields and Green Acres, two gardens that are not owned by one individual, but are peopled by the presenters and maintained by a team of unseen gardeners. There is nothing wrong with this; indeed, it must make life much easier for the presenters to have so much back-up, but what is missing for the viewer is the degree of prurience that comes with seeing behind the scenes on a real person's garden – Percy Thrower at The Magnolias, Arthur Billitt at Clack's Farm, Geoff Hamilton at Barnsdale and yours truly at Barleywood.

'Look at the state of that lawn, Muriel. You think he'd have a better one than that, wouldn't you?'

'Never mind the lawn. Have you seen the colour of those kitchen curtains?'

For this reason I always tried to avoid filming in the house, or showing too much of the exterior in shot. I imagined that people would either think I ought to have something better, or that I was showing off. Strangely, for someone who appears on television quite a lot, and who is happy to write about himself in books like this, I still value my privacy. Mrs T and I don't do much in the way of red-carpet evenings or celebrity galas, and we politely decline requests from *Hello* and *OK!* magazines. Neither do we have that many 'showbusiness' friends. Fame is a by-product of what I do, not the reason for doing it. And yet, as someone who is passionate about gardening and nature I find it impossible to keep that enthusiasm to myself, and since my garden is my workshop as well as my sanctuary, I have a need to share it.

Nevertheless, after six years I was wondering just how long I could carry on. I knew that I did not want to match Geoff Hamilton's record of seventeen years. The Natural History Unit came to see me at Barleywood to discuss 'possible projects'. It's a vague sort of phrase and I can only assume they'd had an eye on me for a while and wondered if we might work together. Two producers came down, and we sat in my conservatory and talked about what I might like to do with them.

They were surprised when I said that I had little interest in the migration of wildebeest in the Serengeti. Yes, I thought the Galapagos fascinating, but I did not really want to spend three months overseas filming giant tortoises. But this, after all, was what natural history presenters did. Sir David Attenborough, the expert's expert and doyen of natural history presenters, had the most travelled suitcase in the world. But then he is not a gardener.

The problem with being a gardener, and being married to a garden as well as a wife, is that you cannot simply push off and leave it for months on end. More to the point, you do not want to. The NHU were on the brink of giving up on me when I said that what I would really love to do was a series about the wildlife and natural history of the British Isles. It seemed to me that we had enough about meerkats and lemurs, lions and tigers and camels, and all too little about dormice and starlings, red squirrels and Glanville fritillaries – the wildlife on our doorstep and the countryside we need to cherish.

They listened patiently as I explained my feelings, and went away promising to come up with a strategy that would hopefully enable us to work together. That was in 2001. The result was *British Isles: A Natural History*, a series exploring the foundation of our islands, their geology, geography, climate and natural history, over the last few million years. It took two years to make this eight-part series, and I managed to be away from home for only a week at a time, so that my garden would not become totally overgrown.

What this commitment did mean was that I could not possibly continue presenting *Gardeners' World*. And so, at the end of 2002, I relinquished my tenure as 'the nation's head gardener' and moved on. It was not an easy decision to make. My ambitions had never stretched beyond what I was doing but, as they say, if someone throws a ball at you, there is nothing you can do but catch it.

The autumn of 2002 became a turning point in so many ways: in October I stopped presenting *Gardeners' World* and *Ground Force*. On 16 December we moved house and on 17 December we went to Yorkshire for my mother's funeral. Moving house and the death of a loved one are, they say, two of the three most traumatic things that can happen to you. The other is divorce. Yes, well, moving swiftly on . . .

But there were happier things, too. During that same year I worked on a series I had longed to present, one that would go right back to basics and make gardening easy to understand. *How to be a Gardener* was made in several small gardens local to me in Hampshire, since I knew that we would be moving and could not base it at Barleywood. It turned out to be a great hit. I showed folk how to sow seeds and take cuttings, but also explained the 'Why?' as well as the 'How?' The book that went with the series became the fastest-selling gardening book of all time. I don't mean to be sound boastful; I was just chuffed really. It seemed to suggest that a straightforward and simple explanation of the gardening basics was what a lot of people needed.

Of all the gardening series I have ever made, it is *How to be a Gardener* of which I am most proud. It was produced by Kath Moore, whose way of bringing out the best in a presenter has yet to be equalled. 'Give me a bit more heart,' she'd say, tapping her chest with her fist. 'Just a bit more heart.' I gave *How to be a Gardener all* of my heart, and it ran for two series.

So did my natural history programmes. *The Nature of Britain* followed *British Isles: A Natural History* in taking a closer look at our different wildlife habitats – from mountain and moorland to streams and rivers, fields and hedgerows – explaining the interdependency of plants, animals and humans in an ever more pressurised world. But I have always believed in being positive about natural history, not being the prophet of doom. Drone on at folk for too long about how this is threatened and that is on the verge of extinction and they will switch off, believing that there is little they can do to redress the balance. A celebratory, though not head-in-the-sand, approach is, I reckon, far more effective and pragmatic than the tired old 'ten seconds to midnight' stance, which leaves people despondent and breeds inactivity. Get them engaged, without browbeating them, and they will do their bit for conservation and stewardship of the countryside. Of course people need to know how fragile is the land on which they live, and how its future lies in our hands, but show them how they can make a difference, and explain the adaptability and opportunism of the wildlife that inhabits it, and they will see that it is not a hopeless cause but rather something they might feel able to participate in.

Making the series was tremendously enriching. I walked on snowy mountain peaks in the Cairngorms, travelled the Norfolk

Broads by boat and explored coastal caves for seals and Scottish rivers for salmon. I travelled from Shetland to the Channel Islands, from the Norfolk coast to Pembrokeshire – the entire length and the entire breadth of Britain. It confirmed my long-held suspicions that there is nowhere else on earth I would rather live, and no other country endowed with so rich a variety of scenery and natural history.

There are, of course, scary moments when you're making programmes in rugged terrain. Throughout the four years that it took to make *British Isles: A Natural History* and *The Nature of Britain*, I had one or two close encounters of the hair-raising kind. I escaped a helicopter that crashed adjacent to Hadrian's Wall (it plummeted to the ground a few yards in front of me; mercifully, the crew escaped with only minor injuries). I was lucky on two counts – first in that they missed me, and second in that I was due to go up with them on the next flight. As it turned out, that was the end of the filming day – the cameraman had cracked a rib and the camera was written off. Well, if it wasn't written off during the crash it was certainly written off afterwards when the fire brigade covered it in foam.

We were cut off by the tide on a rocky coastline in Devon, thanks to a producer who wanted 'just one more shot' and found it hard to believe that, although I would reluctantly do as he asked, the waves were less biddable. I ended up legging it over some craggy rocks while the crew sat tight with their equipment and waited for the tide to recede.

We got back to London that night to discover that the *Evening Standard* had got wind of it. It is curious, in cases like this, to observe the sort of 'Chinese whispers' way that stories have of growing out of all proportion, and changing with the telling. The bald facts are that our escape across the sand was cut off, but that we were high enough up on the rocks to be well above the high-water line. We were not in danger at any time. All we had to do was wait until the tide went out again. The guys had a camera, tripod and sound equipment to carry and so stayed put. I had nothing except myself to worry about and so I clambered – carefully – over the rather jagged rocks to safety.

The first version that appeared used the words 'hero' and 'rescue' when referring to my actions. In the second version the word 'ill-advised' appeared. And by the time the third edition came out we were on to 'foolhardy'. You've got to smile.

The two series were well received by viewers and got high ratings. One or two critics, however, could not see any link between gardening and natural history and questioned my involvement. And so it is that gardeners labour on in a world where some think that plants have nothing to do with natural history, which is all about birds and animals and fishes. Heigh-ho . . .

When it was revealed that I was about to present a natural history series the papers reported that I was to be 'the new David Attenborough', which is a sure way of raising expectations too high, not to mention hackles. It was a ridiculous assertion. There never will be 'a new David Attenborough'. I am content to be 'the new Alan Titchmarsh', which is, in some ways I suppose, preferable to 'the old Alan Titchmarsh'. Or is it? You know, I'm not so sure . . .

Perhaps those critics were right, in that the longer I live the less I realise I know and the more unsure I become of so many things – things that, when I was young, seemed irrefutable. Copper bottomed. Guaranteed.

The other thing I have learned is that it does not do to become too self analytical or too precious. As Dame Margot Fonteyn said, 'To take one's job seriously is imperative; to take oneself seriously is disastrous.'

Looking back, the one thing I know for certain is that I have been extraordinarily blessed. It doesn't do to say so, of course. It makes you sound soppy and sentimental. But I consider myself so very fortunate in the things I have been allowed to do and the people I've encountered on the way who were confident enough in my abilities to encourage me in my endeavours. To the friends who have stuck by me through thick and thin, and a family who could not be more supportive, I can never express my gratitude profoundly enough.

I have made my way in life, as Sir David Frost put it, 'by trowel and error'. Last year I had the honour of being the High Sheriff of the Isle of Wight. It is an ancient office, and one which allows you to commission a personal coat of arms from the College of Arms in London. Those arms contain a motto. Mine is short and sweet: *et stilo et rutro*. Translated from the Latin: 'by pen and spade'. Two implements that haven't done badly for me, all things considered.

Tailpiece

Sir, I admit your general rule
That every poet is a fool:
But you yourself may serve to show it,
That every fool is not a poet.

'Epigram from the French', Alexander Pope

Just so. But how to sum up? I fly in the face of Mr Pope and offer no more than the following, which I must confess, in the interests of chronological accuracy, was written three years ago:

I started at this gardening lark
When I was young and green,
Upon my grandad's cabbage patch
Neath rows of runner bean.

And then when I was fifteen years
I learned it as my trade;
I mowed the grass, worked under glass
And dug and hoed and sprayed.

When I was one and twenty
I travelled down to Kew

Where, 'mongst the palms, in maiden's arms,
My passion for them grew.

When I was one and thirty
I wrote in book and mag,
And garden folk, from Cheam to Stoke,
Sent problems by the bag.

When I was one and forty
I gardened on the telly,
And then the post, from town to coast,
Grew heavier and more smelly.

Now that I'm one and fifty
(Alright then, fifty-seven)
Bugs and beasts and floral feasts
Are my idea of heaven.

But when I'm one and sixty
I'll toddle out the door;
'Cos now that I'm a sex-god
It don't matter any more.

You know, it really is very dangerous when you start believing
things that are written about you . . .

Picture Acknowledgements

Illustrations by Alan Titchmarsh

Photographs from the author's collection: 1 top, 2 top, 3 top right, 5 top, 7 bottom. Additional sources: *Amateur Gardening* May 1983: 5 bottom. ©BBC: 4 bottom, 6 top right. *Boltons* catalogue: 6 top left/photo courtesy Garden Answers. The Francis Frith Collection: 2 bottom. Getty Images: 1 bottom. Karen Graham: 8 top. Tudor Harwood: 3 bottom. Rex Features: 8 bottom/photo Mikael Buck. Michael J. Stead: 7 top. Alison Titchmarsh: 4 top. TopFoto: 3 top left, 6 bottom.

Text Acknowledgements

'How does a Gardener Grow?' by Fay Inchfawn. Reproduced by permission of Lutterworth Press.

Cider with Rosie by Laurie Lee, published by Chatto & Windus. Reprinted by permission of The Random House Group Ltd.

Much Obliged, Jeeves by P.G. Wodehouse, published by Hutchinson. Reprinted by permission of The Random House Group Ltd. Copyright © P.G. Wodehouse. Reproduced by permission of the Estate of P.G. Wodehouse c/o Rogers, Coleridge and White Ltd., 20 Powis Mews, London W11 1JN.

'In Westminster Abbey' from *Collected Poems of John Betjeman* by John Betjeman. Reproduced by permission of John Murray (Publishers).

'The Barrel-Organ' by Alfred Noyes. Reproduced by permission of The Society of Authors, Literary Representative of the Estate of Alfred Noyes.

From the song: 'Lets Face the Music and Dance', words and music by Irving Berlin ©. Reproduced by permission of Warner Chappell Music Ltd. and EMI Music Publishing Ltd. London W8 5SW.

And Now All This, by W.C. Sellar and R.J. Yeatman. Reproduced by permission of Methuen Publishing Ltd.

'The Life of Galileo' by Bertolt Brecht. Reproduced with kind permission.

'How to be a Champion' from the book *The Best of Grantland Rice* by Grantland Rice. Published by Franklin Watts, 1963.

'Woodstock'. Words and Music by Joni Mitchell, © 1969 (Renewed) Crazy Crow Music. All Rights Adminstered by SONY/ATV MUSIC PUBLISHING, 8 Music Square West, Nashville, TN 37203. Used by permission of Alfred Music Publishing Co., Inc.